Civilizations

Civilizations

ten thousand years of ancient history

Jane McIntosh and Clint Twist

Contents

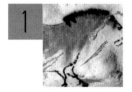

PREHISTORY   8

This chapter briefly examines more than 2 million years of human development before focusing upon the last 10,000 years when the adoption of agriculture quickened the pace of change and laid the foundations of civilization. Special features take a closer look at stone tools, which first extended people's physical capabilities, pottery (developed worldwide as a storage medium) and irrigation, which greatly enhanced agricultural productivity.

CITIES AND STATES   34

The emergence of civilization in Mesopotamia, Egypt, India and China after 3000 BC opened a new chapter in human development, and by 1000 BC West Asia and the eastern Mediterranean were home to many competing states. Cities emerged, the focus of hierarchical societies led by priests or kings, who were often accorded lavish burials after death. Thriving crafts included the working of copper and bronze and later iron. International relations developed, involving both trde and warfare. The creation of writing not only facilitated the administration of these states but also led to the recording of their history and culture.

CLASSICAL CIVILIZATIONS

After 600 BC new states emerged, climaxing in four empires that controlled the greater part of the Old World, stretching from Spain to China and from Britain to southern India. Linked by trade over land and sea, they provided fertile ground for the development of great religions, philosophy, mathematics, science, technology and the arts. Coinage promoted commerce, while many economies depended on slavery.

EMPIRES OF THE NEW WORLD

Civilizations in the New World developed quite independently of the Old. Mesoamerica and the central Andes were the main centres by around 1200 BC. Superb craftsmanship included the manufacture of fine textiles. Temple pyramids marked widespread adherence to religions whose practices included blood-letting and human sacrifices supported by warfare, and which promoted a detailed knowledge of astronomy.

Timeline

	10,000–8000 BC	8000–7000 BC	7000–6000 BC	6000–5000 BC	5000–4000 BC	4000–3000 BC
SUBSISTENCE WHAT PEOPLE ATE	• The Ice Age ended; glaciers retreated over much of the northern hemisphere, which was rapidly recolonized. • Worldwide, everybody lived by hunting and gathering, but in some areas food plants began to be tended; wild wheat and barley now a major source of food in the Near East. • Coastal resources becoming important in many areas as sea levels rose. • Dogs domesticated in Eurasia and the Americas, probably to help with hunting.	• By 8000 BC Some communities in Levant planting as well as harvesting barley, emmer and einkorn wheat. • c.7500 BC Sheep and goats being herded in mountains of western Iran. • By 7000 BC first farmers in area from Turkey to Pakistan produced domestic crops of wheat, barley, beans, lentils and peas and kept domestic sheep and goats. • c.7000 BC Horticulture developing in New Guinea.	• 6500–6000 BC Millet cultivated on the Yellow River and rice on the Yangzi River, China. • 6500–6000 BC Cattle domesticated in Anatolia, North Africa and Pakistan. • By 6500 BC plants including beans, squash, peppers and medicines being cultivated in highland Peru. • By 6000 BC agricultural communities in southeast Europe and Mediterranean. • Some plants planted and tended by Mesoamerican hunter-gatherers.	• c.6000 BC Farming began in Nile Valley, with West Asian and local crops and animals. • By 5000 BC farming communities across most of Europe. • c.6000–5500 BC Irrigation agriculture developed in Mesopotamia and farmers spread into southern Mesopotamia. • Domestic pigs kept by farmers in China, Europe and West Asia; Chinese farmers also keeping chickens.	• From c.5000 BC extensive exploitation of rich marine resources of Peruvian coast. • c.4750 BC Maize cultivated in Mesoamerica. • c.4500–4000 BC Agricultural intensification in Mesopotamia: ploughs; animal traction; dairying. • c.4400 BC Horses domesticated on steppe margins in eastern Europe. • By 4000 BC Farming communities from West Africa to Ethiopia, growing sorghum, yams and other local crops.	• By 4000 BC much of Europe's woodland cleared by fire and axe for farming and grazing. • By 4000 BC domestic guinea pigs, and llama and alpaca domesticated in Andes. • c.4000 BC Irrigation techniques in use in Pakistan. • By 3500 BC more intensive agriculture in China – agricultural area expanding. • By 3500 BC domestic cotton grown in Peru – twined cord used for textiles and nets.
TECHNOLOGY WHAT PEOPLE MADE	• Sea levels rose, separating (among other places) North America from Siberia, Australia from New Guinea and Tasmania, and Britain and Ireland from European mainland. • Stone tools used worldwide. Many now made from small blades, often embedded in wooden handles to make a great variety of tools. • Pottery made in Japan from c.11,000 BC.	• Pottery being made in North Africa and China by 7500 BC and in West Asia by 7000 BC. • Ground and polished stone used to make axes, grindstones and containers in many parts of the world.	• By 6500 BC linen textiles manufactured at Çatal Hüyük, Anatolia. • Pottery made throughout West Asia, in Sahara and Nile Valley, in China and parts of South-East Asia, and in areas around the Mediterranean. • c.6500 BC copper smelting began in parts of Near East.	• By 5000 BC pottery being made in most of Europe and in Pakistan. • By 5000 BC copper being smelted in southeast Europe and gold being worked. • Before 5000 BC, mould-made bricks used for buildings in Anatolia.	• Earliest American pottery used in Amazon Basin c.5000 BC. • c.4500 BC Introduction of slow wheel (turntable) for making pottery in West Asia. • By 4300 BC domestic cotton grown in Mesoamerica and Pakistan. • From c.4200 BC copper mining in Balkans, Europe. • c.4000 BC Jade traded as luxury material in China. • Sailing boats in Mesopotamia from 4500 BC and by 4000 BC in Egypt.	• c.4000 BC Plough agriculture in northern China and Europe. • c.4000 BC Lacquerware being made in China. • 3800 BC Invention of the wheel in Mesopotamia; spread to steppes by 3650 BC and to Europe by 3200 BC. • 3200 BC Substantial bronze production in Mesopotamia. • c.3500 BC In West Asia fast wheel used for making pottery. • By 3000 BC South Americans used seaworthy balsawood rafts.
CIVILIZATIONS THE GROWTH OF CITIES	• Permanently settled villages appearing in some areas, such as Near East. Year-round occupation allowing ownership and accumulation of possessions, including non-portable tools such as heavy grindstones and fragile objects.	• By 7500 BC Jericho (Palestine), a large farming settlement, had stone walls and a massive watch tower. • Links and networks developing between communities as permanently occupied villages emerged, exchanging plants and animals, prized raw materials such as obsidian, ornaments such as seashells, and ideas.	• Permanently occupied villages supported by agriculture developing in many parts of the world, with a great variety of houses whose forms reflected local materials and environmental conditions. • 13-hectare (32-acre) village of Çatal Hüyük in Anatolia, a remarkable indication of potential size and prosperity of early farming communities. • Increasing variety of non-portable and fragile objects such as pottery, being made and accumulated by inhabitants of permanent villages.	• c.5500 BC Temples being constructed in southern Mesopotamian settlements. • After 6000 BC stamp seals used in Mesopotamia to mark ownership of property.	• Towns developing in Mesopotamia and other parts of West Asia. Uruk founded before 4000 BC – later became world's first city. • By 5000 BC megalithic tombs being constructed in Europe. • Temple pyramids constructed in Peru from c.4000 BC.	• By 3300 BC Uruk, the world's first city, covers over 200 hectares (500 acres). • From c.4000 BC trading towns developing across Iranian plateau. • 3500 BC First writing in the world began in Mesopotamia; cuneiform developing by 3100 BC. • 3400 BC Walled towns in Egypt. • 3200 BC Earliest hieroglyphic writing in Egypt. • 3000 BC Permanent settlements on Peruvian coast.
PEOPLE WHO DID WHAT	• By 9000 BC colonists had spread to the southern tip of South America.					• 3000 BC unification of Upper and Lower Egypt, traditionally by king Narmer.

3000–2000 BC	2000–1500 BC	1500–1000 BC	1000–500 BC	500–1 BC	AD 1–500	AD 500–1500
• 3000 BC Cultivation of vine and olive transforms Greek agriculture. • 3000 BC Millet farming spread from China to Korea. • 2900 BC Silkworm domesticated in China and by 2700 BC silk industry greatly developed • By 2000 BC permanent farming settlements in Mesoamerica, growing maize, beans and many other plants. • By 2500 BC potatoes cultivated in the Andes and by 2000 BC sweet manioc cultivated in Amazonia.	• By 2000 BC irrigation well established in coastal Peru. • c.2000 BC Beginning of horseriding which, combined with wheeled transport, allowed nomadic pastoralism to become a way of life and vast steppe region of Eurasia to be colonized. • From c.2000 BC local plants such as sunflowers cultivated in eastern America. • 1900 BC Fayum oasis drained and brought under cultivation. • 1500 BC Wet rice cultivation spreads into Korea from China.	• From 1500 BC skilled navigators, fishers and farmers growing taro, yams and fruit began colonizing Melanesia. • 1490 BC Hatshepsut sent expedition to Punt, which brought back incense trees. • c.1200 BC Agricultural terracing constructed in Peru. • c.1200 BC Soya bean cultivation spread from Manchuria into China and thence throughout East Asia. • By 1000 BC horseriding pastoralists spread across steppes to Chinese borders.	• By 1000 BC bitter manioc cultivated in Amazonia and complex preparation necessary to remove its poison developed. • By 1000 BC maize, beans and squash introduced from Mesoamerica being cultivated in southwest America. • From c.700 BC settled farming villages developed in southeast North America (Adena). • By 500 BC rice cultivation had reached Japan from Korea. • By 500 BC farmers and cattle herders over northern half of Africa, including Lake Victoria.	• From c.500 BC Chinese used iron for agricultural tools, including ploughs and sickles. • Persians constructed underground aqueducts (qanats) for irrigation. • From c.200 BC Bantu farmers moving southward in Africa, introducing domestic animals, crops, pottery and iron. • By 100 BC networks of canals, reservoirs and dams with sluice gates developed in Sri Lanka for irrigated agriculture. • By 100 BC Maya creating raised fields in Yucatán.	• Construction of Persian underground aqueducts continues and expands under Parthians and Sasanians. • By 1st century AD flourishing maritime trade in spices from Southeast Asia and India to the west. • Intensive agriculture in Maya heartland, with canals, raised fields and hillside terracing. • 1st–3rd century AD Chinese agricultural productivity improved by innovations, including seed drill, harrow and wheelbarrow.	• AD 600 Nazca and Huari constructing agricultural terraces and aqueducts. • By AD 600 Tiwanaku state constructed drainage channels and raised fields around Lake Titicaca. • By 16th century AD Aztecs constructing floating gardens (chinampas) in and around Tenochtitlán.
• c.3000 BC Potter's wheel invented in China and by 2500 BC high-temperature firing of fine pottery. • c.3000 BC Papyrus used in Egypt as writing material; by 2800 BC wooden plank boats being built; mummification in use by 2500 BC. • 2600 BC Sophisticated wells and drainage constructed in Indus towns and cities. • 2200 BC Bronze working in China. • By 2000 BC heddle looms being used in Peru.	• 2000 BC Development of swords, carts and chariots with spoked wheels in West Asia. • 1900 BC Beginning of iron working in Anatolia. • Cold-hammered copper objects made in eastern North America from Great Lakes copper. • By 1800 BC Chinese producing bronze ritual vessels. • 16 October 1876 BC Eclipse takes place, accurately forecast by Chinese. • c.1600 BC Glass vessels begin to be made in West Asia.	• By 1500 BC Bronze working spreads to Korea from China. • 1500 BC Bronze working begins in Southeast Asia. • 1200 BC Rapid spread of iron-working technology through western Asia and Europe. • Before 1000 BC iron working begins in India. • By 1000 BC cavalry used in Near Eastern warfare.	• 7th century BC Coinage first used in China and Greek Asia Minor. • c.900 BC Etruscans working iron. • From 7th century BC iron working in north and west Africa. • 6th century BC Iron working in China; casting iron by 500 BC. • By 500 BC bronze metallurgy had reached Japan from Korea. • 850 BC Shrine of Chavín de Huántar in Peru constructed – included sophisticated arrangement of water channels.	• 4th century BC Hippocrates lays foundations of western medical practices and ethics. • From 500 BC iron working in Southeast Asia. • 4th century BC Copper coinage in China; 220 BC Chinese circular coins standardized. • By 200 BC coinage in widespread use in Eurasia. • From 500 BC impressive mounds constructed in southeastern North America. • 3rd century BC Great Wall of China built by Shihuangdi.	• AD 105 Traditional date of Chinese invention of paper. • AD 120 Construction of Pantheon in Rome, using concrete and creating largest ancient dome. • AD 130 Chinese invent seismograph. • Military innovations by Central Asian nomads include stirrups and scale armour, adopted by their settled neighbours. • AD 300 Clinker-built boats in northern Europe.	• Moche invent process for chemically electroplating metal objects. • Moche and other Andean cultures construct fine roads, impressive pyramids and massive burial mounds. • 5th century AD Mixtecs of Mesoamerica creating fine goldwork. • From 15th century AD Inca create roads, bridges, irrigation canals and structures of massive stones. Invented quipu for keeping records.
• 2700 BC First Egyptian pyramid built at Saqqara; Great Pyramid of Khufu at Giza built 2550 BC. • 2600 BC U-shaped shrines constructed in Peru. • By 2600 BC Indus script fully developed; 2500 BC Sumerian script modified for writing Akkadian language; in Egypt simpler hieratic script in use as well as hieroglyphic script. • c.2500 BC Egyptians establish fort at Buhen to control Nubia. • c.2100 BC Ziggurat of Ur constructed by Ur-Nammu.	• 2000 BC Emergence in Crete of palace-based Minoan civilization; 1800 BC Cretan scripts began. • By 1800 BC Indus civilization in decline. • 1760 BC Law Code issued by Babylonian king Hammurabi. • 1700 BC First use of alphabetic signs in the Levant. • 1600 BC Chinese writing on oracle bones began. • 1600–1400 BC Mitanni empire. • 1600 BC Shaft grave warrior burials at Mycenae.	• c.1650–1100 BC Mycenaean civilization in mainland Greece; took over Crete c.1450 BC after fall of Minoans and adapted script as Linear B. • 1500–1450 BC Egyptians gain control of Nubia and in 1460 BC of Levant; lose control of these c.1100 BC; end of New Kingdom c.1070 BC. • 1200 BC Olmec civilization emerges in Mesoamerica. • 1200 BC Emergence of Chavín civilization in Andes. • 1027 BC Fall of Shang dynasty in China to rival Zhou.	• 900-669 BC Assyrian empire expands: conquers Babylonia, Levant and Egypt. • 800 BC Greeks add vowels to the first alphabet, giving rise to all later European scripts. • By c.800 BC the Phoenician trading empire spreads throughout Mediterranean. • By 800 BC Greek city-states developing; 750-600 BC Greeks establish many overseas colonies. • 500 BC Simple writing system developing in Mesoamerica; Brahmi script in India.	• c.500 BC foundation of Monte Albán city and state in Mesoamerica. • 490–479 BC Greeks defeat might of Persian empire; democracy established in Athens; city enjoys 'Golden Age' until it falls to Sparta in 404 BC. • From c.400 BC Teotihuacán empire developing in Mesoamerica. • 321 BC Most of India unified under rule of Maurya dynasty. • 250 BC Emergence of Nazca culture in southern Peruvian coast; constructed Nazca Lines.	• 1st–2nd century AD Kushan dynasty rules much of India and western Central Asia. • c. AD 300 Korea and Japan adopt many elements of Chinese culture, including Buddhism in AD 336. • c. AD 300 Beginning of Classic Maya civilization, using full writing system; heyday of Teotihuacán empire. • Jesus lived 4 BC– AD 30; Christianity an official religion of Roman empire by AD 337. • c. AD 400 Emergence of Tiwanaku state.	• AD 600 Nazca taken over by Huari in South America. • AD 650 Fall of Teotihuacán empire in Mesoamerica. • AD 800 Rise of Mississippian towns in southeast North America. • AD 900 Demise of Classic Maya city-states; rise of Toltecs in Mesoamerica; construction of pueblos in southwest North America. • AD 1350 Mixtecs gain control of Oaxaca Valley. • AD 1410 Inca empire expanding; reaches greatest extent by AD 1527.
• 2800 BC Kings gaining control of Mesopotamian city-states. • 2600 BC Emergence of Indus civilization. • 2700–2200 BC Old Kingdom Egypt. • 2350 BC Sargon unites Sumer and Akkad in first Mesopotamian empire. • 2112 BC Ur-Nammu founds Ur III empire in Mesopotamia, which lasts till 2004 BC. • 2050 BC Mentuhotep reunites Egypt – beginning of Middle Kingdom.	• 1800 BC Old Babylonian empire founded. • 1800 BC Emergence of Shang dynasty in China. • 2050–1750 BC Egyptian Middle Kingdom – c.2000 BC conquered northern Nubia. Hyksos rulers from 1750 BC. • 1650 BC Unification of Anatolian city-states to form Hittite empire.1590 BC Hittites sacked Babylon, but did not pursue their advantage. • 1550 BC Ahmose I reunites Egypt, founding the New Kingdom.	• c.1500 BC Egyptian king Tutmose I defeats Mitanni. • 1350 BC Egyptian king Akenaten introduces heretical worship of the sungod Aten. • c.1300 BC Inconclusive battle between the Egyptians and the Hittites at Kadesh; c.1200 BC fall of Hittite empire. • 1200–1100 BC Sea Peoples destructively active in the Mediterranean; 1186 BC defeated by Egyptians under Ramses III. • c.1100 BC Phoenician trading cities emerging in Levant.	• c.1000 BC Zoroastrianism founded; 550 BC adopted as official Persian religion. • 776 BC First Olympic games. • 771 BC Collapse of centralized Zhou rule in China. • 6th century BC development of Confucianism and Daoism in China and Buddhism in India. • 550 BC Cyrus II founded Persian empire. • 519 BC Romans expel Etruscan kings and found Roman Republic.	• 338 BC Philip II of Macedon becomes master of Greece. • 336–323 BC Conquests of Alexander the Great. • From 264 BC First Punic War between Rome and Carthage. • From 4th century BC warring states of China gradually taken over by Qin state; 221 BC Qin dynasty unite China under Shihuangdi; 202 BC beginning of Han dynasty. • 146 BC Romans win Third Punic War and raze Carthage. • 27 BC Start of Roman Empire.	• 1st century AD Buddhism spreads to China via Silk Road trade route linking Roman, Indian and Chinese empires • AD 116 Roman empire reaches maximum extent. • AD 220 Fall of Han dynasty. • c.AD 320–500 Guptas rule much of India. • AD 350 Huns driven westwards from Chinese borders, menacing India and Europe by 5th century AD. • AD 476 Fall of western Roman empire to barbarian invaders.	• After the death of Mohammed in AD 632, Islam rapidly established over much of Southwest Asia and North Africa. • AD 987 Legendary Toltec ruler Topiltzin traditionally founded Chichén Itzá state in northern Yucatán. • AD 1345 Aztecs founded city of Tenochtitlán; 1427 Aztecs begin conquering neighbours. • AD 1519 Spaniards under Cortés invade Mesoamerica; Aztecs conquered by 1521. • AD 1532 Spaniards under Pizarro destroy Inca empire.

1

PREHISTORY

TAKING OVER THE WORLD

The roots of human civilization can be traced back some 10,000 years – to the very beginnings of agriculture. It was then that many communities started to establish permanent settlements, and from these beginnings there emerged the first urban civilizations, around 5,000 years ago. This is only a tiny fragment of our story, as humans have been around for at least 2 million years. Nevertheless, this small slice of time is the most exciting part of our history, as it was at the moment when humans began to practise agriculture and live in permanent settlements that the pace of change accelerated, leading rapidly to the very different world in which we live today.

How have we reached this point? It is impossible to understand the achievements of recent times without tracing the story back to the very beginning – to the moment when our remote ancestors began to shape their own destiny instead of leaving it to nature.

Previous page. The cultivation of cereals – wheat, barley, millet, rice, maize and others – which began in many parts of the world between 9000 and 1000 BC, revolutionized the way of life of human societies and set in train irreversible changes to the environment.

MIND OVER MATTER

Through time, all living organisms have evolved by adapting to changes in their environment. Humans are no exception to this, although more than any other creature we have adapted not so much by evolving different physical characteristics, but by actually changing our environment to suit ourselves, sometimes for the better, sometimes for the worse.

Early humans began making stone tools more than 2 million years ago. Tools allowed them to perform actions that their lack of claws and their feeble teeth made otherwise impossible – cutting through tough animal hides to get meat, digging up plant tubers and roots and making other tools of wood. They later learned to use fire – to make their food easier to chew and digest, to keep them warm and to ward off dangerous animals. They also began to construct shelters to protect them against cold and heat.

The first humans lived in Africa and were creatures of the tropics. By 1.8 million years ago they had spread well beyond this region, as far as eastern and Southeast Asia, and more than half a million years ago they were living in much cooler areas too, such as northern Europe. Their innovations had already made them phenomenally successful, allowing their populations to grow and making it possible for them to cope with a wide range of climates and environments, many different kinds of

Ten thousand years ago there were only 10 million people in the world. By 2000 BC there were around 100 million, and now there are a staggering 6 billion.

COLONIZATION OF THE WORLD

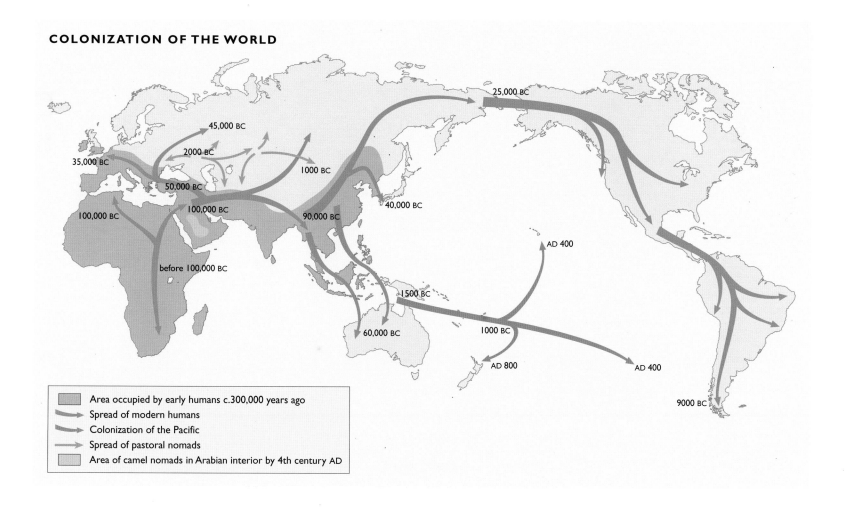

25,000 BC

45,000 BC

2000 BC

35,000 BC

1000 BC

50,000 BC

100,000 BC

40,000 BC

100,000 BC

90,000 BC

before 100,000 BC

AD 400

1500 BC

60,000 BC

1000 BC

AD 800

AD 400

9000 BC

Area occupied by early humans c.300,000 years ago
Spread of modern humans
Colonization of the Pacific
Spread of pastoral nomads
Area of camel nomads in Arabian interior by 4th century AD

plants and animals for food and other uses, and a great variety of natural hazards.

Modern humans

Around 120,000 years ago the first anatomically modern humans developed – people indistinguishable from us and different in some ways, often subtle, from the other types of human that had existed before. Appearing first in Africa, they are believed to have spread also into Asia and Europe. At first they were little different in behaviour from the other humans with whom they coexisted, but they proved capable of rapid and far-reaching innovations. Perhaps as early as 60,000 years ago, and certainly by 50,000, they had colonized Australia – crossing the sea to do so, which means that they were already able to make seaworthy boats. By 40,000 years ago they were beginning to spread throughout Europe and were starting to make new kinds of objects and behave in new ways, reflecting spiritual and social as well as technological needs.

Individuals and society

The period from 40,000 years ago until the end of the last Ice Age around 10,000 BC is known as the Upper Palaeolithic – the last phase of the 'old' Stone Age. It is during this time that we first come face to face with our earliest direct ancestors and can recognize them as people who were as human as ourselves. Chance had preserved the remains of earlier humans, but the Neanderthals probably deliberately buried their dead. The burial practices of modern humans were more systematic than those of their Neanderthal predecessors. They laid the bodies carefully in graves or under heaps of stones or plant material and placed with them things that the deceased might need if they were going to another world – the clothes and

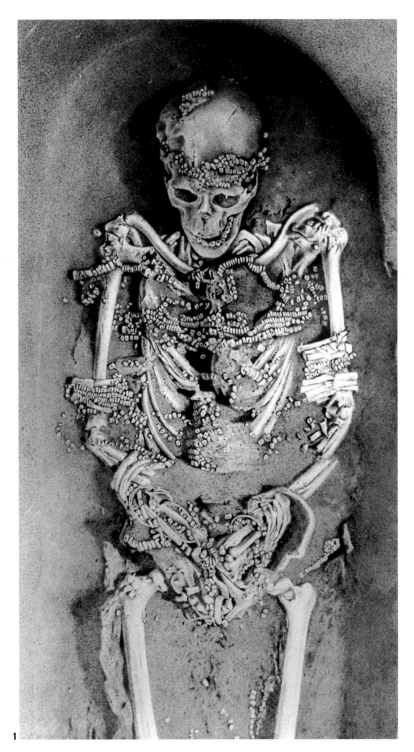

1. The Palaeolithic bodies buried at Sungir in Russia, dated around 23,000 BC, are covered in carved ivory beads. It is likely that originally these were attached to clothing sewn from animal skins, including a cap or hood.

ornaments they wore, the tools they had used and things to eat and drink. Sometimes they scattered red ochre over the body – perhaps symbolically giving new life to the deceased. This implies that they were now thinking of people as individuals and wondering what happened to them after death.

We don't know when earlier humans began to clothe themselves – although it is likely they used skins to keep themselves warm and dry. But these modern humans were certainly making leather clothing, which they cut with sharp stone tools and stitched with bone or ivory needles. They may have dyed these garments, often decorating them by sewing on patterns of shell or bone beads. They also made headdresses, pendants and other jewellery. Like modern fashion, these made a personal statement, showing who people were within their community and which community they belonged to when they encountered other groups.

Tools and technology

Early stone tools had served many purposes, and had remained basically the same for hundreds of thousands of years. Gradually, however, tools became more varied and more specifically designed to do particular jobs. They also became smaller, making them more manageable and using less raw material. The Upper Palaeolithic people made many different tools from long flint blades – knives, spearheads, scrapers, awls and engraving tools. They made others from wood, bone, antler and ivory. Not only were these tools suited to their purpose but, increasingly, they were also a vehicle for artistic expression. Much energy went into producing tools that were beautiful, perfectly shaped and pleasing to look at and to handle, and sometimes decorated. For example, long bone rods used for throwing spears more efficiently often had the hook at the end fashioned into the shape of an animal.

Ice Age homes

Much of the Upper Palaeolithic period coincided with the last Ice Age – a time when world climate was generally colder and drier. Much of the earth's moisture was locked up in the ice sheets that covered substantial parts of Europe, North America and northern Asia, so sea levels were up to 100 m (330 feet) lower and much land that is now underwater was exposed. In the areas of arctic tundra just to the south of the ice sheets, such as France and parts of Russia, people needed shelter from the elements. Caves and rock shelters provided convenient homes, in which other structures were often erected, made from wood, stone and skins. Substantial houses of skins were constructed over mammoth-bone frameworks in eastern Europe and Russia, while in warmer areas or during the summer months, people lived in tents of skin and wood.

2. Palaeolithic people lived in caves and on open-air sites, where shelters were constructed of whatever materials were available. At some sites, such as Mezhirich in the Ukraine, huts were built of skins over a framework of mammoth bones and tusks.

HUNTER-GATHERER LIVES

One of the keys to human success has been the development of an omnivorous diet, making it possible for people to find food in a rich diversity of environments. Our early ancestors scavenged meat from animals killed by other predators, but by half a million years ago people were also hunting game. In the Upper Palaeolithic period hunting was well developed and often involved storage – for example, some groups filleted meat and dried or smoked it so it would keep. Storage made it possible for people to colonize cold northern latitudes around this time.

Often communities concentrated on particular species of animals – reindeer in southern France, mammoth in North America, gazelle in the Middle East, for example. Great herds of these animals generally moved with the seasons in order to find food where it occurred at different times of year. Often the people who hunted them also moved seasonally, following the herds for meat and gathering plant foods, such as fruits, berries, leaves, seeds and tubers, available in different regions at different times of year. Fish, such as salmon, might also have been part of the diet.

Seasonal migrations not only maintained a year-round food supply but also had other advantages. They would have brought together different communities, allowing them to renew kinship and friendship ties and to cement these with new marriages. Seasonal movement also gave people access to useful raw materials such as stone for tools, either directly when source areas were visited or indirectly by exchange of gifts when communities met up.

An unbroken thread

In some parts of the world, such as northern Europe, these seasonal migrations involved movements over long distances. In other areas, the distances travelled might be far smaller, and in regions of particular abundance, human groups might not have had to move at all. This hunter-gatherer way of life, in all its diversity, was universal until around 8000 BC, when farming began to develop in some regions.

Gradually farming took over as the main way of getting food over much of the globe, and in some regions hunter-gatherers were

 STONE AGE ARTISTS

Many Upper Palaeolithic works of art served as tools, but there were also many objects made that were not functional. These may reflect the religious beliefs of these Palaeolithic people – the 'Venus figurines', such as the one illustrated, representing mother goddesses and a fertility cult, for example – but we cannot know for certain what they signified.

The same is true of the magnificent paintings and engravings created by these people on the walls of caves and rock shelters or portable plaques of stone or bone. Some small engravings on wood or ivory rods may have been calendars, devices for counting the days in a lunar cycle or recognizing the approach of individual seasons. Such information would have been important for planning – for instance, marking when to prepare for a seasonal migration following herds of animals that they hunted or for the arrival of spawning salmon.

Other pieces of art may have played a role in different parts of life. Engravings found deep in the inaccessible recesses of cave complexes may have been created for ceremonies initiating children into adulthood. The art on cave and rock-shelter walls is justly famous – magnificent paintings of bulls and bison, horses and other animals such as lions and rhinos, bring vividly to life the world in which our ancestors lived.

eventually pushed into marginal areas, such as the Kalahari Desert, where farming was not possible. In some areas, notably India, a symbiosis between hunter-gatherer and farmer developed, farmers providing grain, domestic animals and manufactured goods in exchange for forest products such as honey that the hunter-gatherers could more easily collect. But in many areas, such as North America and Australia, hunting and gathering remained the main way of life into recent times.

Surviving or historically documented hunter-gatherer groups give us some insight into the way of life of our ancestors (though the ways of coping with any environment are legion and so no human society is ever identical to any other in the lifestyle it adopts. Modern Inuit (Eskimos) allow us to glimpse

the problems encountered by our Ice Age ancestors and suggest ways they may have dealt with them. Australian Aborigines reveal the strategies, skills and ingenuity needed to win a living from the hostile arid interior of their continent. Nineteenth-century records of Pacific coast Native Americans show the richness of a sedentary hunter-gatherer life made possible by the seasonal abundance of migratory fish, particularly salmon.

Apart from the sculptures known as 'Venus figurines', Palaeolithic artists rarely depicted people. Paintings usually concentrated on the impressive animals that shared their world.

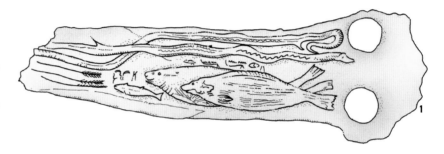

1. In this 'rolled-out' version of the decoration on a baton from Montgaudier in France, characteristic features of spring are shown, such as a salmon coming up-river to spawn, and animals paired for mating.

2. Although the rock art of France and Spain is best known, the Palaeolithic period was a time of prolific artistic creativity worldwide. In southern Africa, from which this painting of men and kudus comes, the tradition continued into recent times.

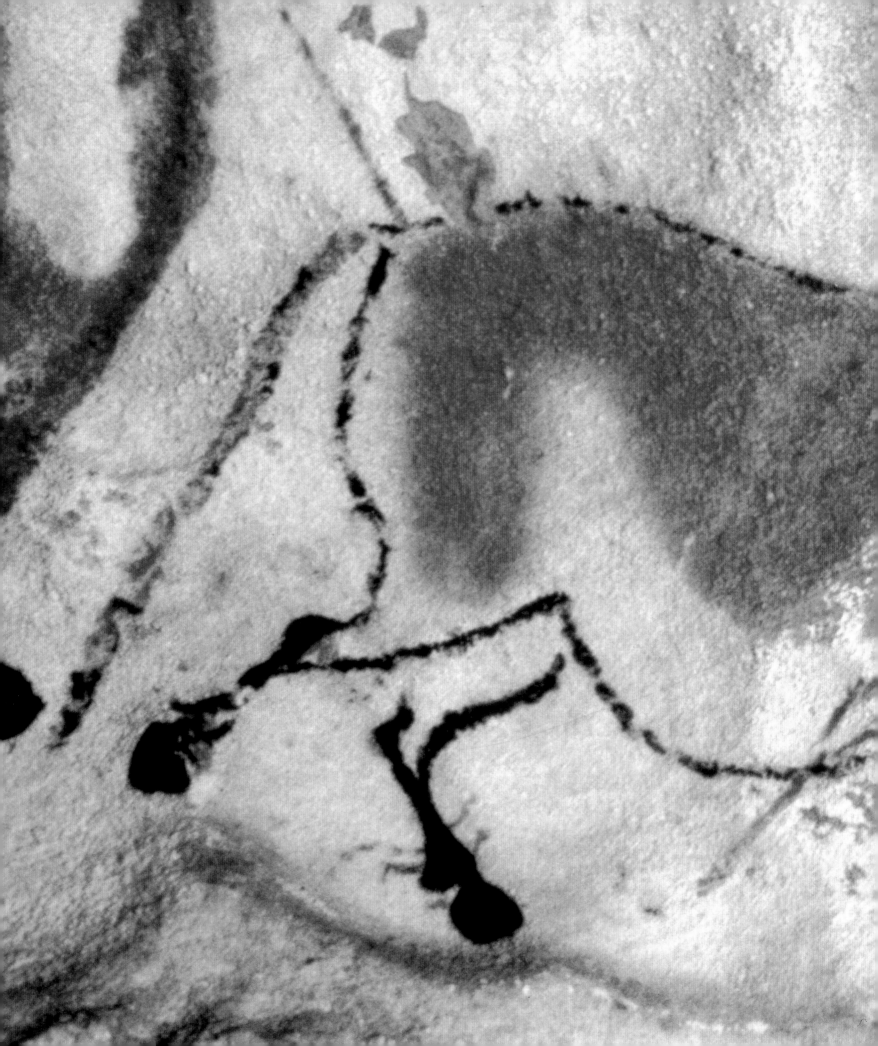

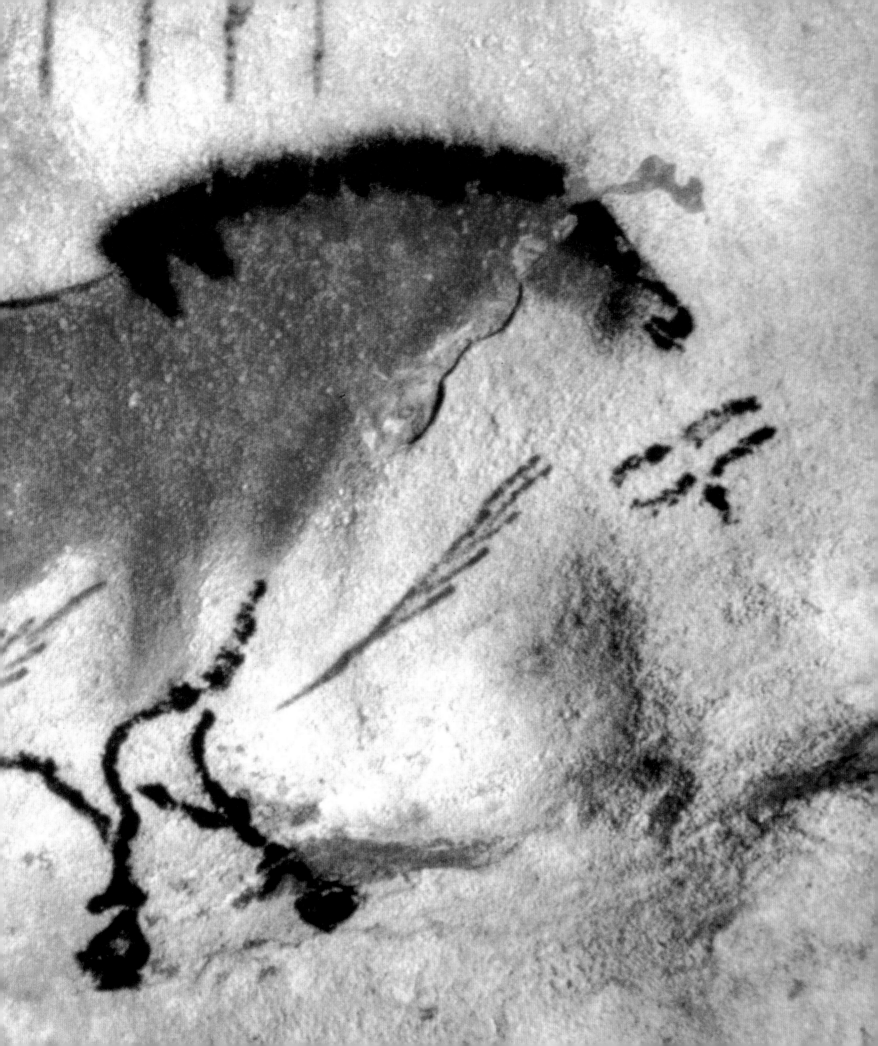

Previous page. Ice Age masterpieces such as this horse from Lascaux in France convey the impression of power and movement in a few simple lines and blocks of colour, using natural pigments including charcoal and red ochre.

1. There are still many groups in the modern world, including the Australian Aborigines, whose livelihood depends on wild resources such as game, wild plants, insects, birds and fish, and who therefore move with the seasons, with few permanent possessions. **1**

COLONIZING THE GLOBE

The first humans were few in number and confined to certain parts of Africa, but populations rapidly grew, due to our success in devising technologies to overcome our physical limitations. By 1.8 million years ago humans had spread out of Africa as far as China, Java and the Caucasus, later colonizing much of Europe. Modern humans repeated the process after 100,000 years ago, becoming established throughout Europe (outside the glacial regions of the north) by 40,000 years ago. Asia was also colonized and from there people reached across the sea to Australia. Gradually they also moved into the cold regions of northern Asia and towards America.

At the height of the glacial conditions the lowered sea level exposed a land bridge across what is now the Bering Strait between Siberia and Alaska. This land bridge, known as Beringia, linked the Asian and American continents, so gradually people also colonized the extreme north of America. However, a massive ice sheet covered the northern part of North America, blocking the way further south.

It was probably only when the ice sheets began to melt, around 12,000 BC, that it was possible for people to move south into the Americas. Once the opportunity arose, however, their spread was extremely rapid, colonists reaching the southern tip, Tierra del Fuego, by or before 9000 BC.

Big-game hunting

European settlers recorded a hunting strategy, now vanished, but practised on the North American plains for thousands of years. Although generally small parties hunted a few animals at a time, on occasion a number of tribes or groups would come together for a bison drive. An advance party would locate a herd and by careful movement slowly drive the bison into a restricted area. Here many other hunters lay in wait, ready to stampede

the herd when it was in position. The panicked animals were then driven into a natural trap: into a dead-end gorge or over a cliff, for instance. Hundreds of animals were killed. The rest of the assembled tribespeople waited around the kill site, ready to swoop in to butcher the animals, stripping off and treating the hides, roasting some of the meat and preserving the rest. Similar game drives are known from other parts of the world – in the Levant and probably Europe towards the end of the last Ice Age, for example.

Penetrating the extremes

Although the first colonists of the Americas were accustomed to a cold environment, the Arctic was initially too hostile. Over many thousand years, however, dwellers in the extreme north developed technologies that gave them mastery over this icy region, even enabling them to hunt large sea mammals in the polar waters. In equivalent latitudes of Asia and Europe, now separated from the Americas by the postglacial rise in sea levels, other human groups like the Lapps also developed a way of life suited to the frozen north. Elsewhere, other difficult regions were gradually conquered. The domestication of the horse made it possible for herders to move into the steppes of Central Asia by 1500 BC, exploiting its scattered pastures. Camels, domesticated in North Africa by the 7th century BC, later opened up the deserts of North Africa and Arabia to herders and traders.

The coasts of Australia and New Guinea had been colonized by 50,000 years ago, and over the millennia people adapted their way of life to settle in the interiors – the deserts of Australia and New Guinea's mountains. People also settled on surrounding islands, developing their seafaring skills in the process. From 1500 BC they began to colonize the scattered islands of the Pacific, reaching the farthest, the Chatham Islands off New Zealand, by AD 1000. The Antarctic to the south was too inhospitable for human life until the development of 20th-century technology.

The 20th century also saw the first venture of humans beyond the earth, landing people on the moon. Human ingenuity has overcome our physical limitations and devised the means to maintain human life in environments that are ever more different from that in which our ancestors evolved. It is this ingenuity that has got us to where we are, and that leads us on into the future.

PACIFIC VOYAGERS

Around 1500 BC, people were living in the Pacific islands as far east as the Solomon Islands. A new wave of colonists now began to move out from the Philippines, reaching New Caledonia, Fiji and Samoa within 500 years. These people were skilled navigators so seafood played a large part in their diet, but they also kept domestic animals – pigs, dogs and chickens – and grew garden crops such as taro (a plant with edible roots), bananas and breadfruit. They made attractive pottery with stamped decorations, but stopped doing so about 2,000 years ago.

By this time, settlers had also reached eastern Micronesia. The islands of eastern Polynesia, tiny dots scattered over a vast area of open sea, were progressively settled over the following centuries – the Marquesas and Society Islands by 150 BC, Easter Island and Hawaii by AD 400 and New Zealand by AD 800. The settlement of the Pacific was a staggering achievement. Colonizing expeditions were sent out from settled islands in large outrigger canoes (small examples are shown right): they carried not only men and women but also their plants and animals. They sailed into the unknown, relying on their intimate understanding of ocean currents, winds, wave and cloud patterns, the stars and the movements of birds and other natural phenomena to enable them to find other islands.

STONE TOOLS

Our ancestors began using deliberately shaped stone tools at least 2 million years ago, and they doubtless made and used tools of wood and bone as well. However, stone tools provide most of the available physical evidence about early human culture, because stone endures the ravages of time almost unchanged while wood and bone soon decay. Broken stone remained the only source of a strong, sharp cutting edge until bronze tools were developed in western Asia around 3200 BC and later in other parts of the world (▷ pp. 44–5). It is important to realize that all the basic elements of civilization – cities, writing and even metalworking – were developed by societies that were still largely dependent on stone tools.

2

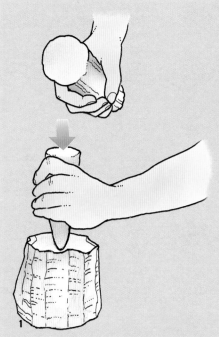

1. Indirect percussion – hitting a punch set against the stone core instead of striking the stone directly – gave the stoneworker greater control, allowing him to create long, parallel-sided blades.

Hunters' toolkits

For most of the prehistoric period, stone tools were mostly associated with the main activity of obtaining food, usually by the hunting and butchering of large animals. By about 40,000 years ago modern humans had developed an efficient and portable stone technology based on chipping away a series of sharp blades from a carefully shaped core of suitable stone. These blades could be made and used straightaway to skin and slice up an animal carcass, or they could be modified to produce specialized tools such as projectile points, scrapers for removing hair from animal hides, or borers for making holes.

Stone-working skills steadily improved, and by about 20,000 years ago some groups were producing exquisitely fashioned spear heads, each one painstakingly shaped by pressing the edge with a piece of deer antler to remove small flakes of stone.

Towards the end of the Ice Age (about 14,000–10,000 BC), as people in many parts of the world began exploiting a greater variety of food sources, there was a further development in stone-blade technology. Instead of producing a few large blades, the stone workers now concentrated on producing thousands of small, sharp blades, which could be embedded in wooden handles to make a wide variety of tools. One of the most important of these was a long knife (often curved) for harvesting wild cereals.

Farmers' tools

Exploiting cereals also required the development of an entirely new stone tool – the grindstone – to process the hard, ripened grain into a more digestible form. This tool consisted of a large stone tray on which grain was placed and then crushed and ground with a smaller rounded stone.

The adoption of a settled lifestyle, which is marked by the development of heavy and

cumbersome grindstones, stimulated a further development of stone working. Some stone tools, especially axes, were now shaped by slow grinding and polishing. This technique produced a much stronger edge than that produced by chipping or flaking. It was mainly the polished stone axe that was responsible for the rapid clearance of Europe's forest cover (some 25 per cent by 4000 BC) as agriculture spread across the continent. Some of these polished axes became prestige items, and are found in burials.

In Eurasia, stone tools were generally replaced by the introduction of bronze and then iron, although this process of change was much more rapid in some regions than others. In the Americas, however, metal remained a rare, prestige material, and stone tools were in everyday use right up to the Spanish conquest.

Material value
The most commonly used material for stone tools was flint, a hard, fine-grained rock that is widely distributed across the globe, occurring as pebbles in rivers and on beaches, and as nodules in softer rock. However, good flint

may be scarce locally, and 'tool-quality' stone sometimes had to be obtained from sources 50 km (30 miles) or more distant.

A much rarer material was obsidian, a type of volcanic glass that can be worked to an extremely sharp edge. Deposits of this highly prized dark stone were a valuable resource, and in both Eurasia and the Americas obsidian was distributed over networks extending for hundreds of kilometres.

2. The earliest cutting tools were simply broken pebbles with sharp edges; but more than a million years ago our ancestors began making elegantly shaped handaxes.

3. This pre-dynastic Egyptian ceremonial flint knife demonstrates the superb craft skills of ancient workers in stone.

4. Jade and greenstone are very hard and have been valued by many societies. Often they were used to make ceremonial tools and weapons, like this adze used by a Maori (New Zealand) chief.

FIRST AGRICULTURAL REVOLUTION

About 10,000 years ago, in the region of the Near East known as the Fertile Crescent, people began to develop a new relationship with a few plants, particularly wheat and barley. For the first time, these plants became more than just a convenient source of food to be gathered from the wild. Now they were tamed and gradually altered to suit human requirements – they became domesticated. In different parts of the region, the same process was successfully applied to various wild animals. Later, people in other areas of the world, including China, the Americas and parts of Africa, independently domesticated a variety of other food plants and animals. Farming also spread into many other regions. The development and use of domesticated plants and animals, often called the Neolithic Revolution, marked the beginning of a whole new way of life as people settled down in permanent villages – the first step towards civilization.

THE ORIGINS OF AGRICULTURE

Farming began after the last Ice Age. This not only places the event in time, it is also an explanation. When the glaciers began to melt about 12,000 years ago, huge quantities of fresh water that had been locked up as ice were released into the biosphere. As average temperatures rose, rainfall increased and vegetation flourished. Ten thousand years ago much of the area bordering the Sahara Desert was a region of grassland, woodland and even swamps.

The general improvement in conditions enabled some hunter-gatherer groups to adopt a settled existence in particularly lush environments where food and water were plentiful. The most favoured locations were those that gave easy access to more than one type of habitat (a hillside on the edge of a valley, for example), because a wide variety of foodstuffs was a safeguard against seasonal variations and sudden shortages. Nevertheless, some groups came to depend on one or two food sources in particular. Some coastal groups, for example on the Pacific coast of North America, caught huge numbers of fish during the spawning season, while others were able to concentrate on nutritious plant foods, such as the seeds of certain local grasses.

Adopting a settled existence changed the nature of the food-supply problems facing the group. In most parts of the world plant and animal productivity is seasonal. Fruit, seeds, and easy-to-catch young animals are only available for a few months each year. Instead of travelling with the seasons, a settled group had to have food available locally at all times. The best solution to this problem was to gather seasonally abundant foods that could be stored for up to a year. Plant products in general, and seeds in particular, store much better than animal products,

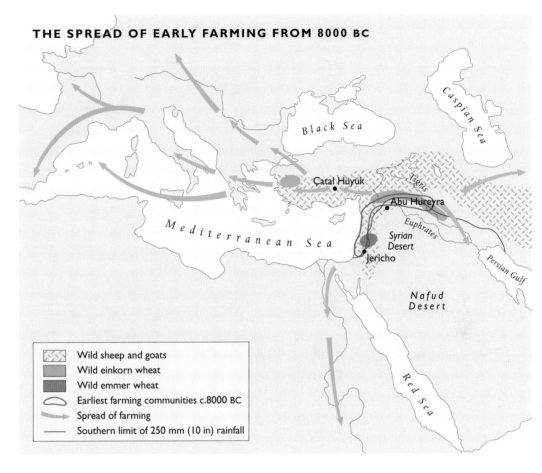

THE SPREAD OF EARLY FARMING FROM 8000 BC

Legend:
- Wild sheep and goats
- Wild einkorn wheat
- Wild emmer wheat
- Earliest farming communities c.8000 BC
- Spread of farming
- Southern limit of 250 mm (10 in) rainfall

which tend to decay quickly unless specially treated. Cereals (grass seeds) were a much better bet for long-term survival than dried fish or venison.

Population pressures

As long as food continued to be plentiful, these newly settled communities flourished and more children were born. When food supplies were interrupted by bad weather or some other natural mishap, those communities with the best food selection and storage strategies tended to survive while others failed.

At some point, and certainly dozens of times in dozens of places, people began to apply rudimentary farming skills. They kept other plants (now regarded as weeds) from

choking their food plants, or even from using their precious water; they stopped a variety of insects, rodents and birds (pests) from eating their food, either in the fields or when stored; and they learned to tame wild animals caught when young. They also began applying their knowledge that seeds could be planted where they didn't grow before, to produce additional food.

By planting and tending their chosen crops, successful groups could grow enough food to feed additional mouths, and populations increased way beyond levels that could be sustained by hunting and gathering. Groups that depended on particular crops, especially if they enhanced productivity by rudimentary farming, became trapped in the new artificial lifestyles they had created. The trap would soon be tightened by the development of the first 'unnatural' life forms – domesticated plants and animals – which were dependent on humans.

Hard work

The development of farming was never an easy option. The transition from food collectors to food producers meant working harder for every mouthful. To nomads, children were a necessary hindrance, almost a luxury; to farmers, children were just small workers and were treated accordingly.

There were other unpleasant surprises in store. People living permanently, and unnaturally, in the same place enabled diseases to develop and spread among them. When they began keeping domestic animals, they caught some of their diseases too. Their diets, which depended on one or two foods, were not as healthy as those of their hunter-gatherer ancestors – for example, tooth decay and abscesses became much more common – and food production and preparation put unnatural strains on their bodies. To add to their woes, settlements with a good store of food attracted the attentions of hungry outsiders. All in all, farming represented a hard-work, high-risk strategy compared with hunting and gathering.

Tools, culture and trade

The beginning of agriculture has been described as the 'Neolithic (New Stone Age) Revolution'. However, the tools and implements used by early farmers were those developed by their ancestors. Two smooth stones were as good for grinding cultivated grain as for grinding grain gathered from the wild; and digging sticks that uprooted plants could be modified into spades or hoes for their nurture. In several parts of the world people devised special long knives, often curved, for cutting through plant stems when harvesting a crop – the first sickles.

In other aspects of life, change was more evident. Dwellings became more weatherproof and more spacious as settlements grew in size and experience; and pottery – too heavy and fragile for peoples on the move – soon became a mainstay of food storage and preparation. Change took place in people's spiritual lives as well as their physical lives. The development or adoption of agriculture seems to have shifted people's perceptions of themselves. No longer part of the natural flow across the landscape, they now found themselves engaged in a life-or-death struggle

DOMESTICATION

Plants were domesticated through a process of unnatural selection. By choosing plants with the biggest edible grains to provide the next year's seed, farmers learned to improve the yield of their crops. But grain size was not the only important factor. Wild grasses must scatter their seeds easily. Human farmers, however, wanted seeds that would stay on the stems while they were harvested and transported back to the farm.

Some natural mutations of wheat produced seeds that stayed on the stem. These were selected by early farmers, and what had started as an occasional mutation gradually became established as a characteristic of cultivated wheat. This could only reproduce successfully with human assistance, by being harvested and then sown; in the wild, domesticated wheat could not compete with wild plants that spread their seed easily.

Animals were also selected for breeding, and again productivity was not the only aim. Early stock breeders learned to select for early maturity in order to produce animals that were not as large, aggressive or dangerous as adult wild animals. In the process, the animals became less able to evade predators and fend for themselves than their wild ancestors, and more dependent on human care.

with their immediate environment, which was interpreted in new ways. Many early farming settlements set up permanent shrines and produced large numbers of figurines, often of 'mother goddesses' and apparently 'sacred' animals.

Initially early farming settlements were almost completely self-sufficient, but as the habit of living in settlements became more widespread, so did interactions between them. Decorated pottery might be exchanged with neighbours for surplus animals, or for some bunches of tasty herbs that had in turn been traded from even further away. Among the most commonly traded commodities at this time were a few highly specialized, domesticated plants and animals, in addition to items such as flint, obsidian and shell. Everywhere that farming first emerged, it took firm root and spread rapidly.

THE 'FERTILE CRESCENT': THE WILD CEREAL BELT

As well as experiencing very favourable climatic conditions following the end of the last Ice Age, the region of western Asia arcing from the Levant across the Euphrates and Tigris rivers to the Zagros Mountains had an unusually high number of plant and animal species that were suitable for domestication.

By about 8000 BC, barley and two varieties of wheat (known as einkorn and emmer) had been domesticated, possibly in the western part of the region, and shortly afterwards pulses such as broad beans, chickpeas, lentils and peas were established as crops. The first animals were domesticated by peoples who had already adopted domesticated crops. Experts are now agreed that animal domestication (pastoral farming) did not develop independently of crop cultivation (arable farming). Sheep and goats were first herded in the mountains of western Iran around 7500 BC, and cattle were domesticated about a thousand years later, possibly in Anatolia (modern Asiatic Turkey).

The most famous of the early farming settlements is the village of Jericho just to the north of the Dead Sea. By about 7500 BC Jericho was surrounded with a high stone wall with a watch tower. The inhabitants of the village followed the traditions of their ancestors, who had harvested wild cereals with curved sickles edged with sharp flakes of stone. They lived in small beehive-shaped huts with sunken floors, beneath which they buried their dead.

Through trial and error, the early farmers in western Asia established a mixed-farming 'package', consisting of one or two cereals and pulses plus herds of sheep and goats.

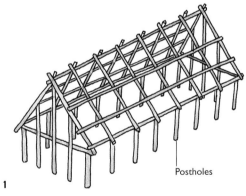

Postholes

1

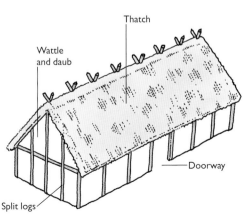

Thatch

Wattle and daub

Doorway

Split logs

2

1. Longhouses built by the first farmers in Central Europe were not only dwellings for people but also included stalls for their animals.

2. A massive tower was built in the wall surrounding ancient Jericho, providing a view over the countryside around and inspiring awe in visitors.

POTTERY

Pottery – vessels and containers made of baked clay – was once considered to be a universal indicator of agriculture. In fact, pottery was made and used by people when they needed it: many peoples have farmed without pottery, while others have made pottery without being farmers.

The earliest true pottery was actually made by a hunter-gatherer people – the Jomon of Japan – around 11,000 BC. The technology of baking clay goes back much earlier: baked-clay figurines had been made by various Palaeolithic (early Stone Age) groups in Europe and Asia since about 25,000 BC.

Early potting techniques
In general, because of its fragility and its primary use as a method of food storage, pottery is associated with a settled lifestyle. Pottery came into fairly widespread use in the Middle East, northern Africa and central China between 8000 and 7000 BC. The earliest American pottery was made in the Amazon basin in around 5000 BC.

All early pots were made in the same way, by slowly building up a container from lengths of wet clay that were carefully smoothed together inside and out. The finished pot might then be decorated in a number of ways before being fired overnight. Often they copied the shape of baskets or wooden containers. One popular method was to wind cord around the unfired pot to leave an impressed spiral design. Other decorative techniques involved scraping lines into the surface of the pot with shells or combs. Some pots, perhaps with a ritual purpose, were sculpted to resemble animals or other natural forms.

Pots were also painted, either before or after firing, and this gave craft workers much greater scope for their creativity. Most early painted designs are purely abstract, but food animals such as antelopes and goats were often represented. As societies evolved, they developed their own distinctive traditions of pottery making and decoration. These traditions were remarkably conservative, and a sudden change in pottery style is often interpreted by archaeologists as evidence of invasion or conquest.

The potter's wheel
About 4500 BC the slow wheel (or turntable) was developed in northern Mesopotamia. The slow wheel enabled potters to rotate their work in front of them, but pots were still built up from pieces of clay in the traditional manner. The introduction of the fast wheel in around 3500 BC was, however, a major breakthrough.

Powered by the potter's feet, the fast wheel could be turned fast enough for a potter to 'throw' a pot from a single piece of clay. In addition to speeding up production, the fast wheel also permitted the production of a wider variety of shapes, all of them elegantly symmetrical. The new wheel was so efficient that it required a team of workers to make the best use of it, and this no doubt encouraged the development of specialist pottery workshops in larger settlements.

Other methods of pottery production were also developed by the early civilizations. In some cities of Mesopotamia (roughly modern Iraq), pots were mass-produced in moulds to make disposable ration bowls. Moulds were also used to make decorative handles and other embellishments, which were applied to pots before firing.

1. The potter operated the fast wheel or 'kick-wheel' by rotating it with his foot, allowing him to shape the pot evenly as it turned. This efficient device was widely used and continued in use into recent times, virtually unchanged.

2

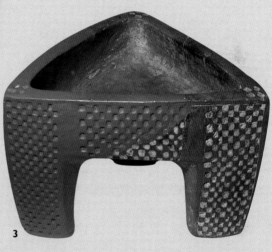

3

2. An infinite variety of geometric and naturalistic painted designs were used to decorate pottery, like this early dish from Arpachiya in Mesopotamia.

3. As well as containers, pottery was made into many different objects, such as figurines and this pottery altar from Neolithic Karanovo in the Balkans.

Pottery and trade

After the introduction of metals, pottery was generally replaced in the houses of the wealthy by vessels of bronze, silver or even gold. Most people, however, continued to make do with pottery.

Cooking pots were usually made locally, perhaps even within the household, although fine-quality tableware might be obtained from further afield. The Roman Samian ware, which made extensive use of moulded decoration, was produced in two great factories in Italy and southern France, and exported throughout the Roman empire. Glazed tableware from the imperial factories of Han China was distributed over a similarly wide area.

Pottery containers were also a mainstay of many other export industries. Countless numbers of pottery amphorae (tall, narrow-necked jars) were made to carry wine and olive oil around the ancient world, and many other substances – from perfume to fish sauce – were traded in specially made pots.

⭐ Poppies were among the first medicinal plants, cultivated in southern Europe by 5000 BC for their pain-relieving sap.

1. The earliest sheep kept by Near Eastern farmers were similar in appearance to goats. Only later were they bred to produce the now-familiar thick woolly coats.

2. Zebu cattle like these were bred from the indigenous cattle of India, while those of the Near East and Europe were descended from the massive and ferocious aurochs.

Village farmers

With good soils and climate, mixed farming could meet nearly all of a village's basic needs. This can be seen, for example, at the village of Abu Hureyra, near the upper course of the Euphrates river, which was rebuilt in about 7000 BC. Previously the inhabitants had farmed cereals, but had obtained their meat from wild gazelles. After the rebuilding, however, most of their meat came from domesticated sheep and goats. In the new village, rectangular mud-brick houses, separated by lanes and courtyards, replaced the older round huts. The interiors of the new houses were plastered, and sometimes decorated with coloured designs.

The basic mixed-farming package was so successful that by 5000 BC it had spread right across western Asia, and beyond. In the west, agriculture was well-established in Anatolia and the Balkans, and pioneer farmers were beginning to colonize central Europe. In the east, farming had expanded onto the Iranian plateau and into Afghanistan and Central Asia.

EARLY AGRICULTURE IN OTHER REGIONS

Beyond West Asia there were fewer plants and animals suitable for domestication. Nevertheless, the general improvement in global climatic conditions led to the independent development of agriculture in several parts of the world in a relatively short period.

By about 6500 BC early farmers in northern China had domesticated the foxtail and broomcorn millets that grew on fertile soils produced by melting glaciers. By 5000 BC people lived in villages of small, semi-underground houses made of hammered earth. Pigs, probably domesticated locally, were the main farm animal; sheep, cattle and goats never became very important in China. Rice was probably domesticated before 6000 BC, on the Yangzi River; it was cultivated using bone spades fixed to wooden handles.

In the Americas, early farmers in Peru had by 6500 BC domesticated beans, squash and peppers. By 4000 BC they also had domestic guinea pigs and llamas. In Mesoamerica, though some domesticated plants were used by hunting groups, the farming lifestyle took longer to become established. Maize was grown here by about 4000 BC but initially the cobs were tiny. By 2000 BC, however, natural genetic mutations – probably amplified by human intervention through selective breeding – led to maize becoming the basis of a permanently settled lifestyle.

In India and Egypt, agricultural techniques were initially imported from West Asia around 6000 BC, although India also domesticated local plants and animals such as sesame, zebu cattle and water buffalo. In these six regions where agriculture was first developed and organized – the Fertile Crescent, China, South America, Mesoamerica, India and Egypt – the world's primary civilizations developed and grew.

 ÇATAL HÜYÜK

During the initial spread of farming, settlements generally remained small – no more than a few dozen houses. Especially favourable circumstances could, however, produce exceptions to this rule. In the Konya Basin of what is now central Turkey, the early farming village of Çatal Hüyük grew unusually large because it was able to exploit local deposits of highly desirable obsidian, a rare volcanic glass that gives a fine cutting edge. The miners and stone workers of Çatal Hüyük supplied high-quality stone tools, and other items such as polished obsidian mirrors, to most of the other villages within a 300-km (190-mile) radius.

By 6000 BC Çatal Hüyük contained hundreds of mud-brick houses built very closely alongside each other. The inhabitants no doubt spent the daylight hours in the fields and used the open rooftops for storage and for moving around the settlement, and as a place to sleep in the summer. In addition to their food crops and animals, the villagers also tended fields of flax, from which they wove linen cloth. They were also among the first to adopt copper metallurgy in about 5500 BC.

The religion of Çatal Hüyük has aroused considerable interest. Several of the buildings in the village appear to have contained shrine rooms, decorated with paintings and sculptures of cattle horns, female figures and birth images. Although the details of the religion remain obscure, the imagery suggests a focus on agricultural and human fertility, productivity and growth.

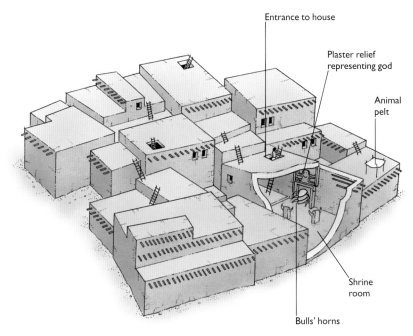

Entrance to house

Plaster relief representing god

Animal pelt

Shrine room

Bulls' horns

1

★ The first farmers in the Indo-Iranian borderlands used baskets lined with bitumen for storage, long before they started making pottery.

AGRICULTURE – THE SECOND REVOLUTION

During the period 5000–3000 BC, agriculture in the Fertile Crescent intensified and was transformed from a subsistence activity into an industry. This transformation was marked by a series of innovations, many of them involving domestic animals. Some animals entered into a new relationship with humans, becoming much more than a handy source of meat and hides.

Perhaps the most important innovation was the 'discovery' of animal power. People realized that animals such as cattle and donkeys could not only carry loads tied to their backs, but that they could also pull ards (primitive ploughs). Animals could also pull sleds, and – after their invention in around 3500 BC – the first wheeled wagons. Animal power increased the energy that could be applied to farming and increased the distances that goods could travel.

Around 4000 BC some farmers in Mesopotamia (the lands watered by the Tigris and Euphrates rivers, in what is now Iraq)

developed dairying and the technology needed to make butter and cheese. As well as greatly extending the range of foods obtainable from cattle, sheep and goats (and consequently their value), dairying also provided a method of storing animal protein, such as butter and cheese, in a form other than preserved meat.

The value of sheep was increased even further when wool became a major agricultural commodity after 3400 BC. Until that time sheepskins were like goatskins – good for leather when the animal was killed. The development of woolly sheep, with a thick coat that could be sheared annually, provided a ready source of a wonderful new high-value textile (▷ pp. 216–17).

Cash crops

Along the Levant coast, olives and figs were domesticated by about 3000 BC, and vine cultivation was developed into a fine art. All three crops provided highly desirable products with good storage properties, which made them excellent trading commodities and a means to

1. This stone mosaic frieze from Tell Ubaid in Mesopotamia, dated around 2500 BC, shows cows with their calves and men milking them – early evidence of dairy farming which provided important new sources of food such as milk and cheese.

accumulate wealth and support dependants such as artisans and soldiers.

Outside the Fertile Crescent, other innovations occurred. In both Peru and India cotton was domesticated by about 3500 BC, while in China silkworms and the mulberry trees they feed on were domesticated a little later, creating further high-value textile industries. In southern Russia horses were domesticated in around 4000 BC, initially for meat, although later they would become one of the main sources of animal power. In the Andes llamas and alpacas were also domesticated around 4000 BC, providing wool and later being used as pack animals.

Some of these innovations, such as wheeled vehicles, spread very rapidly – wagons were being used in Switzerland only 500 years after they were invented – while others, such as silk, remained geographically confined. In many cases, the effect of what has been called the 'Secondary Products Revolution', was to accelerate those tendencies in societies, such as the accumulation of wealth and the centralization of control, that were driving them towards civilization.

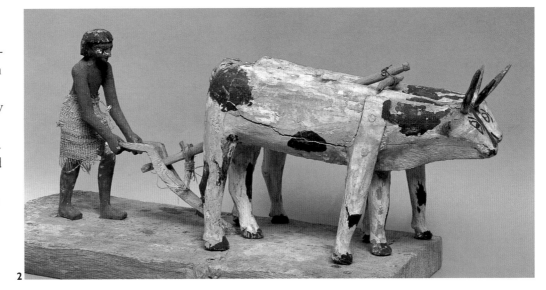

2

3

2. Using animals to pull ploughs (as in this Egyptian model), two-wheeled carts, sledges and four-wheeled wagons increased the efficiency of agriculture.

3. Przewalski's horses, the closest living relatives of the wild creatures from which horses were domesticated – a development which opened up the steppe region to human exploitation.

WATER AND INTENSIVE FARMING

Agriculture began where the water needed for crop growth occurred naturally – on the margins of lakes or rivers and in areas where rain fell in sufficient quantity at the right time of year. As farming spread and more and more people became dependent on it, people began to move into areas where these conditions were not fulfilled. To grow crops in these more arid places and maintain yields in areas where water supplies were adequate but unreliable, people developed various techniques of irrigation.

Providing water...

The simplest means of irrigation were employed first. Various methods were used in different parts of the world. In the Oaxaca valley of southern Mexico shallow wells were dug and the water carried in pots to the plants. At a few early sites in central Mesopotamia small channels were dug to bring water to the fields from rivers or streams.

Building on their experience, people then began to construct more complex systems of irrigation – networks of canals to channel and store the waters from the seasonal inundations of major rivers like the Euphrates and the Nile. Where water was available at the wrong time of year or would rapidly flow away, they learned to build dams and reservoirs. Some cultures, like the Romans, built aqueducts to bring water over long distances, while others, including the Chinese and the people of Sri Lanka, built sophisticated networks of canals for the same purpose.

... and taking it away

In some regions, however, the problem was not too little water but too much. Most crops require adequate drainage. The seasonal floods of the Tigris and Euphrates in Mesopotamia came at the wrong time of year – just as harvest approached – and it was necessary to divert the flood waters using canals. The water was then stored to irrigate the following season's crops.

In many regions of Central and South America, such as the Maya lands, ingenious systems were devised to drain fertile swamps. A network of drainage channels defined small, square garden plots whose surface was raised above the water level by piling on the silt from the channels – adding greatly to their fertility. A bonus of this system was that fish could be farmed in the channels.

1

2

Raising water

Water for irrigation usually had to be lifted from wells or channels to get it onto the fields. It is hard work to lift water by hand, and many devices were invented to make the task easier, such as the shaduf and Archimedes' screw. Animals could be harnessed to a wheel that raised a string of buckets; sometimes the power to drive such a wheel was provided by flowing water.

Worth it or not?

Irrigation not only allowed new areas to be cultivated, but also raised productivity. Yields were higher than with rain-fed agriculture since the amount of water provided was controllable – and often it was possible to raise two or even three crops a year on the same piece of ground. More people could therefore be supported from a given piece of land. But of course it was harder work than simple agriculture – productivity was higher, but more effort was required for every unit of output. Canals and dams had to be constructed and maintained. In some regions, such as southern Mesopotamia, constant irrigation caused the deposition of salts that eventually rendered the land uncultivable. Permanent bodies of water also encouraged mosquitoes to breed, spreading malaria.

Not all land is equally suitable for irrigation. Contrasts in land values promoted competition and conflict, and were closely associated with developing differences in social status. Disputes also arose over the use and maintenance of canals, and in some places, such as Mesopotamia and Sri Lanka, officials were appointed to deal with such matters. In indirect ways such as these irrigation and water control led to changes in societies.

3

1. This Assyrian relief shows a shaduf being used to raise water from a lower to a higher channel.

2. The shaduf's bucket is pulled down into the water. The heavy counterweight on the other end of the pole raises the full bucket when it is released.

3. Floating gardens and raised fields are still used in the Americas. Silt dredged from their drainage channels maintain their high fertility.

2

CITIES AND STATES

A momentous development in world history took place between 4000 and 2500 BC – the emergence of the first cities. The increasing sophistication of agriculture – for example, the use of irrigation and of draught animals – had enabled populations to grow in certain areas. At the same time, societies became more structured, reflecting the wider range of interactions between people, while settlements grew not only in size but also in complexity.

By 2500 BC urban civilizations had emerged in Mesopotamia, Egypt and the Indus valley, and slightly later in China. Over the centuries states rose and fell in these areas, while in other regions new civilizations appeared – the Hittites in Anatolia, the Minoans and Mycenaeans in the Aegean. Farmers and pastoralists moved into new areas, such as the Asiatic steppes, while new skills and technologies opened up other opportunities, such as long-distance trade and communications.

Previous page. The 'standard of Ur' is perhaps the sounding box from a musical instrument. Made of lapis lazuli set in bitumen and inlaid with shell, one side depicts Ur's victorious army, while this side shows the subsequent celebrations.

ON THE BRINK

Early agriculture in the Near East was initially confined to areas where annual rainfall was sufficient to water the growing crops. By 6000 BC, villagers on the fringes of this zone were beginning to construct simple irrigation channels to enable them to cultivate land where the rainfall was inadequate. Their success led to a move further south, into the lower Euphrates valley. Here water control was essential since the annual floods occurred around harvest time – but farming in this area proved exceptionally productive. Communities grew rapidly, supported by high crop yields and large herds of domestic animals, not to mention fish from the river and its tributaries. Surplus agricultural produce provided these communities with the means to support other activities, such as building temples, manufacturing textiles, pottery and other craft objects, and engaging in international trade.

The early Indus and predynastic Egypt

Similar developments took place in the Nile and Indus valleys. Agricultural communities had emerged in many parts of the Iranian plateau, and by 3000 BC prosperous towns had begun to appear in the Indo-Iranian borderlands. These towns were supported by high agricultural yields from fields irrigated from reservoirs; the reservoirs were made by building dams, and collected rainfall and water running off the surrounding hills.

Armed with this expertise in water control, pioneers from this region moved east, out onto the plains of the Indus and Saraswati rivers (the latter now dry). Here they built towns with massive brick walls to protect them against flooding by the unpredictable rivers. The river flood plains were very different terrain to the semiarid mountains from which they were colonized, but the farmers who adapted to this new environment were able to produce abundant crops with relatively

FIRST CIVILIZATIONS OF THE OLD WORLD

First civilizations
- Sumerian
- Egyptian
- Indus
- Shang

1. Magnificent houses made of bundles of reeds are the homes of the modern inhabitants of the southern Iraqi marshes. Similar structures were built by their Mesopotamian predecessors 7000 years ago.

1

In ancient Mesopotamian legend Ziusudra, the good man, like Noah, builds an ark and is saved when the gods cause a great deluge to destroy wicked humanity.

little labour. Settlements multiplied and expanded as the population rapidly increased.

Agricultural villages had been established along the Nile during the 6th millennium BC, mainly growing wheat and barley introduced from the Near East. Of the three regions, the Nile had the easiest regime for agriculture. Each year the Nile rose, inundating the plain on either side of the river. As the floodwaters retreated farmers sowed their crops. Here, as on the Indus and Euphrates, villages grew in size and complexity, gradually uniting into larger confederations that traded (and fought) with each other along the river.

Early China

Early farming in China emerged around two different rivers: the Yellow River (Huang He) where millets were grown from around 6000 BC, and the more southerly Yangtze (Chang Jiang) where rice was the principal crop. Rice cultivation also spread into other regions. By 3500 BC villages on the Yellow River and the east coast were becoming increasingly large and prosperous. Trade brought them luxury goods and materials such as jade from other regions, while fine pottery was produced locally. There was increasing social differentiation within communities, and competition between them. Before 2000 BC villages began to be defended with massive tamped-earth ramparts. Often a number of human sacrifices were buried within the ramparts, reflecting the increasingly elaborate religious rites that were also emerging, frequently involving the use of sophisticated bronze vessels.

A more complex world

These four regions – the valleys of the Euphrates, Nile, Indus–Saraswati and Yellow Rivers – were the most highly developed in the period between 4000 and 2000 BC. However, similar developments were taking place elsewhere.

As productivity was increased in many areas by more intensive agriculture – involving such practices as ploughing, weeding and manuring as well as irrigation and complex animal husbandry – so populations in these regions rose and the density of settlement increased.

Certain people emerged as leaders because of their ability to organize their community for its advantage. They promoted trade for both essential and luxury goods, such as metals, and brought about the construction of major religious monuments. They also led their community in competition with others, expressed more often in the splendour of the chief's possessions than in active warfare. Although in these regions everyone – with the possible exception of chiefs and priests – was still engaged in agriculture, some individuals also spent a part of their time working as craftsmen, making metal tools or ornaments, for instance.

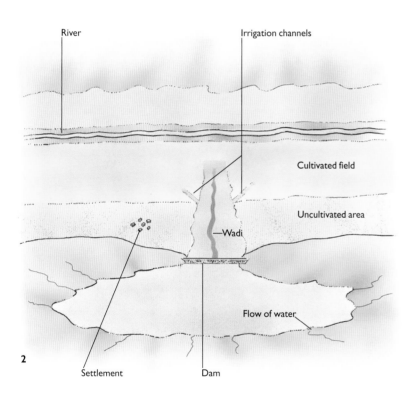

2

River

Irrigation channels

Cultivated field

Uncultivated area

Wadi

Flow of water

Settlement

Dam

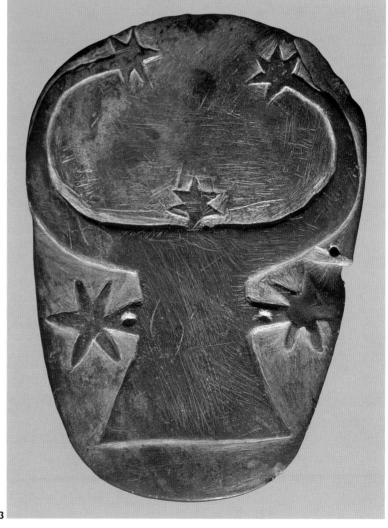

2. In dry regions, such as Baluchistan, water conservation was vital for farming. The local people impounded the water that flowed off from the hills by building a dam at the narrowest point. The water was released from this reservoir when it was needed and flowed along irrigation channels into the fields.

3. The ox-head carved on this slab of stone was probably adopted as an identifying symbol by one of the early village confederations along the River Nile.

3

⭐ Beer was the staple drink of the ancient Sumerians of Mesopotamia, who used up to 40 per cent of their grain harvest for brewing beer.

1. Pottery, useful for storage and easily made, was an early innovation among farming communities across the globe. It rapidly also became a medium for artistic creativity, like this fine early Chinese jar.

THE URBAN REVOLUTION

Civilizations emerged at different times in many parts of the world. Each had its own distinctive character, but there were also common themes. Perhaps most importantly, civilizations appeared in regions where it was possible to produce or obtain enough food to support large numbers of people in a relatively small area and to enable some of the population to work as specialists in activities other than food production – particularly as priests, rulers, traders and artisans. The world's six 'primary civilizations' – those original civilizations that arose independently of each other, in Mesopotamia, Egypt, the Indus valley, China, Mesoamerica and Peru – depended on intensive agriculture to provide this economic advantage.

Later civilizations were more diverse in their economic base, some owing their prosperity to factors such as trade or the control of key resources.

Honouring the gods

Religion played an important role in most societies, and as societies became more complex, so did religious practices and structures. Surplus food production allowed communities to devote some of their energies to constructing monumental edifices to glorify their gods – and themselves, for in many places communities appear to have vied with each other to build the most impressive temples and shrines. Pyramids in

Mesoamerica and ziggurats in Mesopotamia (▷ p. 47), for example, reached up to the skies, elevating the temple to the heavens. The embellishment of religious monuments with fine and often exotic materials was a spur to both trade and craftsmanship.

In pre-urban societies priests not only mediated between people and the gods but also acted as their representatives on earth, organizing and directing the activities of the villagers – for example, selecting the propitious time for farmers to sow their crops. Animals and crops were presented to the priests in good years as voluntary or compulsory offerings to the gods, and these accumulated as the community's stored wealth. This placed priests in a powerful position as guardians of the community's welfare, and the source of aid in lean years. As communities grew in size, the power of the priests increased and the scope of their role as the leaders and organizers of society broadened.

Artisans and trade

Surplus food supplies made it both possible and desirable for some members of society to devote all their time to non-agricultural pursuits, as priests, rulers, traders, soldiers or artisans, for example. Organized production by full-time craftsmen and women of commodities such as fine pottery, textiles and metal objects promoted both efficiency and quality. It also allowed for the development of specialist skills and sophisticated equipment, such as furnaces for smelting metal ores (▷ pp. 44–5).

Artisans were supplied with food and other necessities, and also with the raw materials that they needed for their work, such as wool. Among the most common artefacts found in southern Mesopotamia between around 4000 and 3000 BC are simple 'bevelled-rim' bowls, which may have held a day's ration of food for craftsmen and other specialists. Their labours and the distribution of their wares were coordinated and directed by the priesthood.

Craft products were important not only for people to use themselves but also as goods for trading, along with surplus grain and other foodstuffs. The alluvial plains of Mesopotamia, Egypt, India and China were a fertile environment for growing plants and

STAMPS AND SEALS

One indication of the increasing complexity of settled life was the importance placed on the ownership of property. Before writing was invented, many peoples made use of stamps and seals to mark goods and property as belonging to a particular owner. Made from carved wood, stone or pottery, the earliest stamps (around 5500 BC) had simple geometric designs, and were perhaps originally for applying body paint. Later, stamps were made specifically for impressing a design into soft clay used to seal containers or cover knots fastening a package. Tampering with the contents meant breaking the seal, which could only be reapplied by the legitimate owner.

The demands of civilized life and the needs of city administrators required a much greater range of stamps and seals. In Mesopotamia cylinder seals, like this example, were developed and widely used. Rolling the cylinder across clay produced a single, easily identifiable image. Seals themselves became badges of rank: those of the highest officials were carved from precious stones, and were miniature works of art.

Seals were still used long after writing was invented. Many later Mesopotamian designs also incorporated the owner's name, title and relationship to the gods or ruler. Egyptian seals often took the form of the sacred scarab beetle. The seals made by the Indus peoples provide the main source of evidence for their still-undeciphered script (▷ p. 66).

raising animals, but lacked many of the necessities of life, such as stone and wood for building and tools. Other environments in which civilizations arose were also deficient in certain materials, such as metals. Such materials included those that these civilizations regarded as important for making ritual paraphernalia, badges of office and personal ornaments, as well as everyday commodities. People therefore had to trade with other regions – and the need to provide goods for export acted as a spur to increase agricultural productivity and craft production.

Red tape and literature

Record-keeping became increasingly important as the volume of goods and materials passing through the hands of the administrators increased. This was a spur to the development of writing in some civilizations such as Mesopotamia. In others, including China and Mesoamerica, equally powerful religious reasons were behind the beginning of writing (▷ pp. 56–7). Only Peru lacked writing, although the Incas used complicated knotted strings (quipu) for keeping records.

At first limited in function, writing in many civilizations was soon used to record history, myths and other literature. This gives a more detailed insight into the way societies were developing, and also into the lives of individuals and their perception of the world. In Mesopotamia early literature paints a graphic picture of the social upheaval that saw the emergence of kings and secular authority at the expense of the priesthood, after 3000 BC.

1. On this carved stone vase from the ancient city of Uruk, offerings are being made to the principal city goddess, Inanna, depicted with the king in the top panel. Power struggles between kings and priests developed in the early Mesopotamian civilization.

Cities

As populations grew in size and density, so did settlements. Villages gave place to towns and towns to cities. But these were not merely large agglomerations of people. For a start, city dwellers included not only farmers but also priests, traders and artisans. The emergence of a social hierarchy was reflected in the houses, ranging in size and splendour from the palaces of kings and priests to the simple dwellings of the poor.

Villages were made up largely of houses, with perhaps a communal shrine or other simple religious structure – but cities were generally centred upon a variety of public buildings. Impressive temples and sacred precincts were among the foremost, and in many cases cities sprang up around a place of special religious significance. Structures for storing taxes, offerings and traded goods might form part of the temple or palace complex, as would administrative offices.

Some civilizations, such as that of Egypt, rapidly became unified states while others, like Mesopotamia, were culturally unified but composed of many small city-states. Conflict was common between city-states and between competing groups within states, as well as with outsiders. Most cities, therefore, were fortified. City walls not only defended their inhabitants but were a clear visual demonstration of the might and importance of the city.

URUK

Uruk in southern Mesopotamia (known as Sumer, ▷ p. 47) is claimed as the world's first city, whose origins go back before 4000 BC. By 3300 BC the city housed perhaps 40,000 people and covered 2 square km (500 acres). At its heart was the sacred precinct of Inanna, goddess of fertility, which had a magnificent pillared entrance courtyard decorated with cone mosaics – patterns built up of clay cones with coloured ends pushed into the surface of mud-bricks. Shrines here (and in other Sumerian cities, such as Khafaje, illustrated right) and in the precinct of the sky god An were constructed on high mud-brick platforms approached by staircases. These temple precincts were also administrative centres, and it was here at Uruk that writing was first used – numbers and signs inscribed on tablets, recording food, animals and textiles deposited in or issued from the temple stores.

By 2800 BC the city had more than doubled in size, and a massive defensive wall was built around it. According to epic literature the wall was the work of the legendary king Gilgamesh, who challenged the power of Inanna – a reflection of the power struggle between kings and priests that took place in many Mesopotamian cities around this time. Gilgamesh also defended Uruk against a siege by the king of the rival city of Kish. The stories of Gilgamesh's expeditions to Dilmun (Bahrain) and the Amanus mountains (in modern-day southern Turkey), from which Uruk began to import cedar, reflect the city's involvement in international trade.

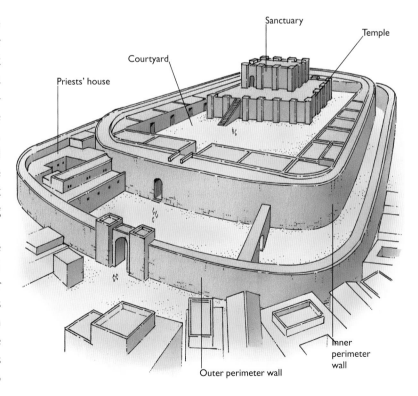

Sanctuary

Temple

Courtyard

Priests' house

Inner perimeter wall

Outer perimeter wall

COPPER AND BRONZE WORKING

Copper is one of the few metals that occurs naturally as nuggets of raw, 'native' metal. Unlike other 'stones', people found that this material could be hammered, bent and cut into shape to make jewellery and other prestige items.

Native copper is very scarce. True metalworking began when people (independently, in several regions) learned that copper could be obtained from certain mineral ores by heating them in a furnace – a process known as smelting.

1

Casting and alloys

Copper ore can be smelted at about 750 °C (1400 °F) and copper metal melts at just under 1100 °C (2000 °F). Both temperatures were well within the range of early pottery kilns, and it is most likely that the two technologies (pottery and metals) were initially closely linked.

The introduction of heatproof crucibles of stone or pottery allowed metalworkers to shape copper by casting – pouring molten metal into a mould. The first – for items such as axe heads – were simple open moulds carved into the surface of stone blocks. These were followed by two-piece moulds that enabled more complex shapes to be formed.

Some copper ores also contain small amounts of other metals, notably arsenic. When smelted, these ores produce an alloy significantly stronger than pure copper, with an attractive silvery colour. Some metalworkers seem to have deliberately selected these ores, and arsenical copper remained popular (especially in Egypt) even after it had been superseded by a superior alloy – bronze.

Bronze is a strong, versatile alloy, made by mixing copper with tin. Deposits of tin ore are much rarer than copper ores – sometimes tin had to be obtained from sources as much as 1000 km (1600 miles) away – but bronze was well worth the trouble. Copper has several advantages over stone as a material for tools – it is heavier, denser and does not break so easily – but it is also softer, and copper cutting edges are quickly blunted. Bronze, however, is the equal of stone in almost every respect, except cost. Making a stone tool can be a

2

quick one-man operation, but making a bronze one required the extraction and combination of two expensive materials, considerable expertise and far more time.

The age of bronze

In about 3200 BC Mesopotamia became the first region to organize sufficient supplies of copper and tin to begin producing bronze in quantity. Metalworking was under state control and virtually all of the production went into prestige personal items and weapons – agricultural tools had a much lower priority.

In Egypt, which was slower to adopt metals, the same pattern of production emerged. whereas in the unwarlike Indus valley, bronze was put to more utilitarian purposes from the outset. In China, bronze working did not begin until about 2200 BC, but developed quickly.

A major innovation – developed indepen-

dently in Eurasia and the Americas – was the lost-wax method of casting, in which a wax model is made and then covered with clay. The clay is then heated, melting the wax, and molten metal poured into the resulting cavity. This method enabled extremely complex and detailed shapes to be made in metal. Casting numerous wax shapes in clay moulds was the first step to mass-production, and was used in Mesopotamia to manufacture identical bronze arrowheads by the thousand.

The thirst of early civilizations for metals, especially tin, was a major stimulus to trade and exploration. Long-distance overland trade networks had to be established and protected to guarantee a reliable supply of raw materials. As demand for bronze increased, overseas sources of metals began to be exploited, and a regular sea trade developed.

1. This large panel of beaten copper backed by wood originally decorated a temple in Ur, built by A-Anepada, king around 2500 BC.

2. By about 1500 BC Chinese workers were able to cast massive bronze ritual vessels using complex multi-part pottery moulds.

3. Copper and bronze metallurgical techniques developed independently in various parts of the world at different times.

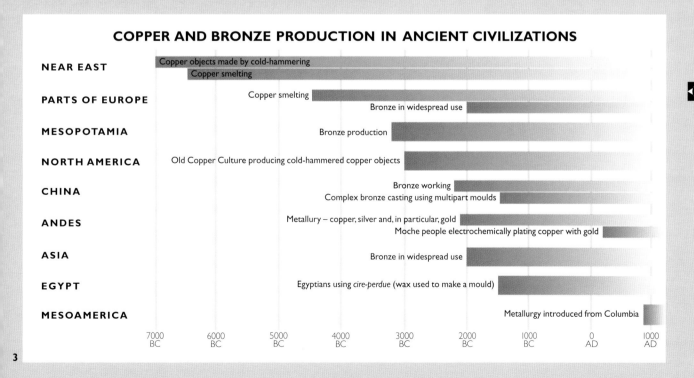

COPPER AND BRONZE PRODUCTION IN ANCIENT CIVILIZATIONS

NEAR EAST	Copper objects made by cold-hammering / Copper smelting
PARTS OF EUROPE	Copper smelting / Bronze in widespread use
MESOPOTAMIA	Bronze production
NORTH AMERICA	Old Copper Culture producing cold-hammered copper objects
CHINA	Bronze working / Complex bronze casting using multipart moulds
ANDES	Metallury – copper, silver and, in particular, gold / Moche people electrochemically plating copper with gold
ASIA	Bronze in widespread use
EGYPT	Egyptians using *cire-perdue* (wax used to make a mould)
MESOAMERICA	Metallurgy introduced from Columbia

7000 BC   6000 BC   5000 BC   4000 BC   3000 BC   2000 BC   1000 BC   0 AD   1000 AD

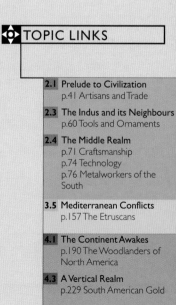

THE LANDS BETWEEN THE RIVERS

Mesopotamia, 'the land between rivers', is the fertile region between the Tigris and Euphrates, in what is now Iraq. It was here, from around 3300 BC, that the world's first cities were built. These were themselves the world's first states, each controlling an area of surrounding agricultural land, and often housing the greater part of the state's population. Between these territories lay uncultivated areas inhabited by roaming groups of pastoralists. From 2800 BC the cities were increasingly governed by kings – originally war leaders in the power struggles between city-states.

After 2000 BC southern Mesopotamia suffered increasingly from invasion and conquest by emerging states further north. Some, like the Assyrians, developed great empires that extended far beyond Mesopotamia itself. Nevertheless, throughout the many dynasties, foreign and native, the fundamentals of Mesopotamian civilization remained relatively unchanged.

MESOPOTAMIAN CIVILIZATION

Although culturally united, southern Mesopotamia was made up of two distinct regions: Sumer in the south, where the Sumerian language was spoken, and Akkad further north, whose population spoke Akkadian. In 2350 BC the regions were united into the first Mesopotamian empire, under the Akkadian king, Sargon. The Akkadian empire lasted a little over a century, and for a time the region broke up again into a number of individual city-states. In 2112 BC southern Mesopotamia was again united, under the Sumerian 3rd dynasty of Ur (the 'Ur III' dynasty).

Writing developed first in Sumer, and the script was therefore designed to render the Sumerian language; modifications had to be made when it was used to write Akkadian from around 2500 BC onwards. In later times,

Sumerian remained the 'classical' language, used for inscriptions and traditional texts, while Akkadian was used for everyday purposes. We owe much of our knowledge of Sumerian to long lists of word-equivalents in Akkadian and Sumerian, laboriously copied by scribes and schoolchildren.

Sacred and secular rule

The first Mesopotamian cities were ruled by priests, and the temple complexes acted as the main centres of administration, where the city's wealth was stored and records kept. The temple authorities employed herdsmen to tend the temple flocks and craftsmen to turn their wool into cloth as well as to manufacture other goods. Merchants were also employed by the temple, which issued them with commodities to trade, although they were also allowed to carry some goods to trade on their own account.

From around 2800 BC kings gradually came to rule the city-states, taking control of the rich revenues of the temple – which remained the largest landowner and the city's main economic and administrative centre. As kings ruled on behalf of the gods, the priesthood retained substantial influence in the running of the state. Kings themselves had many religious duties to perform for the good of their people.

Gods and temples

Although, as in the great city of Uruk (▷ p. 43), several gods and goddesses might be venerated within a single city, one deity was its special patron, worshipped in the city's principal shrine. Enki, lord of the earth, was the principal god of the city of Eridu; Inanna, Uruk's guardian deity, was the most important goddess in the Sumerian pantheon; while Ur was under the protection of Nanna, the

1. Ur was one of the foremost Sumerian cities. Situated in the far south of Mesopotamia, it was a major port for trade through the Persian Gulf.

2. A diorite statue of Gudea, king of Lagash, one of the city states that became powerful in the interlude between the Akkadian and Ur III empires.

1

These massive defences were built to withstand sieges, as described in the legendary literature of the time. Ur-Nammu was also responsible for the building of canals and new buildings in the city, including a palace in the temple precinct to house the chief priestess, a position henceforth held by the king's daughter. Kings often made their mark on their city by erecting new buildings, and Sargon is credited with an entirely new foundation – his capital city, Akkad. Temples, palaces and treasuries were the main public buildings in these cities, but harbours were also constructed in cities like Ur, which at that time lay near the sea.

Mud-brick houses one or two storeys high, arranged around a courtyard, were home to families of various sizes, from simple house-holds of a married couple and their children, to large extended families with slaves. Land was commonly held by the extended family since it was more efficient to farm large areas rather than individual plots. Poorer citizens rented ground from large landowners, paying in labour or in produce, either a fixed amount or a proportion of the harvest; temple lands were farmed on a similar basis.

1. The ziggurat built by king Ur-Nammu at Ur: massive tiered platforms of mudbrick, with a protective outer casing of fired bricks.

2. This head carved of diorite is believed to be a portrait of Hammurabi.

moon god. The chief deity in Sumerian times was Enlil, lord of the air, and his city of Nippur enjoyed a special status among the Sumerian city-states.

Temples generally consisted of a long central hall flanked on either side by a row of small rooms. An altar lay at the far end, and the temple was entered from the side, sometimes through a courtyard. Earlier temples were built on the summit of raised platforms; Ur-Nammu, the first king of the Ur III dynasty, elaborated on this, constructing his principal temples on top of a series of superimposed platforms of diminishing size – the first ziggurats. This became a standard feature of major Mesopotamian temples in later centuries.

Warfare and politics

Land tenure might also entail the duty to perform military service when required. Conflicts between neighbouring cities probably arose initially as boundary disputes, but by 2500 BC ambitious kings were seeking to extend their authority over larger areas, culminating in Sargon's conquest and unifica-tion of Sumer and Akkad in 2350 BC. His successors further extended Mesopotamian dominions, for a time controlling the adjacent highland region of Elam, a realm often in conflict with Mesopotamian empires. However, in 2004 BC, the tables were turned when the Elamites sacked Ur and brought to an end the Ur III empire.

⭐ In about 800 BC Assyrian commandos used inflated animal skins as flotation aids to swim across rivers while weighed down by full battle kit.

Sumerian cities

Ur-Nammu also rebuilt Ur's massive city walls, which, like those of other cities, were originally constructed in the period from around 2800 BC when the Sumerian city-states began to engage in inter-city warfare.

2

THE LANDS OF HAMMURABI

The downfall of the Ur III empire marked the end of Sumerian rule in Mesopotamia, but not the end of Sumerian civilization. Although the region now came under the control of a succession of outside groups, most of the basic styles and forms of Sumerian civilization were preserved. The city of Babylon, to the north of Uruk and Ur, emerged as the new centre of power under the control of Amorite kings. The Amorites were originally nomadic herders from the northern Levant, who quickly adapted to city life and sophisticated warfare. By around 1800 BC they controlled most of northern Mesopotamia.

The sixth Amorite king, Hammurabi, conquered the south and created a unified empire – with Babylon as its capital – that extended from Mari in the west to Elam in the east. In about 1760 BC he issued his famous Law Code, copies of which were carved in stone in all the major cities of the empire. Hammurabi's laws, with their stress on violent retribution – 'an eye for an eye' – reflect the harsh justice of a nomadic people, and are markedly different from earlier Sumerian law, an urbanized and more humane system that made provision for financial compensation in cases of bodily injury.

Under a series of less able successors, Hammurabi's empire gradually declined both economically and politically. Many cities and vast areas of farmland in the south were abandoned, and Babylonian power was reduced to a small core area around the capital. In 1590 BC, Babylon itself was sacked

 ROYAL GRAVES AT UR

The Sumerian King List catalogues the cities chosen in turn by the gods to exercise dominion over the others. Ur was granted this supreme role from the reign of king Mes-Anepada, around 2550 BC. During this time of great prosperity for the city, its kings and queens were interred in a remarkable cemetery. More than two thousand people were buried here, mostly ordinary individuals with a few personal possessions. Seventeen graves, however, contained monarchs, including Meskalamdug, father of Mes-Anepada. Buried in stone-built chambers constructed within large grave pits, the royal dead were decked in their finest robes and jewellery, such as this gold headdress (right). Around them were arranged many treasures – expensive cosmetics, chests of clothes, gaming boards, carts and sledges with gold and silver decorations, complete with the oxen that had pulled them – and statues coated in gold and lapis lazuli.

They did not go alone into the afterlife. Many of their attendants also entered the pit, apparently willingly: grooms to hold the oxen, soldiers to guard the grave pit's entrance, and many young women, often carrying exquisitely decorated lyres. Each carried a cup from which they must have drunk a drugged potion that killed them or rendered them unconscious while the grave pit was filled in.

⭐ If a Sumerian couple were unable to have children, a slave girl might bear the husband's children, who would legally become the children of his wife.

1. At the top of this magnificent stele, the god Shamash instructs king Hammurabi to give justice to his people. Below is the text of the king's Law Code, which covered many aspects of public and private life.

2. The palace at Mari had more than 300 rooms, arranged around two courtyards and surrounded by a strong outer wall. This statue of a goddess was found in the antechamber to the throne room.

in a Hittite raid, and southern Mesopotamia then came under the control of a Kassite dynasty from western Iran.

Under Kassite rule, Babylonia began to regain some of its former power. Abandoned farmland was gradually reclaimed and irrigated once more, and some cities were restored to their former glory. The Kassites also restored many Sumerian shrines and generally encouraged a revival of Sumerian culture. Peaceful relations were maintained with the more distant powers of Egypt and the Hittite empire (▷ p. 101), although relations with neighbouring Assyria were more difficult.

Northern rivals

The decline of Babylonian power created opportunities in northern Mesopotamia, and between 1700 and 1200 BC a three-sided power struggle developed. The Hittites, based in Anatolia, contested with the native Assyrians and the foreign Mitanni for control of the region.

The Assyrian state developed around the city of Ashur, a centre for trade with Anatolia since Sumerian times. Donkey caravans carried tin and textiles to towns in Anatolia and brought back gold and silver. During periods when external control lessened, the city acted independently and gradually extended its territory. After the decline of Babylonian power, Assyria was briefly absorbed into the Mitanni empire.

The Mitanni created a powerful state which, through their mastery of chariot warfare, by 1600 BC dominated an area that stretched from the Levant coast to the Tigris river. By around 1400 BC, however, the Mitanni empire had disintegrated, challenged to the south by the emerging power of New Kingdom Egypt (▷ p. 89), in the north by the equally expansionist Hittite empire (▷ p. 101), and in the east by Assyria.

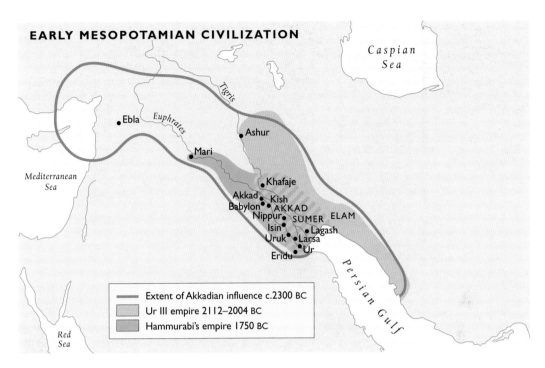

EARLY MESOPOTAMIAN CIVILIZATION

Legend:
- Extent of Akkadian influence c.2300 BC
- Ur III empire 2112–2004 BC
- Hammurabi's empire 1750 BC

MARI

Thanks to its position at a crossroads of traditional trade routes between Mesopotamia and the Levant, the city of Mari was a thriving commercial centre, dealing in copper, tin, silver, timber and textiles. By 2100 BC Mari had more than 25,000 inhabitants, many of them skilled craftworkers who produced high-quality jewellery and ivory carvings. Its Amorite kings ruled from a great palace situated just outside the city. In the royal archives scribes kept a meticulous written record of many aspects of palace life, such as the collection of taxes and tolls on river traffic, correspondence with the rulers of Babylon and other cities, and the activities of officials responsible for maintaining quality among the city's craftworkers. The archives also stored the personal correspondence of the royal family, such as a furious letter from prince Yasmah-Addu to his father the king, asking when 'daddy' will start treating him like a responsible adult.

In 1757 BC Mari was attacked and destroyed by Hammurabi, who burned the palace to the ground. The heat of the flames baked the clay tablets in the archive, and they were preserved beneath the collapsed palace until they were discovered by modern archaeologists.

> ★ Assyrian reliefs show kings holding lions by the throat as they kill them with swords. The lions of the region, now extinct, were smaller than modern lions.

After the Mitanni collapse, Assyria was able to expand westwards to the Euphrates, creating its own empire. Assyrian kings also began to interfere in the affairs of Kassite Babylonia to the south, and in 1227 BC Babylon itself was captured and incorporated into the empire.

This first Assyrian empire was, however, extremely short-lived. Beginning around 1200 BC a series of migrations, raids and disruptions caused the sudden collapse of the Hittite empire, and many cities of the Levant were destroyed. Throughout Mesopotamia groups from the surrounding hills began occupying the best farmland, and central authority was considerably weakened. The Assyrians lost control of Babylon, and later sacked the city in around 1100 BC. Assyria itself barely survived as an independent state, and remained weakened for some time.

THE NEO-ASSYRIAN EMPIRE

After about 900 BC the Assyrian state gradually regained its strength. Having become expert in the use of cavalry, the Assyrians were able once again to defeat and conquer their neighbours, with the exception of the mountain kingdom of Urartu. By 800 BC they had created a revived and enlarged Neo-Assyrian empire in northern Mesopotamia, with a new capital at Nimrud.

For the next two centuries a series of warrior kings further expanded the Neo-Assyrian empire into the largest the world had yet seen. Tiglath-Pileser III (ruled 744–727 BC) led military expeditions southwards that conquered the whole of the Levant and added Babylonia to the empire. Sargon II

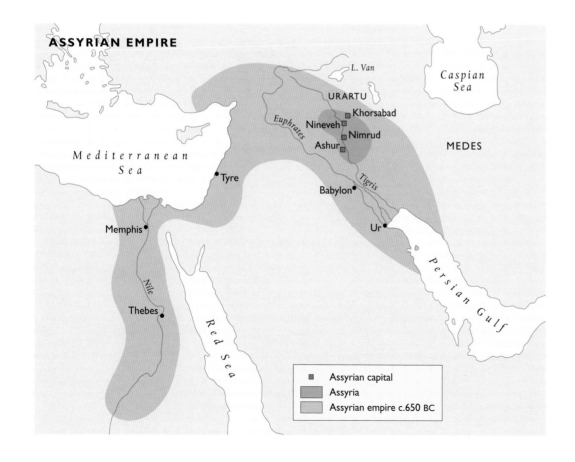

ASSYRIAN EMPIRE

L. Van
Caspian Sea
URARTU
Euphrates
Khorsabad
Nineveh
Nimrud
Ashur
MEDES
Mediterranean Sea
Tyre
Tigris
Babylon
Memphis
Ur
Persian Gulf
Nile
Thebes
Red Sea

■ Assyrian capital
Assyria
Assyrian empire c.650 BC

1. (opposite) The Assyrians were masters of siege warfare. Here, they attack the walls of an enemy city with a battering ram, while their archers shoot arrows at the city's defenders from a tall siege tower.

1. King Ashurbanipal spears a lion, one of several which have been caught and released into the royal park to provide the king's sport – although Assyrian kings also hunted lions in the wild.

(ruled 721–705 BC) finally defeated the people of Urartu in the north, and gained control of the island of Cyprus. In 669 BC Egypt was invaded and incorporated into the empire, which now stretched from the borders with Nubia in the south to Lake Van in the north, and west to east from the Mediterranean to the Persian Gulf.

During these campaigns the Assyrian army developed into the most feared fighting machine of its day. Although its main tactic was the cavalry charge by men armed with swords, spears and axes, the army became proficient in most aspects of warfare. No city could hold out for long against an Assyrian siege. No matter how strong the city walls, they soon fell – smashed by great battering rams and undermined by sappers. Defeated enemies were deported to other parts of the empire.

Control and collapse

Within their empire the Assyrians were concerned only with political and economic control, and made little attempt to extend Assyrian culture to their subject peoples. Most of their construction projects were dictated by military necessity, or were devoted to the beautification of the Assyrian capital – first at Nimrud and later at Nineveh. Their palaces were decorated with magnificent reliefs, many of them showing the king hunting lions, which was both an enjoyable sport and the traditional royal duty of Mesopotamian rulers. The last of the Assyrian kings, Ashurbanipal (ruled 668–627 BC) was a renowned scholar as well as a great warrior, and built a great library at Nineveh to house some 25,000 clay tablets containing great works of Mesopotamian literature, mathematics and astronomy.

The more distant regions of the empire, such as the Levant and Egypt, were ruled by native princes whose main responsibility was the annual collection and payment of tribute to their Assyrian overlords. Any signs of dissent were crushed immediately by Assyrian troops, and punishments for rebellious cities and provinces were severe – in 689 BC Babylon was sacked, and in 663 BC the Egyptian capital, Thebes, was destroyed. The Assyrian empire was eventually overthrown by a combination of enemies from within and without.

In Iran the Medes had their own loosely organized empire. They were originally a nomadic people from around the Caspian Sea in the far northeast of Iran, who since about 1000 BC had gradually expanded southwards, establishing control over the local populations. In 625 BC rebellious Babylonians allied with the Medes and decisively defeated the Assyrians. The main Assyrian cities were destroyed, and a Neo-Babylonian empire was established over most of the former Assyrian domains.

The greatest of the Neo-Babylonian kings was Nebuchadnezzar II (ruled 605–562 BC), who extended the empire to the Levant coast and sacked Jerusalem in 586 BC.

Nebuchadnezzar was also responsible for building the magnificent Ishtar Gate in Babylon, which was decorated with brightly coloured glazed tiles. However, the new empire of Babylon lasted less than a century, and in turn was superseded by the empire of the Persians.

2. The magnificent Ishtar Gate at Babylon (left) was one of eight entrances to the inner city. It stood on the processional way from the akitu temple to the temple of the city's principal god, Marduk. The gate was decorated with glazed bricks with relief figures depicting bulls (3, below) and dragons.

THE BEGINNING OF WRITING

The earliest writing, dated around 3500 BC, comes from Mesopotamia. However, writing has been independently invented several times in different parts of the world. The representation of language by means of two-dimensional symbols permitted communication between individuals separated by some distance. It also allowed the long-term storage of information, such as genealogies, tax records and legal decisions. Hitherto, such information had depended for its survival on human memory, with all its frailties.

1. The formal Egyptian hieroglyphic script always remained pictorial. In this king list from the temple of Ramses II, the names of the kings are enclosed in cartouches (name rings).

One route to literacy

The early writing system of Mesopotamia seems to have arisen from traditional, preliterate methods of keeping count. One of the simplest methods of counting sheep is to drive them through a narrow gate and place a pebble in a bag for every sheep that goes through the gate – the number of sheep equals the number of pebbles. If there is a mixture of adult sheep and lambs, different coloured pebbles can be used to keep a tally of the two sorts of animal.

During the Neolithic period some of the peoples in the larger villages of northern Mesopotamia began using small clay tokens of simple geometric shapes to keep tallies of flocks, herds and jars of produce. If animals were to be sent to another village, the person driving the flock would be given the tokens representing the animals in the flock. As towns, trade and cities developed, so did the system of tokens, and by 4000 BC it had become fairly standardized.

Writing was invented in about 3500 BC when some individuals in southern Mesopotamia, probably traders or profes-

sional administrators, began sealing their tokens in a clay envelope, and scratching a summary of the contents on the outer surface. They used a combination of tally marks and symbols representing tokens to show what the envelope contained.

Within a few hundred years the envelopes and tokens had been replaced by simple clay tablets inscribed with a greater range of symbols. The first symbols were pictures of the things that the words represented (pictographs), but these quickly became stylized and unrecognizable as objects. In

3

2. The pictographs of early Mesopotamian writing soon gave way to stylized cuneiform signs that developed through time. This tablet recording astronomical forecasts dates from the 7th century BC.

3. The writing on this early Sumerian tablet still uses recognisable pictographic signs, such as the conical jar which stands for 'beer'. The tablet records quantities of malt and beer; the round holes represent the number 10.

parallel with this, symbols and combinations of symbols generally came to represent the sound of the word for an object, rather than the object itself, and true writing was created. The clay tablets were inscribed using the cut end of a marsh reed, which produced a distinctive wedge-shaped mark, and such writing is known as cuneiform.

Separate developments

The first Egyptian writing – hieroglyphics (sacred writing) – was also pictographic, perhaps based on religious and cult symbols.

The earliest examples, which date from about 3200 BC, are found on carved bone labels attached to goods in graves, and it is probable that Egyptian hieroglyphs also developed from preliterate systems of record keeping. By around 2500 BC, Egyptian administrators had developed a shorthand form of writing hieroglyphics, known as hieratic.

In China writing began around 1600 BC as questions scratched onto 'oracle' bones. The bones were then heated by touching them with a hot metal poker. From the pattern of cracks this produced, sages and diviners would interpret answers to the questions. Soon afterwards writing using the same system was inscribed on bronze ritual vessels. In Mesoamerica rudimentary writing was invented by 500 BC. Only the Maya developed true writing – they mainly used their ornate glyphs to record the dates, lineages and victories of their kings on public buildings.

◆ TOPIC LINKS

2.1 Prelude to Civilization
p.41 Stamps and Seals
p.42 Red Tape and Literature
p.43 Uruk

2.2 The Land Between the Rivers
p.47 Mesopotamian Civilization

2.3 The Indus and its Neighbours
p.66 The Mystery of the Indus Script

2.4 The Middle Realm
p.73 Oracle Bones

2.5 The Gift of the Nile
p.83 Building a State

4.2 Builders of Mounds and Pyramids
p.195 Teotihuacán and Monte Albán
p.199 Maya Writing

Around 2600 BC a civilization emerged in the Indus valley that rivalled the great empires of Mesopotamia in wealth and sophistication. This civilization was highly organized, and built a number of carefully planned cities.

The Indus people traded overland both to west and east, and also played a major role in the flourishing sea trade along the Persian Gulf with the cities of Mesopotamia. These cities were rich in agricultural produce, but they lacked many valuable raw materials such as stone, wood and copper ore, as well as luxury materials like gold. This had encouraged them to intensify the eastward trade that had already existed for thousands of years. Substantial towns emerged along these trade routes, stretching across the Iranian plateau to the Indo-Iranian borderlands, from where pioneer communities settled the Indus valley itself, leading to the emergence of a sizeable and peaceable urban civilization.

THE CITIES OF THE IRANIAN PLATEAU

By 3300 BC many towns had sprung up across the Iranian plateau. Their existence was largely due to the westward trade with Mesopotamia, where they sent valued materials such as copper ore and steatite (soapstone). In an ancient story a legendary Sumerian king, Enmerkar of Uruk – having failed to obtain what he wanted by threats of military action – sent donkey caravans of barley to Aratta, 'beyond seven mountains' in eastern Iran, to procure gold, silver, carnelian and lapis lazuli.

Prosperous towns, such as Shahr-i Sokhta, were located near the source of raw materials or at strategic points on the trade routes. They were often industrial centres where raw materials were worked into fine luxury objects, such as steatite bowls. Seaborne trade also took place among the coastal communities that dwelt along the Persian Gulf.

One of the most treasured materials sought by the peoples of West Asia was lapis lazuli, a beautiful blue stone. Before the entry of the Indus civilization into the trade networks the only known source of lapis lazuli was in the hills near Badakhshan in Afghanistan. The local people mined the lapis and traded it with their neighbours. It changed hands many times before it reached Sumer, where it was used to decorate valued objects (▷ p. 49).

There are no weapons and no scenes of fighting from the Indus civilization. Unlike all the other ancient civilizations, the Indus people lived in peace.

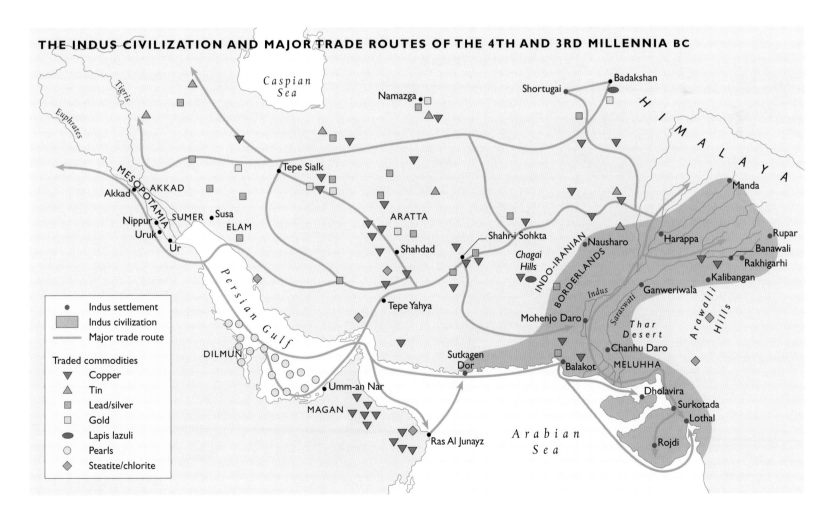

THE INDUS CIVILIZATION AND MAJOR TRADE ROUTES OF THE 4TH AND 3RD MILLENNIA BC

Legend:
- Indus settlement
- Indus civilization
- Major trade route

Traded commodities
- ▼ Copper
- ▲ Tin
- ■ Lead/silver
- ☐ Gold
- ● Lapis lazuli
- ○ Pearls
- ◆ Steatite/chlorite

⭐ The Indus people made minute beads of steatite (soapstone) that measured only 1 mm across – we still don't know how. Two small pots found together held 34,000 beads.

THE INDUS CITIES

The eastward trading routes from Mesopotamia extended beyond the Iranian plateau to the Indo-Iranian borderlands, in what is now eastern Afghanistan and western Pakistan. People from this mountain region colonized the Indus valley, establishing villages and small towns. Around 2600 BC most of these towns were replaced by planned cities such as Mohenjo Daro and Harappa.

The cities were laid out in a grid pattern with wide main streets running north–south and east–west. Smaller lanes opened from these streets, and it was here, away from the dust raised by bullock carts and the hustle and bustle of public life, that the houses had their doors. Entering the house, the visitor turned along a narrow passage, emerging into a courtyard, which was the centre of domestic life. Here grain was ground, meals were cooked and children played. This was also where thread was spun, and clothing was made, washed and hung out to dry. The family might sleep in the courtyard or climb the stairs to upper rooms or the roof. A bathroom was an important feature of most houses, with a floor paved with bricks. Used water ran away into the efficient public system of covered drains, which were regularly cleaned and inspected. The drains ran along the streets, and the houses also had toilets that were separately emptied.

Tools and ornaments

Workshops were to be found throughout the Indus cities. Here craftsmen made a great variety of fine objects, for everyday or special use, and for trade. Everyone needed pottery to store and cook their food and to eat from, and this was probably made locally in every

1. Mohenjo Daro, like other towns and cities of the Indus civilization, was built of millions of baked bricks made in a standard size. Wooden doors and lattice windows of wood or occasionally carved stone relieved the plain façades.

2. (opposite) Lapis lazuli, gold and other valued materials were used by the Sumerians to make wonderful objects such as gaming boards and this bull's head decorating a lyre from a royal grave at Ur.

1. Terracotta models included various two-wheeled carts drawn by bullocks. These strongly resemble farm vehicles still in use in the area, underlining the continuity between past and present in many aspects of life.

settlement, along with everyday tools of stone. Fine pots with beautiful painted decoration, however, were created in city workshops. Other specialist craftsmen were also concentrated in the cities, where they made a great variety of complex and sophisticated goods – copper and bronze tools, jewellery of gold, silver and semiprecious stones, exquisite steatite (soapstone) seals, and many objects of shell, such as bangles, trumpets and fine inlays. Shellfish were collected by coastal fishermen and some of the task of sawing and polishing the shells was undertaken in coastal settlements like the small town of Balakot. Finer work was created in the major cities like Mohenjo Daro and Harappa.

Women wore lots of bangles made of pottery, shell and sometimes metal, and plentiful strings of beads, made particularly from beautiful stones such as red agate, carnelian and green serpentine. Their only clothing seems to have been a short skirt. Men also wore some jewellery and a cloth tied around the waist. These clothes would have been made of cotton or wool and were probably brightly coloured and patterned – but they have all decayed away so we cannot know for sure.

Trade

The entry of the Indus civilization into the established long-distance trade networks brought about a major alteration in the pattern of international relations, deflecting trade from the towns of the Iranian plateau. Indus merchants plied the sea lanes of the Persian Gulf, and some even resided in the distant cities of Mesopotamia.

The Indus people also traded closer to home. Although they made some tools from fine flint, others were made from copper, which they also occasionally alloyed with tin to make bronze. Some of the copper and tin they obtained from their neighbours, fisherfolk who lived near the rich copper deposits of the Aravalli hills to the southeast of the Indus region. Hunters and gatherers who moved with the seasons through the arid and forested regions to the south and east supplied the Indus people with things like honey and ivory. In exchange they received Indus tools, such as copper fishhooks, as well as grain and domestic animals.

Farming

The fertile plains of the Indus are even today a major area of wheat cultivation. In ancient times, however, the area suitable for farming was much larger because then there was another river, the Saraswati, that ran parallel to the Indus, to its south, flowing through what became the Thar desert when the Saraswati later dried up. Indus farmers grew abundant crops of wheat and barley, oil seeds like sesame, pulses such as peas and lentils, and various fruits and vegetables, as well as cotton for making cloth. By 2000 BC they were also growing rice and various types of millet in some regions.

Settled farmers kept domestic animals, including water buffalo for milk and bullocks to pull their ploughs and carts, as well as sheep and goats and perhaps rabbits for meat. There were also specialist herdsmen who drove their animals into the hills during the hot summer months, returning in the winter to the plains where the animals grazed in the rough lands beyond the fields. These pastoralists also used their animals as beasts of burden, carrying goods between the Indus cities and villages.

The gift of the rivers

The rivers were the lifeblood of the Indus civilization, watering the fields, providing fish for food and carrying traders and travellers across the land, from the timber-clad slopes of the Himalaya to the sea. We know from pictures on ancient seals that the Indus boats 4,000 years ago were very similar to the wide, flat-bottomed craft still used on the river today, floating gently downstream or sailing upstream against the current.

But the rivers were not always so benign. They could be capricious, and often changed their course. From the earliest days of the Indus settlements massive walls were constructed around the towns and cities to protect them against river flooding.

A peaceful civilization

The magnificence of the city walls may also have been intended to impress visitors from the countryside or from foreign lands. But, contrary to earlier ideas about the Indus

 BEAD AND BANGLE MAKING

The Indus craftsmen made exceptionally fine beads and bangles. Seashells were sawn into pieces using fine copper saws, then ground and polished to make single large, thick armbands or many slender fine bangles. Most beads were of stone. An appropriate piece was first heated to make it easier to work, then roughly shaped by sawing and chipping. Tiny drills of very hard stone were used to perforate the beads. Finally, each was finished by grinding and polishing. It probably took a craftsman 10 to 15 days to make a single bead. Long biconical stone beads were particularly difficult to produce and required the highest skill. Various brown, red and green stones were used, particularly banded agate. Craftsmen skilfully cut beads from this material to expose beautiful symmetrical designs, including eye shapes, perhaps thought to bring good luck. Carnelian, a rich orange-red stone, was decorated with white bleached lines to give a similar effect. Important individuals wore beads made from ivory, gold and silver, while ordinary people wore strings of pottery beads, often imitating the highly valued long biconical stone beads. Necklaces were often put together from an attractive selection of beads of different shapes and materials.

1. Terracotta figurines of women or goddesses were common, but few bronze figures are known. This one, often called the 'dancing girl', wears many of the bangles that were a characteristic ornament worn by Indus women of all ranks.

2. Indus stone sculpture was rare. This superb figure is often called the 'Priest-King' and may well depict a ruler.

civilization, it is not now thought that the walls were built to prevent attacks. The city gates had guardrooms, but these were not designed for defence – they may have merely functioned as customs posts, where taxes were collected on goods being brought into or out of the city.

In fact, there is no evidence of warfare of any kind from the Indus civilization: spears and arrows were for hunting only, and there are no signs of soldiers or armies or of violent destruction. Such a peaceful civilization is almost unique in history.

Who ruled the Indus?

What was the nature of Indus society? Who were its rulers? What was its religion? One might expect the remains of the public buildings in the cities to provide clues to help answer these questions, but the great variety of different types makes it hard to piece together a coherent picture. Nevertheless, there is striking uniformity in the objects used by the Indus people and in many other aspects of life – such as town planning and urban sanitation – from end to end of the Indus civilization: this was clearly a unified state, in which many different groups played integrated roles.

One part of each town and city was set apart, often on a higher mound. In some cities, such as Mohenjo Daro and Harappa, this 'citadel' mound was separate from the rest of the city, with its own surrounding wall. In others, such as Dholavira in the south, the citadel is a walled area within the main city. In addition, the range of public buildings found within each citadel is often different in each town and city.

Mesopotamia and most other early civilizations have splendid palaces in which the rulers lived, rich royal graves and splendid temples. There are no structures of this kind in the Indus civilization. The rulers may have lived in some of the buildings on the citadel or in large houses in the town, but they did not have an obviously wealthy lifestyle. It is likely, therefore, that the rulers were not kings, but high priests of some kind.

Indus religion

On the citadel at Mohenjo Daro there is what appears to be a religious complex. At its heart, surrounded by small bathrooms, is the 'Great Bath', built of tightly fitted bricks and bitumen to make it watertight. In later Indian religion bathing and ritual purity play an important role, and it seems likely that ritual bathing was also important to the Indus people. The Great Bath may have been used for major ceremonies of purification.

Other cities also had bathrooms on their citadels, and at a number there were pits and fireplaces with offerings of sacrificed animals, often called 'fire-altars'. In addition to the Great Bath, the citadel of Mohenjo Daro also included a pillared hall, while in the lower city there is a building that may have been a temple housing a sacred tree. A reverence for trees and other natural phenomena, such as snakes, are, like ritual bathing, features of later Indian religion.

The Indus civilization contains other hints of later developments, strongly suggesting that many aspects of Hinduism have their roots in Indus religion. A seal from Mohenjo Daro, for example, shows a figure very similar to the Hindu god Shiva, seated in a yoga position and surrounded by wild animals. A goddess pictured on other seals, often with a tiger, may be a prototype of his wife Durga. The numerous Indus figurines of women, sometimes carrying babies, were possibly used in ceremonies or as offerings and are likely to be representations of a mother goddess, a popular figure in later Hindu folk religion.

Organizing life

Our inability to read the Indus script makes it hard to unravel the details of Indus social organization, but we have some clues. There is a strong indication that the caste system, by which later Indian society has been structured into occupational classes, has its roots in the Indus civilization. There was also an efficient distribution system that ensured that the inhabitants of the towns and cities were provided with high-quality goods and raw materials. Several of the cities had large buildings on their citadels that may have been stores for grain or other goods collected as taxes. The rulers would have used these to pay craftsmen and public workers. They also issued goods to merchants for local and foreign trade, as can be seen from official stamps on sealings from sacks of goods in the warehouse at the coastal city of Lothal. In this town – as in others on the borders of the Indus civilization – there were many workshops where beads, shell bangles and gold and copper artefacts were turned out in quantities far exceeding local needs and therefore destined for trade. Some goods were traded with neighbouring groups of hunter-gatherers who supplied honey and other forest produce in exchange for copper knives, cultivated grain and domestic animals.

Five major cities dominated the Indus civilization: Harappa in the north, Rakhigarhi in the east, Dholavira in the south and Ganweriwala in the centre of the rich plains of the Saraswati, and Mohenjo Daro. Mohenjo Daro was by far the largest, and its central position gave it access to all quarters of the civilization and to the neighbouring Indo-Iranian borderlands. Many distinctive and unique features of Mohenjo Daro, from the Great Bath to the immense diversity of craft production, suggest strongly that this was the capital and seat of government.

The Indus people were the first in the ancient world to have toilets in their houses. Some were 'squatters', but others had seats.

2

PERSIAN GULF TRADE

By 2500 BC the development of the civilizations of Mesopotamia and the Indus had brought about a great change in international trade. Ships sailed from Indus ports through the Persian Gulf and up-river to anchor in Mesopotamian harbours such as Ur, directly linking the two major trading partners. The opening of this sea route bypassed the intermediate towns of the Iranian plateau, and as a result that area began to decline in importance and prosperity.

By contrast, the people of Dilmun (the island of Bahrain and adjacent territories) profited from this new trading route. The sweetness of the water of Dilmun was famous, and ships called there to replenish their supplies. The Dilmunites also sailed to Mesopotamia themselves, bringing their 'fish-eyes' (pearls), as well as goods they had acquired from the people of Meluhha (the Indus) and Magan (Oman) – the latter being a major source of copper ore.

The Indus people did not themselves greatly prize that precious commodity, lapis lazuli – they had many other fine stones to choose from closer to home, such as carnelian. But they were very aware of its value for trade, and so they founded a colony at Shortugai in Afghanistan, 1,000 km (600 miles) from home, from which they were able to exercise a monopoly over the export of lapis. They could also obtain lapis from a nearer source, in the Chagai hills of Baluchistan. Now Sumer could obtain its lapis lazuli only from the Indus people.

The traders and merchants of the Indus also supplied Sumer with ivory, fine beads of carnelian and other semiprecious stones, and many types of wood – used for constructing boats and buildings, and for making furniture. Some of these objects have survived to provide evidence of their origin, and we also know from Sumerian texts what they imported, and how they ran their trade. However, it is still a mystery what the Indus people imported from Mesopotamia – we cannot read their writings, and no obvious imports survive. Perhaps they were interested in luxury manufactured goods, such as fine woollen textiles and perfumed ointments.

 ## THE MYSTERY OF THE INDUS SCRIPT

Most early civilizations developed some form of writing, and the Indus people were no exception. The mature and sophisticated Indus script was used to write on seals, pots, copper tablets, bangles, amulets and probably many other artefacts that have now vanished, such as textiles and palm-leaf manuscripts. But, unfortunately, the Indus script has resisted all efforts to decipher it. There are a few clues. Some signs are pictorial, such the fish sign on the elephant seal illustrated here, though most are very stylized and difficult to interpret. Writing on amulets may well be magical formulae intended to protect the wearer, while that on pottery vessels probably describes their contents. The inscriptions on seals, usually only a few signs long, are likely to give the name or title of their owner. Although the seals cannot be read, they were clearly used in an official capacity – to identify individuals who worked for the state (as bureaucrats or merchants, for example), and to stamp goods to show that they were officially recorded.

The Indus script will probably never be deciphered – the texts that survive are too short, giving little to work on. In addition, we do not know what language the Indus people spoke – although most scholars think it was an early form of the Dravidian languages now spoken in southern India.

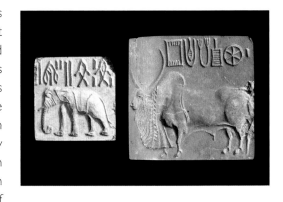

THE END OF THE INDUS CIVILIZATION

Around 1800 BC the Indus civilization went into a decline, and the highly organized life of the cities disappeared. Writing was abandoned and people came to rely on locally made goods rather than the specialized craft products of the former age. No one knows for sure what caused the decline, but there have been a number of suggestions.

The Indus decline coincides with political upheavals and economic problems in Mesopotamia, which in turn brought an end to the long-distance seaborne trade through the Gulf. Another factor may have been disease. Skeletons found at Mohenjo Daro show that many people in the cities suffered from serious illnesses such as malaria.

Environmental change also played its part. The great Saraswati river, which had watered an extremely fertile and productive farming area, began to dry up, cutting crop yields. Farmers in

the east and west were cultivating rice and millets, and these, unlike the wheat and barley grown in the Indus region, were crops highly suited to the lands further to the east and south, including the Ganges valley. Many farmers therefore moved east and south, further reducing the food supplies available to feed the city dwellers.

As things went wrong within the cities, nomads from the north moved in to take over some areas of the Indus. These nomads were Aryans, warlike horse-riding pastoralists who spoke an Indo-European language ancestral to the modern languages of northern India. In time, despite their small numbers, the Aryans came to dominate the agricultural communities among which they settled.

Indian village life continued relatively unchanged, but the towns disappeared. It was more than a thousand years before India again had towns and cities with drains and writing and specialized craftsmen, but many features of ancient Indus life survived, to re-emerge in the cities of historical times.

1. The Great Bath was the focal element of Mohenjo Daro's citadel mound. Nothing comparable is known from other Indus cities.

SETTLEMENTS

Hunter-gatherers usually lived in very small communities. Farming allowed more people to be supported by the produce of a smaller area, so settlements grew in size. As agriculture intensified so settlements expanded. Towns and cities were not just overgrown villages, however, but centres containing substantial public buildings and housing people engaged in a variety of occupations. Cities were often major political centres – larger and more complex than towns. In some civilizations, notably that of the Indus, cities were deliberately built to a predetermined plan.

2

Settlement location

People generally required a good water supply and access to adequate arable and pasture land, but a variety of other factors might also be influential in determining the location of settlements. Trading settlements sprang up at key places on trade routes and often became industrial centres, processing local or traded raw materials and manufacturing goods. Other

towns and cities developed as political centres in densely settled areas – in some cases, such as the highland Mexican city of Teotihuacán ($\triangleright$ pp. 196–7), the majority of a region's population might be accommodated within the city. This facilitated administrative control, but was less than convenient for the farmers, who had to travel out to their fields. Religion might also play a part in the original location of a settlement, as houses grew up around a shrine or sacred spot. In troubled times the needs of defence could be paramount in determining where a settlement was built. This could be inconvenient – for instance, the Mycenaeans had to construct substantial tunnels to allow the inhabitants of their fortified citadels to gain protected access to water collected in cisterns outside their walls.

Urban buildings

The variety of houses within a settlement generally reflected its social composition. In cities, housing was often arranged in neighbourhoods of different affluence – the humble dwellings of farmers and artisans, the mansions of wealthy merchants, adminis-

trators and nobles, and the palaces of priests and kings. Palaces not only had private apartments finely and lavishly constructed and furnished, but also often served as a city's administrative centre, with public audience halls, record offices and storerooms.

Such public functions might also be served by separate buildings – in ancient Rome, for instance, there were separate law courts, while political business was conducted in the Senate. Frequently these public buildings lay in the heart of the city and were accompanied by major religious edifices, since religion played a part in most aspects of life. Many ancient Indian cities had Buddhist monasteries within them, centres not only of religious devotion but also of education.

Towns and cities were usually the focus of trade and industrial activity. Some crafts, such as weaving or woodworking, could be undertaken in the home or in workshops within the settlement. Others, like metalworking and potting, caused some industrial pollution and

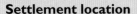

1

1. Wealthy, important individuals, like this Egyptian scribe, Nakht, and his wife, lived in comfortable and elegant houses with private gardens.

3

many societies preferred these to be located on the edges of settlements or beyond. In many cities, such as Teotihuacán, separate neighbourhoods housed different crafts. The large numbers of people within cities provided craftsmen with a substantial market, and trade networks ensured both the distribution of their products over a wider area and the supply of the raw materials they required. Many important Indus cities were located on the edge of the civilization to facilitate trade.

Urban life

City dwellers often had many ways to spend their time. Some societies provided public recreational facilities, such as Greek theatres and Roman bathhouses. Many cities included public parks and private gardens, and in some, like those of the Maya, crops were raised. There was often a public water supply, though in some cities water had to be fetched from outside. A few, such as Anuradhapura in Sri Lanka, had large pools in which the inhabitants could bathe as well as draw water. Sanitation was important – a few societies, such as the Indus civilization and the Romans, had excellent drains and toilets. But in all cities public health was a problem since the density of population maintained many diseases such as smallpox and tuberculosis. Often disease played a significant role in the eventual collapse of a civilization.

2. Some cities had defensive walls while others were protected by a river or moat that also provided a water supply for their citizens, as in this Elamite city, Madaktu.

3. Religious and administrative buildings lay in the heart of the city, as in the Roman Forum where the remains of temples still stand.

2.4 THE MIDDLE REALM

China – known to its inhabitants as 'the middle realm' – was one of the cradles of civilization. From 3500 BC intensive agriculture had enabled communities in the heartland around the Yangtze and Yellow rivers to expand – this brought them into conflict with each other. By 1800 BC this area of northern and central China was culturally unified under the Shang dynasty. The Shang state had many features of civilization – writing, cities, craft specialization and a complex social hierarchy. Under their successors, the Zhou, political unity gradually disintegrated into interstate warfare, but in 221 BC the Qin established the first Chinese empire.

Further south, hierarchical society was slow to develop. By the 3rd century BC, however, richly furnished graves show the emergence of an élite, able to command the services of fine craftsmen. In the steppe to the north, the Chinese came into conflict with warlike nomadic pastoralists, who produced magnificent metalwork and textiles.

THE SHANG

Between 3500 and 2000 BC farming communities in China grew culturally closer, developing many of the features so characteristic of Chinese civilization. Many of the finer objects were now made by specialist craftsmen, including delicate pottery drinking cups, and jars and bowls on tall stems or three legs. These were used in religious ceremonies, conducted in elaborate ceremonial centres. Jade, widely distributed through long-distance trade networks, was of great ritual importance. Jade objects were placed – along with other prestige goods – in the burials of the emerging leaders of society. Competition between communities led to warfare and the construction of massive defensive walls of tamped earth around the villages.

Around 1800 BC much of northern China was united under the leadership of the Shang dynasty. The Shang claimed to have the 'Mandate of Heaven' – they believed that their rule was divinely sanctioned. Texts inscribed on bronze vessels and oracle bones (▷ p. 73) give us an insight into life at this time. For example, people used oracle bones to enquire which ancestors were causing illness and what sacrifices were needed to placate them.

Shang kings ruled from a succession of capitals, of which the last, Yin (modern Anyang), is the best known. Shang cities were often spread over a wide area, with a fortified centre containing palaces, shrines, store-rooms and élite residences. Outside the city walls lay other residential areas, workshops and cemeteries. Kings travelled through their domains with their court, hunting for sport and for food, and observing and administrating their kingdoms. Most people, however, lived in scattered agricultural villages.

Craftsmanship

Workshops lay on the outskirts of the city. Here specialist craftsmen made fine, elaborately decorated bronze vessels, casting them in complex moulds made of many interlocking pieces of pottery. Many of these vessels were used in religious ceremonies, holding offerings of wine or food for the gods or the ancestors. The designs often had a special religious significance, such as the grotesque face known as 'taotie', perhaps intended to ward off evil. The shapes of these vessels reflected those made in pottery in earlier times.

The city craftsmen also manufactured pottery and objects of jade and lacquer. To make lacquerware a wooden base was overlaid with painted layers of the sap of the lacquer tree; this sap was waterproof and heat resistant as well as highly decorative. Shang lacquerware included small objects like boxes and ornaments, but lacquer was also used to decorate structures such as tomb ceilings.

Jade is an extremely beautiful, usually greenish, semiprecious stone, and is exceptionally hard and difficult to carve. To the Chinese it represented the eternal world of the gods and the afterlife. Jade placed in burials ensured the eternal life of the dead, while in life jade ornaments invoked divine protection. Shang jades include a number of ritual objects, as well as exquisite figures of animals and birds.

Royal graves

Fu Hao was the one of the wives of Wuding, a Shang king who reigned from 1324 to 1266 BC. Unlike most women of the time –

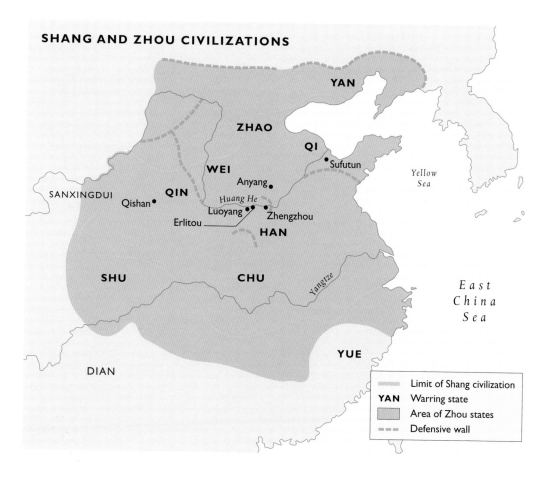

SHANG AND ZHOU CIVILIZATIONS

YAN

ZHAO

QI

WEI

• Sufutun

Anyang •

Yellow Sea

SANXINGDUI

QIN

Huang He

Qishan •

Luoyang •• • Zhengzhou

Erlitou

HAN

SHU

CHU

Yangtze

East China Sea

YUE

DIAN

	Limit of Shang civilization
YAN	Warring state
	Area of Zhou states
- - -	Defensive wall

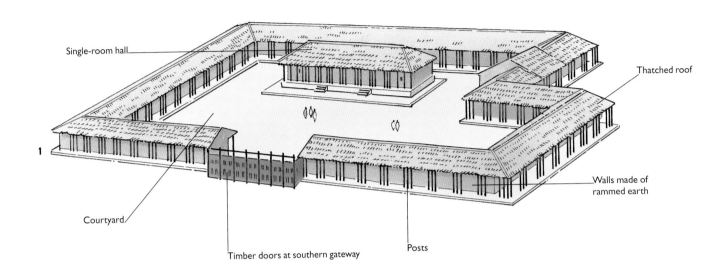

Single-room hall

Thatched roof

1

Walls made of
rammed earth

Courtyard

Posts

Timber doors at southern gateway

1. The palace was the heart of a Shang city. Not only the residence of the royal family, it was also the centre of administration, with halls and offices for dealing with both civil and military matters.

⭐ Chinese peasants thought oracle bones were the bones of dragons, which were believed to be shed just as snakes slough their skins.

who were confined to domestic matters – Wuding's wives had important roles in his government. Fu Hao was a general, leading the army in many campaigns. When she died she was buried in the traditional manner, in a wooden chamber at the bottom of a deep shaft. Six dogs and 16 men, women and children were sacrificed and placed in the grave shaft to serve her in the afterlife. Such human sacrifices were customary: one royal tomb contained 165. In Fu Hao's grave more than 1,600 precious objects were placed for her use in the other world: these included bronze ritual vessels, fine pottery, carved jade animals and birds, imported cowrie shells, rare ivory beakers decorated with turquoise. Since she was a war leader, she also had many weapons.

Neighbours and enemies

The Shang are China's first literate civilization, so we know a lot about them. Other prosperous states existed at the same time but are less well known. However, recent discoveries – such as the ritual offering pits at Sanxingdui in Sichuan, with their fabulous gilded bronzes

and jades – reveal a little of the splendours of the Shang's contemporaries.

The Shang both traded and fought with their neighbours. War captives were important as sacrificial victims, and their bodies were placed in the foundations of major buildings, in offering pits or in the graves of important people. Massive walls of tamped earth surrounded Shang cities as defence against external threats or internal revolts. The palace compounds within the city were also often separately walled. The king maintained a small permanent bodyguard, but peasants had to fight when required, forming armies several thousand strong. They were armed with bows and arrows, spears or halberds, and daggers for fighting at close quarters. The soldiers wore chest armour made from bamboo, and leather helmets. Captains rode into battle in chariots, with a driver to control the horses and a soldier holding a shield to guard the captain's back. The northern nomads fought from agile horses, so were difficult to pin down. Fighting the neighbouring tribes was more straightforward: battles were won by sheer weight of numbers and endurance.

THE ZHOU AND THE WARRING STATES

In 1027 BC the Shang dynasty fell to the rulers of the Zhou state to their west. The Zhou kings claimed the 'Mandate of Heaven', arguing that the Shang dynasty had forfeited it by their decadence. For about 250 years the Zhou dominated northern China, but in 771 BC the western part of their domains was overrun by nomads from the north. The Zhou moved east, founding a new capital at Luoyang (in modern Henan province), but other states that had previously acknowledged Zhou authority now began to compete for dominance.

Warfare became an established way of life for these rival states. Each maintained standing armies and could raise conscript armies of peasants tens of thousands strong.

People took refuge behind the strong walls of towns and cities and their enemies developed siege engines to attack them. States constructed earthen defensive walls along their borders. Many innovations in weaponry appeared, including crossbows and catapults, and saddles were adopted from the northern nomads. Warfare was no longer simply a matter of pitched battles but involved strategy and planning – one general wrote a manual of military advice, The Art of War, which is still highly regarded.

From the 5th century BC the number of rival states decreased as some gradually swallowed up their neighbours. The conflicts in this 'Warring States' period culminated in 221 BC in the overall victory of the Qin state, whose king founded the first Chinese empire (▷ p. 147).

 ## ORACLE BONES

The Chinese developed writing as a means of consulting their gods. Signs engraved on early Chinese pottery were the forerunners of the true script that had developed by the time of the Shang dynasty. These early signs are pictographic – they use simple pictures to convey words and ideas. Although later Chinese scripts became much more stylized, they retained many pictographic signs as well as phonetic elements.

The Shang people wrote questions to their gods or ancestors on the shoulder blades of pigs (right) and oxen or on the shells of turtles. They asked if the harvest would be good, if a planned hunt would be successful or whether it was a propitious time for the king to travel through his realms or to undertake a military campaign. King Wuding (▷ p. 71) asked about the baby his queen, Fu Hao, was expecting.

To answer a question, priests applied a hot metal rod to the bone and observed the pattern of cracks that it caused. They interpreted this as the gods' reply, which they recorded. When the event took place, they also recorded the outcome, which sometimes did not tally with the gods' reply. Wuding received a favourable reply to his question about the baby, but it turned out badly – from his point of view – because the baby that was born was a girl.

Technology

Iron working in China began in the 6th century BC and developed rapidly, since iron was abundant, cheap and more efficient than bronze. The Chinese learnt early how to cast iron, a technique not developed in the West until medieval times. While iron came into everyday use for tools and weapons, bronze continued to be used for ritual vessels and ornaments. A huge copper mine at Tonglushan was worked on an industrial scale through much of the Zhou period, with shafts up to 50 m (165 feet) deep.

Bronze was also used for casting bells. A magnificent set of 65 bronze bells mounted in a lacquered wooden stand was placed in the tomb of Yi, marquis of Zheng, who died in 433 BC, along with many other musical instruments such as flutes, stone chimes, panpipes and a zither. Music and hunting were popular pastimes of the élite in Zhou times.

Silk had been produced since before 2700 BC. By the Zhou period, raising silkworms and spinning and weaving silk were major industries. Despite the endemic warfare, much of the period was one of prosperity for farmers. Roads and canals were built to facilitate troop movements and the supply of food to the army on campaign, and as a by-product the canals also improved the supply of water to agricultural land,

1. This Shang bronze tripod vessel was probably used for preparing sacrificial meat to offer to the gods or ancestors. It is decorated with the face of a 'taotie', a benign monster who was thought to ward off evil.

increasing productivity. The state of Qin – the home of the future ruling dynasty of China – was particularly successful in this respect. Iron tools also made farming easier and more efficient.

Other changes

The Zhou period also saw the introduction of coinage, which aided commerce. Cowrie shells, which had been used as a simple medium of exchange in Shang times, were replaced by miniature bronze knives and spades in the 7th century BC, and in the 4th by copper coins with a central hole to allow them to be threaded on a string or belt.

The 6th century BC saw the emergence of two philosophies that were to be vitally important in Chinese life. Confucius (Kongfuzi, 551–479 BC), adviser to the ruler of the state of Lu, advocated a way of life based on mutual respect, duty and responsibility between people in all walks of life and the maintenance of traditional values. The Confucian emphasis on wise paternalism and clear authority, in both family and state, had a major long-term effect on Chinese rulers and society. In contrast, Lao Zi, who lived around the same time as Confucius, proposed a way of life that maintained links with nature and one that fostered simplicity – Daoism.

2. The Chinese used complicated piece moulds to cast intricate shapes in bronze. This ornament, dating from the late Zhou dynasty, depicts wrestlers, some of the many entertainers who performed for the élite. 2

METALWORKERS OF THE SOUTH

Rice cultivation, which had begun in the Yangtze valley by about 5500 BC, gradually spread southward into southern China, Vietnam and Thailand. Small village communities developed, which produced attractive pottery painted with swirling geometric patterns and stone and shell jewellery. Exchange networks were already operating, giving people access to raw materials from other regions, and these developed greatly after 1500 BC when bronze working began. Copper ores occur widely over the area, while tin – the other metal required to manufacture the alloy bronze – is found in many parts of south Malaya. Bronze bangles and occasionally bronze axes began to be placed as grave goods in the burials of the emerging élite.

After 500 BC iron began to be worked too. Iron ores were far more widespread and abundant than copper and tin, and it was not long before tools of wrought iron came into common use. Iron tools made it possible to clear and prepare land for agriculture, resulting in a rapid expansion of settlement into areas previously only sparsely inhabited. Conflict between communities also began to develop as they expanded, and for the first time weapons as well as tools were made. More marked differences in wealth and status are seen most clearly in the treatment of the dead, from simple graves with few offerings to splendid burials in elaborately carved wooden coffins or plastered cists (stone-slab coffins), with rich grave goods of stone and bronze.

Among the finest and most prestigious objects in the graves of community leaders were bronze drums. Named after the site of Dong Son in northern Vietnam where they were first found, these drums were most common in Vietnam and Yunnan in southern China but were traded into Thailand, Malaya, Java and Sumatra. Made by the lost-wax process (▷ p. 45), they were exquisitely decorated with fine linear designs of animals and geometric shapes, as well as stylized scenes of people engaged in activities such as paddling canoes.

The people of Yunnan, known to the Zhou Chinese as the Dian, also made drums. These had three-dimensional scenes of figures arranged on their surfaces – less finely made than the Dong Son drums but more elaborate. From these we can gain a picture of life in these communities: fishing played a major role in the economy alongside rice cultivation, while sports included bull fighting. These drums were used as containers for valuables such as cowrie shells. Cowrie shells had earlier been traded into northern China where they were used as currency, while pieces of carved jade found their way south.

A leather pouch found in a frozen grave at Pazyryk in the Altai region of southern Siberia was finely decorated with blue and white fur – and still contained cheese.

1. (opposite) The richest grave at Khok Phanom Di in Thailand held a woman adorned with large shell discs and more than 120,000 shell beads.

1. A felt rug from one of the richly furnished graves at Pazyryk in the Altai is decorated with appliqué designs showing a seated goddess.

THE CONQUEST OF THE STEPPES

As well as trading to the south the Chinese also interacted with their neighbours to the north and west, the nomads of the Asiatic steppes. This interaction mainly took the form of constant warfare, but there was also some trade. The Chinese borrowed many ideas and innovations from the steppe nomads, such as wearing trousers for horse-riding.

The steppe zone – which stretches right across Central Asia to the eastern fringes of Europe – is one of rich but scattered pastures. Herders were not able to exploit this region until the domestication of the horse (around 4000 BC in the area north of the Black Sea) and the invention of wheeled transport (around 3500 BC in the Near East) gave them the mobility to move across this vast region. This mobility was increased around 2000 BC by the development of lighter, faster carts with spoked wheels and the adoption of horse-riding. The innovation of keeping animals for milk as well as meat also played a part, promoting pastoralism as a specialist way of life. By 1500 BC, pastoralist groups existed across the steppe region from the Black Sea to Mongolia.

As well as keeping herds of horses, sheep and cattle, and hunting wild game, these nomads raided their settled neighbours, particularly in times of hardship when the grazing was poor. Their mobility made them hard to defeat, so the Chinese attempted to cope with their attacks in other ways: by building walls to keep them out, by buying them off with luxury goods such as silk cloth, and by bribing one group of nomads to keep the others at bay – for the steppe peoples were frequently at war with each other too.

Nomadic life

Although some steppe peoples engaged in agriculture and lived in settlements, the majority moved between areas of pasture, living in tents or covered wooden wagons. Despite their mobile lifestyle they produced a wealth of beautifully crafted objects. These included colourful woollen textiles, woven or made of felt, and horse harness and clothing made of leather and decorated with appliqué designs, particularly of animals. They also made finely carved wooden furniture and horse decorations, and vessels and jewellery of gold and silver decorated in an extraordinarily rich and exuberant style. These depicted not only their own lives – hunting, fighting, milking and sitting around – but also the wild birds and beasts of the steppe, not to mention fantastical creatures inspired by drug-induced hallucinations.

 The ancient Chinese had a special type of ritual bronze axe that they used for beheading their sacrificial victims. One example that has been found is decorated with an execution scene.

▷ NOMAD TOMBS

Most of our evidence of the steppe nomads comes from the graves of their nobles and royalty. In the Altai region of Siberia and Mongolia great mounded tombs have been preserved by freezing in ice. Important people from the steppe tribes were buried in wooden chambers constructed in the base of deep shafts. Once filled in, a huge mound of earth and stones was erected over the top. The tomb often contained the burial of several important people, laid out in all their finery – gold torcs (neckrings) and pectorals (chest ornaments), leather boots decorated with gold leaf, felt stockings and fur robes. The bodies were often placed in a coffin made from a tree trunk. Around them were heaps of their possessions – gold and electrum jars (right), wooden stools, decorated leather bags, felt wall hangings, Persian carpets and Chinese silks. Sacrificed servants were also placed in the grave, along with a number of slaughtered horses laid out with all their finest harness.

The 5th-century BC Greek historian Herodotus wrote about the Scythians, the steppe nomads living in the lands around the Black Sea at the time that the Greeks colonized its coasts. His description of royal funerals closely matches the evidence found in the Altai graves. He wrote that the bodies were gutted and stuffed with aromatic herbs and spices to preserve them. The people found in the Altai graves were embalmed in this fashion, and several bodies are so well-preserved that one can still see the elaborate tattoos with which they were often decorated. The tattoos reflect the same themes as the designs on artefacts – predators hunting their prey, lively horses and swirling patterns.

TOMBS AND BURIAL PRACTICES

For most ancient peoples, the importance an individual had in life was reflected in the manner of his or her burial. In China and across the steppes of Asia, royal and élite graves were often placed under enormous mounds, while in Egypt and Mesoamerica kings and other powerful leaders were interred within pyramids. The domed shape of Buddhist stupas reflected their origin as funerary mounds housing the remains of Buddhist saints (▷ p. 140). In some places the élite had tombstones, while ordinary peasants were buried in unmarked graves.

1. Jade was believed by the Chinese to ensure immortality. Prince Liu Sheng (who died in 113 BC) and his wife Dou Wan were buried in suits of jade plaques fastened with gold in an attempt to preserve their bodies.

Taking it with you

The mounds, pyramids or mausoleums of the élite enclosed elaborate burials in which the corpse was surrounded by a rich range of precious grave goods that would serve and give pleasure to the deceased in the afterlife. More sinisterly, such burials sometimes included the bodies of servants, concubines, soldiers and horses, sacrificed to attend and protect the dead leader in the hereafter. In time, real human sacrifices gave way to the burial of representations – such as the life-size terracotta army guarding China's first emperor, or the 'shabti' figures placed in Egyptian graves.

The grave goods interred with a person usually reflected their position both within

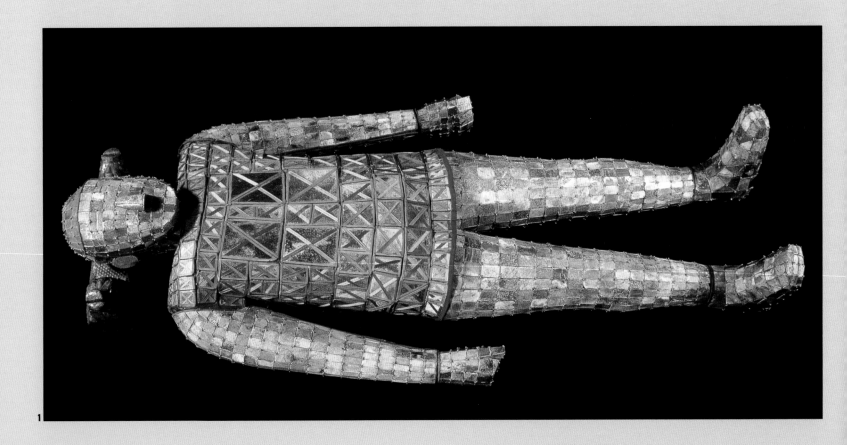

1

their kin group and in society. Some grave goods related to the gender or age of the deceased. Others cross-cut these distinctions to mirror status or occupation. A well-off person below the highest rank might be buried with some metal jewellery, while a skilled craftsman might be interred with the tools of his trade. A humbler member of society might only be accompanied by their clothes and a few possessions, such as a knife or spindle, plus food or drink for the afterlife.

Grave goods are often a major source of information about a past society. The range of goods found in different graves tells us how highly structured the society was, and what was chosen for burial tells us what they regarded as valuable and significant. For example, an iron dagger placed in the tomb of Tutankhamun reflects the high value placed on this new and rare material in the 14th century BC.

Dust to dust or living for eternity

The way the bodies of the dead were treated varied from culture to culture, and also within an individual culture. In some societies, such as those of ancient Egypt, the steppes and South America, important people were mummified. In Egypt the lavishness of this treatment reflected social standing, from the simple untreated burial of peasants to the long and elaborate process used to preserve the royal bodies of the pharaohs.

Other cultures employed a variety of methods of disposal, such as simple inhumation or cremation. Alternatively, bodies might be exposed until animals and birds had picked the bones clean; these were then collected and deposited in a grave or tomb, often along with many others. Such rites were practised as far apart as Neolithic Europe, Iron Age

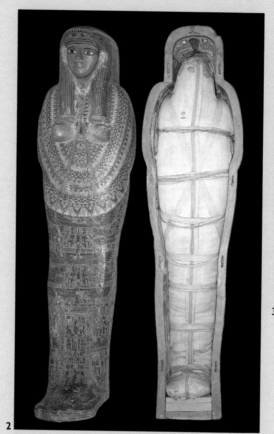

2. The Egyptians gave elaborate rites to their dead, often mummifying the body, which was then wrapped in linen and placed in a painted coffin.

3. Pacal the Great, king of the important Maya city of Palenque from AD 615 to 683, was buried in a magnificent stone sarcophagus deep within this pyramid.

south India and early eastern North America. The construction of such communal tombs emphasized group affiliation to ancestral lands rather than individual identity.

A culture's religious beliefs often played an important role in determining the rites used for disposing of the dead. The ancient Egyptians thought it necessary for the body to be preserved in order for the spirit to have a place to dwell. But there were other cultures for whom the soul could not be released into the afterworld until the body had been cleaned of flesh or destroyed, by being eaten by animals for instance. Burial practices and religion were often closely allied.

◆ TOPIC LINKS

1.1 Taking Over the World
p.12 Individuals and Society

2.2 The Lands Between the Rivers
p.49 Royal Graves at Ur

2.4 The Middle Realm
p.71 Royal Graves
p.79 Nomad Tombs

2.5 The Gift of the Nile
p.90 The Valley of the Kings

3.4 The Great Han
p.148 Tombs

4.1 The Continent Awakes
p.190 The Moundbuilders

4.3 A Vertical Realm
p.214 Royal Graves

THE GIFT OF THE NILE

The magnificent civilization of ancient Egypt, which emerged around 5,000 years ago, was completely dependent on the river Nile. Egypt is almost entirely a land of desert, but the waters of the Nile gave the country great agricultural wealth. This 'gift of the Nile' enabled Egypt's pharoahs (kings) to build massive tombs and palaces as enduring monuments to their power.

Despite several periods of internal upheaval, the Egyptians were able to maintain their independence for more than two millennia. From around 2000 BC warrior pharaohs expanded Egypt's borders first to the south and then to the north, establishing a territorial empire that was one of the ancient world's first superpowers. However, Egyptian independence was ended in the 7th century BC when it fell prey to a more aggressive empire, that of the Assyrians. Thereafter, Egyptian culture became gradually submerged beneath a succession of foreign overlords.

EARLY DYNASTIC EGYPT AND THE OLD KINGDOM

Farming and settlement in Egypt were at first confined to a narrow ribbon on either side of the Nile, whose annual flood watered the fields. For most of Egyptian history, the Nile valley (known as Upper Egypt) remained the main focus of Egyptian culture and political power; to the north, the Nile delta region (known as Lower Egypt) was slower to develop.

Shortly before 3000 BC the confederations of fortified towns in Upper Egypt were united, with Hieraconpolis emerging as the leading town. Hieraconpolis extended its influence northwards into Lower Egypt, which was politically not as well organized as the south. According to tradition, the whole of Egypt was unified under a single ruler by Narmer (also known as Menes) around 3000 BC. This marks the beginning of the 'Dynastic Period' in Egypt – Narmer and all subsequent pharaohs were arranged by ancient Egyptian historians into a series of dynasties according to family or regional connections.

After unification the balance of power within Egypt shifted northwards, creating an underlying tension between Upper and Lower Egypt – some monuments, for example, were duplicated, with both a northern and southern version. This tension was to surface intermittently throughout Egyptian history. During this early period the series of myths and rituals surrounding the Egyptian animal-headed gods and goddesses

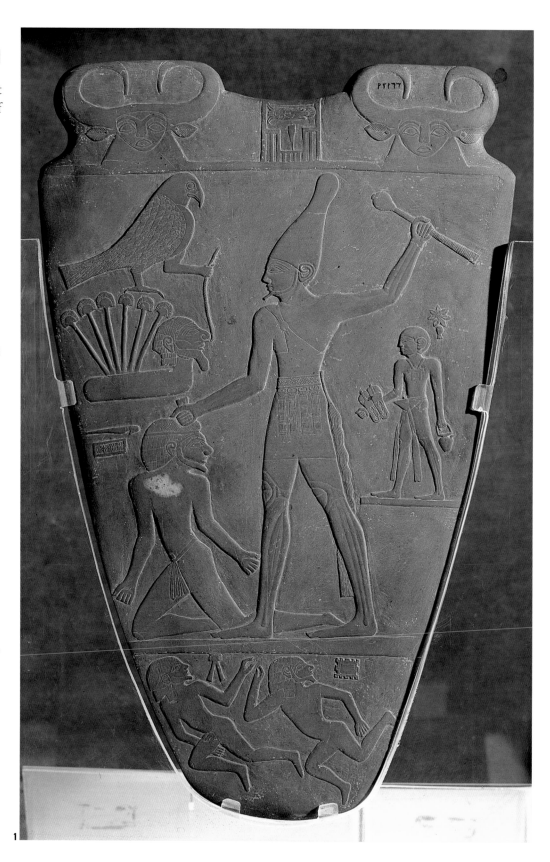

1. This ceremonial plaque of Narmer, the first king of united Egypt, shows him smiting an enemy. The king's name, symbolized by a catfish with a chisel, is set within a rectangular frame that represents the façade of a palace. 1

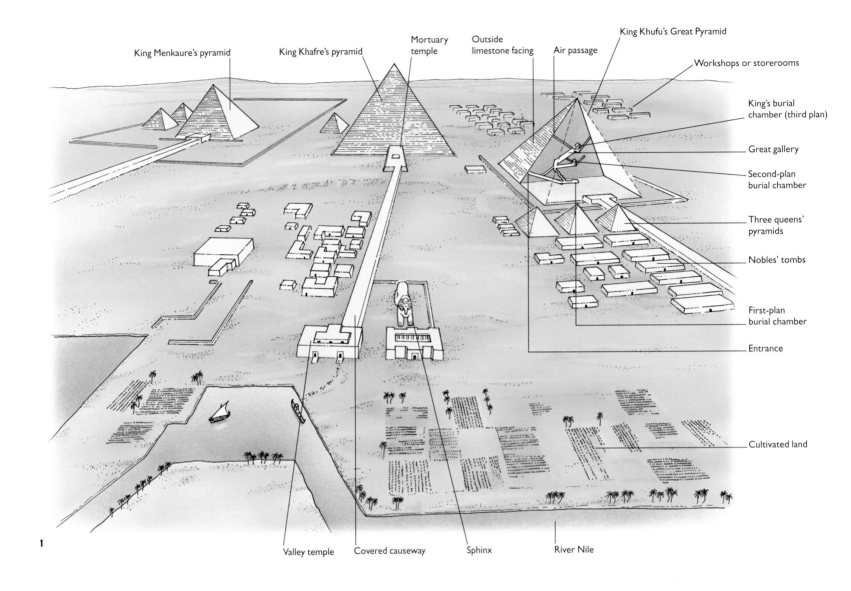

King Menkaure's pyramid

King Khafre's pyramid

Mortuary temple

Outside limestone facing

Air passage

King Khufu's Great Pyramid

Workshops or storerooms

King's burial chamber (third plan)

Great gallery

Second-plan burial chamber

Three queens' pyramids

Nobles' tombs

First-plan burial chamber

Entrance

Cultivated land

Valley temple

Covered causeway

Sphinx

River Nile

1

1. The royal burial complex at Giza was dominated by the Great Pyramid of Khufu (right). Before it stood the three small pyramids of his queens. To its south lay the pyramid of Khafre and beyond that the smaller pyramid of Menkaure.

(who probably originated as the animal totems of individual towns) were merged into a single national religion.

A new capital was established at Memphis, where the narrow Nile valley widens into the delta, and the port of Buto (in the middle of the delta) imported luxury goods, such as wine, from the Levant. The lure of the south, however, was greater. Egypt's southern neighbour, Nubia, was a rich source of cattle and exotic goods such as ivory and animal skins. By the middle of the 3rd millennium BC Egyptian settlers had estab-

lished an outpost at Buhen, in central Nubia.

As Egypt grew in power and wealth, and the Nile delta became more intensively cultivated, the state was able to devote considerable resources to ceremonial projects, chief among which was the burial of the pharaoh. Around 2700 BC, the pharaoh Zoser had the first pyramid – supposedly designed by the architect Imhotep – constructed as part of his funerary complex at Saqqara near Memphis. Unlike later pyramids, Zoser's pyramid did not have smooth sides, but rose in several great steps.

2. The pyramid of Khafre was built of blocks of stone brought to the site by river. In front of the pyramid, the king's mortuary temple stretched almost to the river. Beside it reclined the sphinx, a huge lion-bodied creature with the king's head.

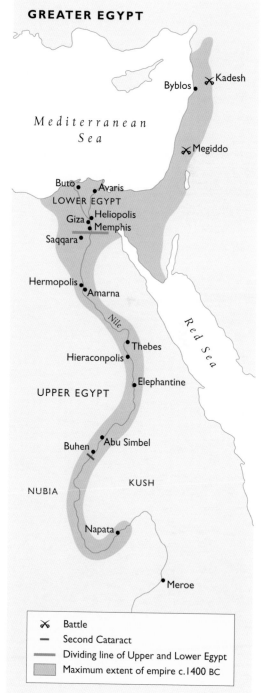

GREATER EGYPT

Kadesh
Byblos
Mediterranean Sea
Megiddo
Buto
Avaris
LOWER EGYPT
Giza
Heliopolis
Memphis
Saqqara
Hermopolis
Amarna
Nile
Thebes
Hieraconpolis
Red Sea
Elephantine
UPPER EGYPT
Buhen
Abu Simbel
KUSH
NUBIA
Napata
Meroe

✕ Battle
— Second Cataract
━ Dividing line of Upper and Lower Egypt
▓ Maximum extent of empire c.1400 BC

Building a state

The reign of Zoser marks the beginning of the Old Kingdom period in Egypt, which was the great age of pyramid building – over 50 were built in all. The three most famous pyramids are at Giza, and were built between 2650 and 2550 BC by the pharaohs Khufu, Khafre and Menkaure. The Great Pyramid of Khufu is the largest ever built. It measures 147 m (482 feet) high and was constructed with more than 2 million stone blocks, each weighing on average 2.5 tonnes; the largest blocks weigh 80 tonnes.

Pyramid construction was extremely important to the development of the Egyptian state. Pyramids were the first Egyptian monuments to be made of stone, as opposed to mud brick, and stone now became the building material of choice for all prestige projects. The use of stone gave a sense of permanence and continuity to Egyptian culture.

Even more important was the process of construction itself. Egypt was not very urbanized at this time, and most people lived in small agricultural villages, their lives revolving around the annual Nile flood. All of the construction work, including quarrying and transporting the thousands of tonnes of stone, was carried out by work gangs of ordinary farmers, who either volunteered or were 'recruited' each year. Most of the work was carried out during the months of flood, when work in the fields was impossible, and when the best possible use of water transport could be made.

The responsibility for organizing and feeding a large temporary workforce of up to 40,000 labourers – supervised by teams of master builders and skilled craft workers – required detailed and efficient administration, particularly as the construction of a single pyramid was spread over 20–30 years. Egyptian officials made extensive use of hieratic writing – a simplified form of hieroglyphics (▷ p. 57) – and papyrus, an early form of paper made from the stems of a river plant.

The construction of the pyramids – intended to help their king become immortal – was a staggering achievement. This achievement was all the greater because it was done largely with stone tools. Although some copper tools (such as chisels) were in use, Egypt was much slower than other parts of the Old World in adopting advances in metallurgy. Bronze tools did not become widespread in Egypt until a thousand years after the Giza pyramids were completed.

THE MIDDLE KINGDOM

The development of an efficient administration and 'civil service' undoubtedly strengthened the central authority of the Egyptian state. The system, however, depended on a number of regional governors ('nomarchs') to organize affairs locally, especially in the more distant parts of the country. Some of these governors became extremely powerful, and founded their own local dynasties.

Around 2200 BC Egypt was devastated by a series of agricultural disasters – the Nile either flooded too much or too little – and central control collapsed. What followed is known as the 'First Intermediate Period'. Local rulers vied with each other for the title of pharaoh, and fierce civil war broke out in the south between Hieraconpolis and the rival town of Thebes. The Thebans eventually

won the struggle, and around 2050 BC the Theban ruler Mentuhotep II reunited the whole country under his rule. For a people who had experienced 150 years of anarchy and unrest, the restoration of a single ruler brought a great sense of relief.

Conquest and trade

The reign of Mentuhotep II marks the beginning of the period known as the 'Middle Kingdom', an era of peace and stability. During the Middle Kingdom, Egypt grew wealthy through trade and conquest, and Egyptian artists and craft workers created masterpieces of jewellery and painting that were to be imitated, but never bettered, by later generations.

Northern Nubia was conquered and settled around 2000 BC, and fortified towns were

BUHEN

Traditionally, Egypt's southern border was located near the town of Elephantine in the Nile valley. To the south of Elephantine was the first of a series of cataracts – rocky narrows – that impeded river travel. When the Egyptians conquered northern Nubia around 2000 BC, they built a series of fortresses in the desert around the second cataract of the Nile. The fortress of Buhen was one of the largest, and presents a very different picture of Egyptian life than that suggested by tombs and temples.

As well as its purely defensive purpose, Buhen was intended to be a symbol of Egyptian military power. Built entirely of fireproof mud brick, it measured 80 m (260 feet) square and had a double wall surrounded by a deep ditch. Numerous bastions reinforcing the outer wall allowed defenders to rain missiles on attackers from the sides. The inner wall was 7 m (23 feet) thick and had a sheer 15-m (50-foot) face. There were large towers at the corners, with smaller towers spaced regularly in between.

Buhen would have been a tough nut to crack, even for a properly equipped and trained army. Against the tribal troops commanded by the kings of Nubia it remained impregnable, until it was eventually abandoned during the Egyptian withdrawal from Nubia around 1100 BC.

1. Models placed in Middle Kingdom nobles' tombs ensured that they would have a properly equipped existence in the afterlife. Here peasants stack their grain in the granary, while scribes record the details.

2. A sculpture showing a royal scribe working under the protection of Thoth, god of writing and knowledge.

established to protect the new southern border. Along the northern borders Egypt began to play an increasing role in the economic networks developing in the eastern Mediterranean. The main trading partner for Egyptian shipping was the Levant port of Byblos (now Jubeil, in modern Lebanon), which had a thriving colony of Egyptian merchants. Land routes into the Levant were fortified, and military expeditions sent to deal with any interruption of trade. Ships from Minoan Crete (▷ p. 95) also called regularly at Egyptian ports.

The internal economy of Egypt developed and improved at this time. Expeditions were sent into the Sinai peninsula to locate and mine copper ores. Around 1900 BC the pharaoh Sesostris II ordered the draining, colonization and cultivation of the Fayum oasis, a large swamp deep in the desert to the west of the Nile valley. This was a huge undertaking, and whole new towns (such as Kuhun) had to be constructed to house the workers and officials involved in the project. The pharaoh himself supervised the start of agriculture on the reclaimed land. His successor, Sesostris III, reformed the working of the administration to reduce the power of local nomarchs.

Some 4000 years ago wealthy Egyptian men and women wore heavy eye make-up containing minerals that helped prevent eye infection and disease.

1. Paintings in the tombs of wealthy and important individuals depict them in many everyday scenes. The governors' tombs at Beni Hasan show them fishing and hunting in the marshes.

2. Relief decoration on the walls of Queen Hatshepsut's temple at Deir-i Bahri give a vivid account of the expedition that she sent to Punt. In this detail we see her soldiers on parade carrying axes and standards.

Hyksos

The Middle Kingdom came to an end in about 1750 BC, when the central government was overthrown by groups of foreigners already living in Egypt. For the previous century or so, peoples known as the Hyksos had been settling in the fortified towns on the Levant trade routes and in the eastern delta region. The Hyksos (which means 'kings from the hills') entered Egypt from the Levant, but they may have originated further east. The Hyksos period is also known as the 'Second Intermediate Period'.

Although they adopted the Egyptian lifestyle, the Hyksos settlers – such as craft workers, and merchants and their retinues (including armed guards) – brought with them advanced bronze metallurgy, and weapons hitherto unknown in Egypt, including the horse-drawn chariot and the reflex bow. The bow, which was made of laminated strips of wood and horn, was shorter and more powerful than conventional bows, and became a favourite weapon of later warrior pharaohs.

The Hyksos took control of the delta region, and established a capital at Avaris. They could not, however, establish control of the Nile valley, and Egyptian resistance rallied around the town of Thebes, which became the seat of a rival 'Egyptian' dynasty. In about 1550 BC, by using their own weapons and tactics against them, the Theban pharaoh Ahmose I was able to defeat the Hyksos and drive them out of Egypt. The country was reunited once more, with a new capital at Thebes. This was the beginning of the era known as the 'New Kingdom'.

NEW KINGDOM GLORY

During the New Kingdom period a series of warrior pharaohs developed a powerful and well-trained army that was used to conquer and control an empire extending far beyond the borders of Egypt itself. By around 1500 BC the Egyptians had regained control of northern Nubia, and 50 years later they invaded Kush (central Nubia) and established the fortified town of Napata near the fourth cataract of the Nile. This push to the south was reinforced by the expeditions of Queen Hatshepsut to Punt (on the coast of modern Somalia) in about 1490 BC. The ships sent by Hatshepsut (by way of the Red Sea) brought back a rich booty of exotic goods, including incense trees, and reopened trade links with the far south.

In the north, Tutmose I (ruled c.1504–1492 BC) invaded the Levant, led his armies to the Euphrates river in Mesopotamia and defeated the Mitanni (▷ p. 51). A second Egyptian victory, outside the city of Megiddo in northern Palestine around 1460 BC, gave Egypt control of the whole of the Levant coast. A peace agreement was concluded, and was cemented by the marriage of the pharaoh Amenhotep III to a Mitanni princess.

Thebes became a capital city worthy of its empire. Amenhotep III built the great temple of Amun, which became a centre of wealth and power in its own right. Thanks to generous grants from the pharaoh, the temple at Karnak controlled about one quarter of all the cultivated land in Egypt. Other magnificent temples also adorned Thebes, such as the one at Luxor, and Hatshepsut's mortuary temple on the opposite bank of the Nile. The tombs of New Kingdom nobles at nearby Deir el-Medina show that the wealth of empire was spread fairly liberally around – at least among the upper echelons of society.

Revolutionary religion

Around 1350 BC the pharaoh Amenhotep IV attempted a radical reform of Egyptian religion. The traditional animal-headed deities were replaced by a single, all-powerful sun god known as Aten. This reform may have been inspired by genuine religious conviction, but it also represented an attempt by the pharaoh to curb the growing powers of the great temples.

Amenhotep changed his name to Akenaten in honour of the new god, and ordered the construction of a huge palace city on a new site at the edge of the desert. For a brief time this new city of Amarna was the capital of the Egyptian empire. Records found at Amarna show that the pharaoh conducted an extensive correspondence with his 'brother' kings in the Near East – the rulers of the Hittite, Assyrian and Babylonian empires.

After Akenaten's death around 1336 BC, both his city and his reforms were soon abandoned. His son, Tutankhamun, died while young, and a new dynasty soon came to power. Most of Amarna was destroyed, and throughout Egypt references to Aten were erased from temples and monuments.

Slow decline

Egyptian control of the Levant was challenged by the emergent power of the Hittites. A series of military expeditions culminated in the great chariot battle of Kadesh around 1300 BC (▷ p. 102). The Egyptians, led by the last of the great warrior pharaohs, Ramses II, claimed a great victory. In 1265 BC, however, Ramses made a treaty with the Hittites, in which he ceded control of the northern Levant. He then devoted himself to building great temples, such as that at Abu Simbel, and a new capital city in the Nile delta.

2

Egyptian military power rallied briefly under Ramses III, who in 1186 BC defeated the 'Sea Peoples' who had been ravaging the eastern Mediterranean region (▷ p. 105). But the Egyptian empire was crumbling. By about 1100 BC control of both the Levant and Nubia had been lost, and Egypt was confined behind its original boundaries. Within Egypt, central authority declined, and corruption and lawlessness increased. The period from around 1070 BC to 664 BC is often known as the 'Third Intermediate Period'.

Withdrawal of Egyptian troops from Nubia allowed local chiefs to consolidate their own power, and by about 950 BC an independent state of Kush had emerged with its capital at Napata. As the power of the pharaohs declined, the rulers of Kush were able to extend their authority over southern Egypt. Around 727 BC the Kushite king Piankhi marched into northern Egypt and took control of the whole country, establishing a Nubian dynasty. Some 60 years later, in 664 BC, Egypt was invaded by the Assyrians and Thebes was sacked. The Kushites retreated to Nubia, where they established a new capital at Meroë. The pharaoh Psamtek, appointed by the Assyrians to rule Egypt, established a new capital at Saïs. Psamtek freed Egypt from Assyrian domination, and his successors went on to defeat the Kushites. Independence was short-lived, however, as in 525 BC Egypt was conquered by the Persians, then in 332 BC by the Greeks under Alexander the Great, and finally in 31 BC by the Romans.

1. (opposite) Two colossal statues of Ramses II flank the Great Pylon, the second gateway into the temple of Amun-Ra at Karnak.

 THE VALLEY OF THE KINGS

Egyptian legal records show that by 1500 BC tomb robbing was a long-established crime. Archaeology has confirmed this: few tombs have been discovered that were not pillaged soon after they were sealed. When they established their new capital at Thebes, the pharaohs decided on a different burial strategy to ensure that their mummified bodies and carefully selected grave goods would remain undisturbed. Instead of being buried beneath a huge pyramid, surrounded by a labyrinth of funerary temples, the Theban pharaohs now opted for stealth, being buried in tombs at the end of one or more long corridors cut into the natural rock walls of a narrow valley now known as the Valley of the Kings. Egyptian queens were buried in a similar valley nearby.

Unfortunately, the strategy did not work. No matter how hard officials tried to keep the locations secret, and despite harsh penalties for those caught, almost all of these tombs were robbed, sometimes before the clay sealing the tomb had dried out. Carvings and paintings inside the tombs have survived, but the contents are long gone. At least one tomb did remain undisturbed, however – that of the boy-king Tutankhamun (seen here with his young wife), constructed around 1350 BC and re-discovered in 1922. Its contents provided a breathtaking glimpse of the luxurious beauty that surrounded an Egyptian pharaoh, even in death.

WARFARE

The Egyptian, Mesopotamian and Chinese states were created through warfare and conquest. By this period military organization had become relatively sophisticated, but warfare itself – organized violence between clearly identified mutual enemies – is certainly older than urban civilization. Some of the earliest farming communities, such as Jericho, were strongly fortified against the threat of attack. During the prehistoric period, however, there is very little evidence of actual warfare. It is almost impossible to distinguish between tools intended as weapons and those made for other purposes, such as hunting.

3

The first armies

The emergence of the world's first cities in Mesopotamia also witnessed the appearance of the first armies. Although originally city 'guardians', these armies soon became instruments in the conflicts between Mesopotamian city-states.

Military prowess and leadership in war were among the duties of a ruler, as important as his devotion to the city's gods and goddesses. Military rank also began to be an important factor in determining an individual's overall status in society. Organized around a professional core (palace guards, gatekeepers, and so on), the bulk of these early armies consisted of ordinary men, drafted into military service for a particular war or battle. Typically, they were issued with a bronze-headed spear, a shield, and perhaps a bronze helmet, all made in palace or temple workshops.

Warfare consisted of one or both armies, and their supplies, marching until they were within sight of each other. If the armies met in the open, battle was a measured or headlong advance to stabbing, hacking and kicking at each other until one side ran away. If one army stayed within its city, this was attacked and sometimes burned. In the Americas, however, battles were to catch the enemy alive so they could be formally sacrificed later. Broadly speaking, this pattern of warfare was found everywhere that civilization developed – with one notable exception. Curiously, the Indus civilization left no evidence of warfare at all.

Innovations

Expertise in metalworking permitted the development of the first true weapon of war – the bronze sword – a fairly fragile weapon that required considerable skill and courage to use effectively in combat. From the outset, in about 2000 BC, swords were an élite weapon, often with elaborately decorated hilts, that conveyed prestige upon their users, who were accorded higher status than the masses who fought with spears. Spearmen in turn generally had higher status than those who hurled slingshots or loosed arrows from a distance.

Slider

Ratchet

Claw and trigger

Winch

Universal joint

Pedestal

0 25 50 75 100

Scale in cm

1

Warfare also began to develop its own rules: formal declarations were issued, and diplomacy evolved. Generally, these rules tended to lessen the destruction caused by wars – cities that surrendered immediately might be spared the horrors inflicted on those that resisted. The idea – if not the reality – of armies and even states being represented by a single champion emerged – David and Goliath, for example.

Horse power entered warfare with chariots, which were developed around the same time and place as iron making – eastern Asia Minor in about 2000 BC. Chariotry spread rapidly and widely, reaching China, Hungary and Egypt within 300 years. The chariot, which brought great power and mobility to the battlefield, also required a team of specialist workers to construct and maintain it – and became a lasting symbol of power and prestige throughout much of Eurasia.

Cavalry – mounted spearmen or archers – appeared on the battlefields of the Middle East about 1000 BC and added another element of mobility and shock power to the battlefield. In some societies, they also added another tier to the hierarchy of military and social status.

As the early empires grew in size and complexity, so did their armies, with many specialized units, often ethnically based with a distinctive style of fighting or weaponry. The great armies of Assyria, Greece, Rome and Zhou China all had regiments of engineers, smiths and other technicians able to survey enemy fortifications and devise and construct great war engines – such as battering rams, siege towers and giant catapults – able to overcome the strongest city walls. Another innovation was the development of naval warfare (▷ pp. 166–7).

3. Initially the chariot just provided transport to the battlefield, where individuals still fought hand to hand. Its later development into a mobile fighting platform transformed warfare.

1. The need for superiority in battle and siege warfare was a great spur to technological development. This catapult was invented in 399 BC to help the Greeks defeat the Carthaginians.

2. The bow, seen in use in this Assyrian relief, was a powerful and popular weapon of war.

◈ TOPIC LINKS

2.2 The Lands Between the Rivers
p.48 Warfare and Politics

2.4 The Middle Realm
p.72 Neighbours and Enemies

2.6 Zone of Conflict
p.101 The Hittites

3.5 Mediterranean Conflicts
p.163 Military Power

2.6 ZONE OF CONFLICT

From around 2000 BC the eastern Mediterranean region became a focus of conflict and upheaval. The older civilizations based in Egypt and Mesopotamia now had to share the region with new civilizations that had emerged at the fringes. In the west, first the Minoans of Crete and then the Mycenaeans of mainland Greece maintained maritime trade networks that developed long-distance links between the Near East and Europe for the first time. In Anatolia, the militaristic Hittite empire developed and successfully challenged both Mesopotamian and Egyptian military power. For the first time, major advances – such as iron making and alphabets – were developed away from the older centres of civilization.

Around 1200 BC, however, much of the established order was swept away by a wave of warfare and destruction. After a few centuries of relative 'darkness', the eastern Mediterranean emerged into a new, wider, westward-looking world.

MINOAN LIFE

The island of Crete was colonized around 6000 BC by settlers from the Near East, who brought with them the mixed-farming techniques developed earlier in western Asia (▷ pp. 25–8). Some 3,000 years later, farming here was broadened by the addition of vines, olives and woolly sheep. By about 2000 BC Cretans had a sophisticated economy centred on a number of palaces, which developed extensive international trading contacts within the east Mediterranean. Archaeologists call the people of this civilization Minoans.

For most of its history, Minoan Crete was divided into a series of regions, each organized with a main palace and several smaller centres. The palaces, which had a number of functions, were the focus of Minoan society. The main palaces housed the local rulers, and were also the main centres of Minoan religion, which involved a series of ritual performances, some private and some public. The palaces were the main storage and distribution centres for basic foodstuffs and export crops – oil and wine. They were also the Minoan equivalent of factories – centres of craft production, with workshops producing everything from basic pottery to intricate gold jewellery.

Sizeable towns grew up next to some of the palaces, and many Cretans lived an urban life, while the rest dwelt in small villages scattered around the mountainous landscape and linked by narrow tracks. Surplus produce may have been delivered to the nearest villa,

which in turn sent it to the main palace. To keep track of the contents of their huge storage jars filled with grain and oil, palace officials devised a system of pictographic writing for important records. Later, perhaps influenced by merchants trading with the Levant, they began using a script known as Linear A. This is still undeciphered since it is written in an unknown language.

The fall of the palaces

Towards the end of the Minoan period, the palace at Knossos may have become the capital of the whole island. Over several centuries Knossos had grown into a sprawling complex,

1

MINOANS AND MYCENAEANS

- ▫ Mycenaean site
- ▪ Approximate area of Mycenaean culture c.1500 BC
- ◆ Minoan site
- ── Approximate limit of Minoan culture c.2000 BC

Euboea

Orchomenos Gla Lefkandi
Thebes

Aegean Sea

Athens

Mycenae
Tiryns
Argos

Pylos

Melos

Santorini
Akrotiri

Rhodes

Sea of Crete

Khania

Crete
Mallia
Knossos Gournia Palaikastro
Haghia Triada Phaistos Kato Zakro

1. By 2500 BC, sophisticated bronze-using cultures were flourishing throughout the Aegean. Marble from the island of Paros was used by the people of the Cycladic islands to carve fine female figurines like this.

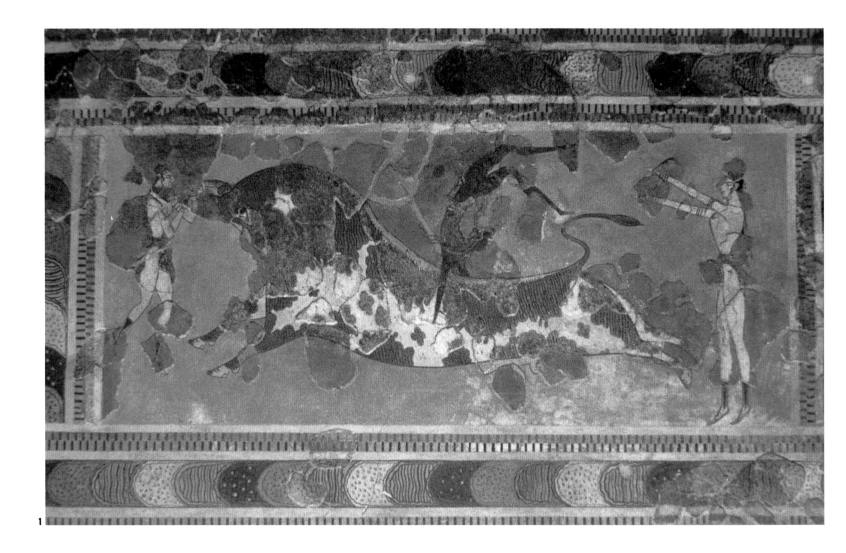

1

1. Paintings in the Minoan palace at Knossos show the dangerous sport of bull-leaping, probably a ritual activity. Bulls played an important role in Minoan religion.

2. The walled acropolis at Mycenae contained the royal palace of the Mycenean kings, as well as shrines, workshops and houses. Outside the walls lay other residential and industrial areas.

3. Bronze daggers inlaid with naturalistic scenes of animals, vegetation and people in silver and gold have been found at Pylos and Mycenae.

by far the biggest in Europe at this time, with hundreds of rooms arranged on several storeys around courtyards, audience chambers and ceremonial areas. Designed as much to meet the needs of Minoan ritual as for practical efficiency, the ruins of Knossos seem to have given rise to myths about a Cretan labyrinth.

Like many island peoples, the Minoans became excellent seafarers. As well as transporting goods around the coast of Crete, their ships traded regularly with Egypt, Cyprus, Asia Minor and mainland Greece, and colonies of Minoan merchants were established overseas. On the nearby island of Santoríni (Thera), a settlement with close links to Minoan Crete may have developed into an independent state before it was destroyed by a volcanic eruption in the 17th or 16th century BC. Fine frescoes on the houses are still preserved beneath the volcanic ash.

In about 1475 BC many of the Cretan palaces were also destroyed, possibly as a result of a massive earthquake, and the Minoan system of rule collapsed. Shortly afterwards Crete came under the control of Mycenaean Greeks.

THE MYCENAEANS

Mycenaean civilization emerged in the south of mainland Greece around 1600 BC as a well-armed military aristocracy ruling from local strongholds. The most important early centre was Mycenae, where a number of warrior-rulers were buried outside the citadel with their elaborately decorated weapons.

The art of the Mycenaeans was influenced by nearby Crete (they probably employed Minoan craft workers) and also by the more distant Levant, for example in the widespread use of carved ivory. Their distinctive weaponry, however, such as the horse-drawn chariot, seems to have come from further east, in Asia Minor (Asiatic Turkey).

2

Seaborne enterprise

The Mycenaeans were experienced sailors. Greece, like Crete, is very mountainous, and sea travel around the coast was often easier than travel over land. Many of the most important Mycenaean settlements, such as Pylos, Tiryns, and Mycenae itself, were situated on traditional land and sea routes.

In about 1450 BC the Mycenaeans expanded into an already weakened Crete, and took over the palaces and villas. In Greece, Mycenaean culture was transformed. Palaces were built at Mycenae, Pylos and other centres, and were decorated with murals like those in Crete. These palaces also became centres of production for perfumed oil and woollen cloth, which were made by slave labour and exported to Egypt and the Levant. The Mycenaeans modified the Minoan Linear A script into Linear B, to write their own language, which was an early form of Greek.

Commercial success encouraged the Mycenaeans to settle even further afield, and trading posts were established on the coasts of the Levant and Asia Minor. Thanks to their location astride traditional trade routes, the lords of Mycenae and Pylos controlled the main channel through which goods from the eastern Mediterranean passed into central and western Europe. For example, Mycenaean perfumed oils were traded with the people of Sardinia for their abundant copper ore.

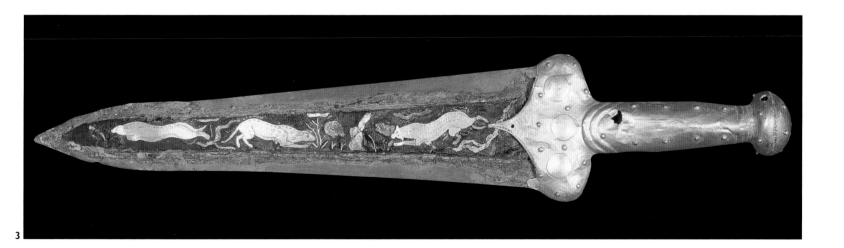
3

IRON TECHNOLOGY

Iron is one of the commonest metals in the Earth's crust, and iron-ore deposits are much more widespread than copper ores. For all of prehistory, however, and for the first millennium or so of Old World civilization, iron was known only from occasional finds of nickel-iron meteorites.

Extracting iron from its ores requires higher temperatures and more complex technology than that needed for either copper or tin – the constituents of bronze (▷ pp. 44–5). The technique of smelting iron ore seems to have been discovered in eastern Anatolia about 1900 BC.

The age of iron

For centuries, the Hittites kept the techniques of iron making a closely guarded secret. After their collapse around 1200 BC, iron technology spread rapidly throughout most of Europe and western Asia. The superior qualities and availability of iron meant that it soon replaced bronze for tools and weapons, although the process was by no means instantaneous.

Initially iron weapons were quite rare and conveyed considerable status. But within a few centuries, iron had become the mainstay of weapon and tool manufacture, while bronze became a specialist metal used mainly for personal adornment and decorative objects.

The advantages of iron

Ordinary iron is much stronger and harder than bronze, and steel (an alloy of iron and carbon) is even harder and stronger, and will also spring back into shape when bent. By any test, iron and steel are superior to bronze for tools and weapons and, once the secret was out, they were much cheaper. Iron could be made from a single locally obtained ore, rather than two costly imported metals, and iron bars (sufficient for one or two tools) became a widely traded commodity.

Iron-making techniques

Smelting iron ore produces a bloom, a honeycomb of iron and impurities, that has to be repeatedly hammered while hot until only metal remains. Iron made by this process is known as wrought iron, and was the most widely made type of iron. By carefully controlling the amount of charcoal in the furnace, and by heating the iron and quenching it (cooling it in oil or water) as it was

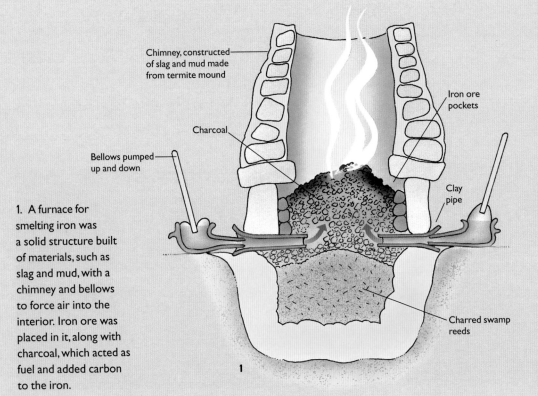

Chimney, constructed of slag and mud made from termite mound

Iron ore pockets

Charcoal

Bellows pumped up and down

Clay pipe

Charred swamp reeds

1. A furnace for smelting iron was a solid structure built of materials, such as slag and mud, with a chimney and bellows to force air into the interior. Iron ore was placed in it, along with charcoal, which acted as fuel and added carbon to the iron.

1

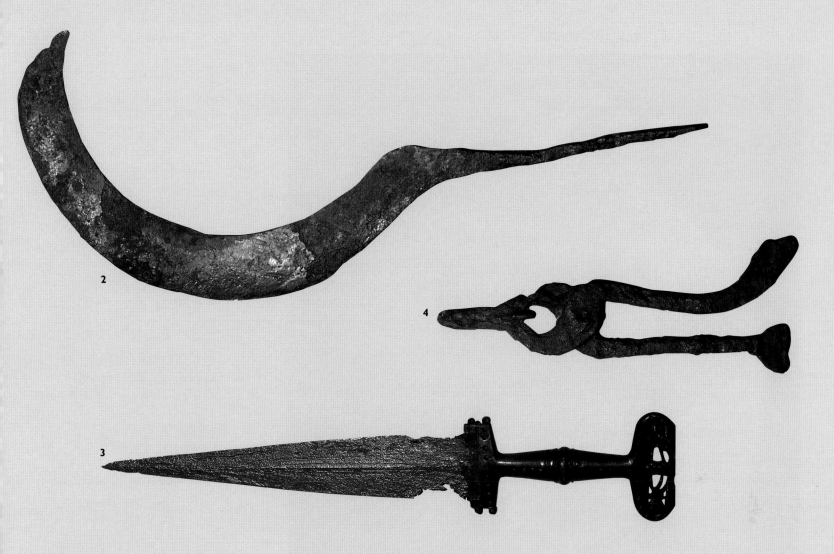

hammered, early iron smiths learned how to make steel, and these skilled workers were highly prized and revered. A few master smiths perfected the techniques of making extremely strong, sharp weapons by hammering together bars of iron and steel of different qualities to make a composite, laminated blade.

Iron around the world

Chinese smiths were able to construct furnaces that could reach the high temperatures needed to melt iron, and by 500 BC had perfected a technique for making cast iron, a material not used elsewhere in the world until after the Roman period. Cast iron is an alloy of iron and carbon (up to five times

more than steel) that can be poured while molten into moulds. In China, stone agricultural tools were replaced not by bronze but by cast-iron implements.

Sub-Saharan Africa made little use of copper, and less of bronze, but after about 700 BC iron working became important and soon spread across the continent. Africans may have learned iron-making skills from Phoenician colonists to the north of the Sahara. However, differences in the techniques used make it equally likely that African iron making developed independently.

The American civilizations, despite their considerable metalworking skills, never discovered the secret of iron making, although they did use polished iron ore for mirrors.

2. Iron was used for many tools. In India, where iron working developed independently, tools such as hoes and sickles (top) were common. The Celts made attractive daggers (3). Iron tongs (4) were used by a Roman smith.

◆ TOPIC LINKS

2.4 **The Middle Realm**
p.74 Technology
p.76 The Metalworkers of the South

2.6 **Zone of Conflict**
p.101 The Hittites
p.104 Westward Expansion

3.3 **The Land of the Buddha**
p.134 Urban Life

3.4 **The Great Han**
p.147 The Han Empire
p.149 Neighbours of the Han

3.5 **Mediterranean Conflicts**
p.167 The Etruscans

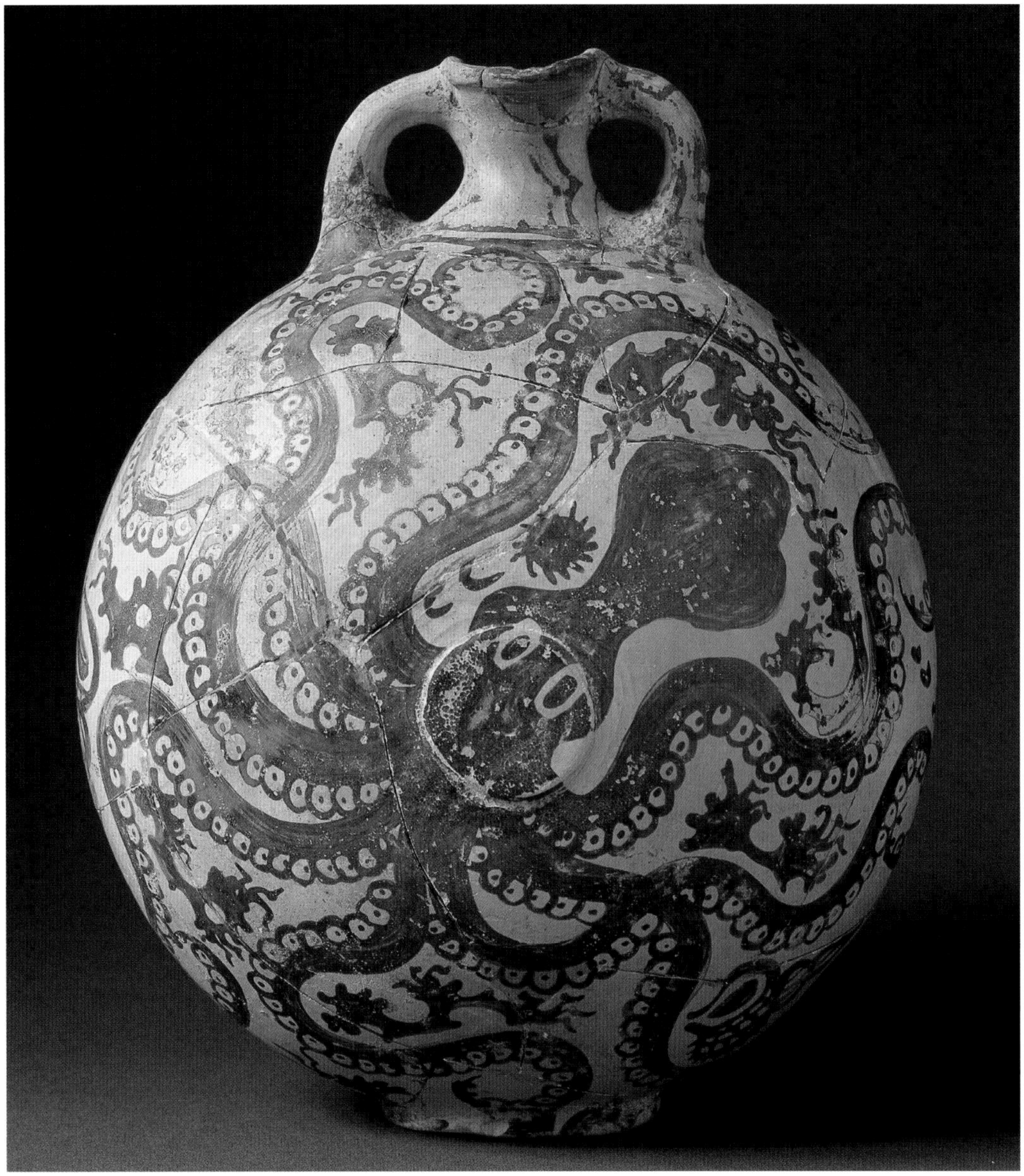

1

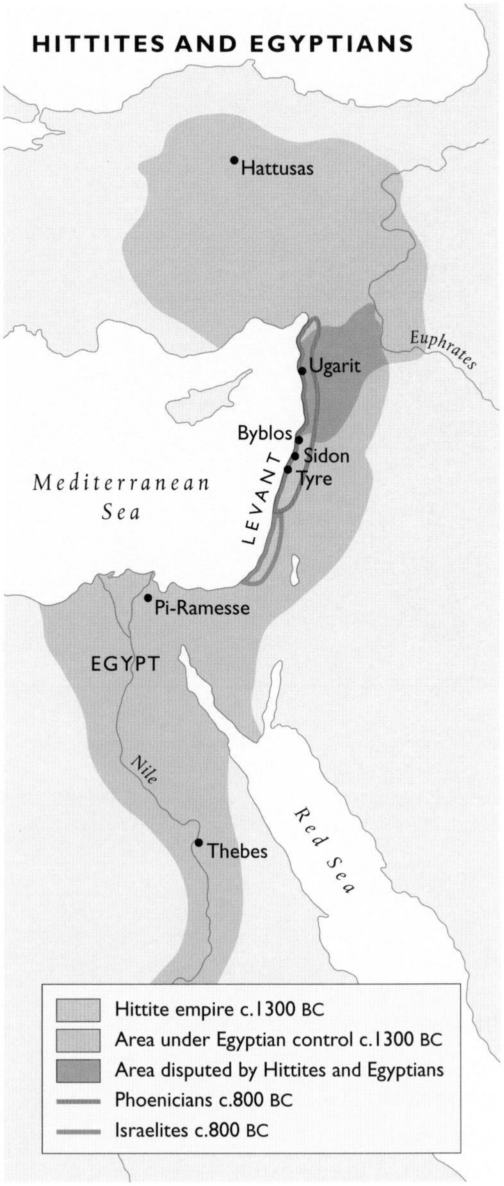
HITTITES AND EGYPTIANS
Hattusas
Euphrates
Ugarit
Byblos
Sidon
Tyre
LEVANT
Mediterranean Sea
Pi-Ramesse
EGYPT
Nile
Red Sea
Thebes
Hittite empire c.1300 BC
Area under Egyptian control c.1300 BC
Area disputed by Hittites and Egyptians
Phoenicians c.800 BC
Israelites c.800 BC

Almost the end

Mycenaean power came to an abrupt end in about 1200 BC, when the palaces and citadels of Greece appear to have been sacked and burned, either by raiders or by the local populace. These events did not happen in isolation, and there appears to have been a wave of destruction and disturbances across much of the eastern Mediterranean region at this time. The sea lanes became filled with a succession of war parties, pirates, and 'boat people' looking for somewhere to settle.

In the 'Dark Ages' that followed the fall of the citadels, a number of Mycenaean settlements were abandoned, and many people emigrated overseas. Some undoubtedly took to the sea as warriors and raiders in their own right, and ended up scattered along the Levant and North African coasts. Others fled to the islands and coastline of Asia Minor.

Some settlements became the first Greek colonies that were to re-establish contact with Greece after the Dark Ages. On the mainland civilization was not completely extinguished. Some larger settlements such as Athens and Lefkandi remained inhabited, and were the first to take up trade with a recovering Levant.

2

THE HITTITES

In the northeast of the Mediterranean region, on the uplands of central Anatolia, a completely separate civilization had developed and flourished. This region had long been in contact with Mesopotamia, chiefly as a source of raw materials, and had several large towns, such as Kanesh, where the Assyrians established a trading post in about 1900 BC. A century or so later this region came under the control of the Hittites, a confederation of warrior-aristocrats who used chariots in battle and were the first to use iron weapons. They established a capital at Hattusas (or Hattush – they called themselves Hatti) in about 1650 BC, and gradually extended their control across Anatolia and into northern Syria.

The habit of warfare, combined with the mastery of making bronze and iron armour and weapons, made the Hittites almost invincible in battle. In 1590 BC an invading Hittite army under King Mursilis sacked Babylon, but did not incorporate it into Hittite territory. Some 200 years later, under King Suppiluliumas, the Hittites finally defeated the Mitanni, who had established a powerful empire in the region (▷ pp. 51). Suppiluliumas installed a puppet ruler and created the Hittite empire. By 1300 BC this empire extended as far south as the Levant coast, where it came into conflict with Egypt.

Metal brokers

The Hittite capital, Hattusas, was enlarged and fortified with massive walls. Several

1. Exhuberant naturalistic designs, frequently with marine themes, adorned the pottery of the Minoans. The Mycenaeans used similar motifs, but executed them with less vigour.

2. Soldier gods armed with sickle swords stride menacingly along the carved rock wall of a shrine in the religious complex of Yazilikaya, just outside the Hittite capital, Hattusas.

new palaces were built and the upper part of the city became a vast ritual area with many temples and processional ways lined with large stone statues. For official accounts and records the Hittites used a form of cuneiform script (▷ p. 57) adapted to write their own language. But for correspondence with foreign rulers they often used Akkadian (▷ p. 47), which had become an international language of diplomacy.

The secret of iron making, which the Hittites kept for 600 years, made them highly desirable trading partners as well as feared enemies. Foreign rulers, such as the Egyptian pharaohs, who wanted some of this new wonder metal, were forced to write begging letters to the Hittite king. The Hittites did not build or sail their own ships, but relied on those of the Levant coast cities, such as Ugarit, which had a semi-independent status under Hittite protection.

About 1200 BC the Hittite barons rebelled against the central authority of the king. Soon afterwards the region was affected by the general disruptions afflicting the region. The Hittite army, which relied on chariots, was ill-equipped to repel attacks from the sea, and Hattusas was burned and abandoned. Hittite power disappeared almost overnight, and much of their empire was absorbed into the resurgent Assyrian empire, although some Hittite traditions were preserved in parts of Syria.

THE BATTLE OF KADESH

The city of Kadesh, situated on the main route into northern Syria, had acknowledged Egyptian overlordship since the mid-1400s BC. Following the Hittite defeat of the Mitanni, the city changed sides and declared itself under Hittite protection.

Around 1300 BC Pharaoh Ramses II led an Egyptian army into the northern Levant to recapture Kadesh. Approaching the city across the plain of the Orontes river the Egyptian column was ambushed by a force of 2500 Hittite chariots. Many of the Egyptian troops panicked and ran, but Ramses (right) was able to rally the survivors and inflict heavy losses on the Hittites. The following day the two sides agreed a truce and the Egyptians withdrew.

On his return to Thebes, Ramses declared Kadesh to be a great Egyptian victory. In the Levant, however, the outcome of the battle was viewed very differently – as an Egyptian defeat. Many of the southern cities rebelled against Egyptian overlordship, and it took 20 years of campaigning before the pharaohs regained control of their Levant empire.

Whatever the outcome (win, loss or draw), the battle of Kadesh represents a major turning point in the balance of power in the region. Ramses's failure to inflict a decisive defeat on the Hittites in effect put an end to any further Egyptian expansion in the Levant, and the Hittite empire was confirmed as the dominant regional superpower.

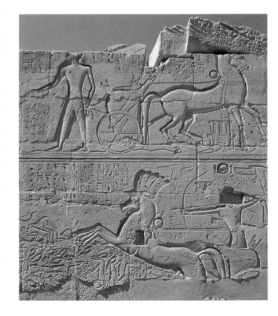

THE PHOENICIANS

The peace that returned to the eastern Mediterranean after the activities of the Sea Peoples (▷ p. 105) was considerably subdued. Two powerful empires – those of the Hittites and the Mycenaeans – had been destroyed, Egypt had retreated from the Levant, and many trade routes had been disrupted or obliterated. The economic recovery of the region was begun around 1000 BC by the Phoenicians, the native inhabitants of city-states such as Byblos, Sidon and Tyre on the Levant coast.

During the power vacuum caused by the collapse of the Hittite empire the Phoenicians were able to establish independent and self-sufficient commercial centres. Unlike inland states, which often became enmeshed in territorial squabbles with neighbours, the Phoenicians were able to expand and compete across open seas that were almost empty of other peoples' shipping.

The Phoenician cities were well located to take advantage of a range of valuable commodities – incense from Arabia, copper from Cyprus and high-grade timber from Lebanon. The city of Tyre also specialized in the production of luxury textiles coloured purple with a dye made from local shellfish. As Phoenician prosperity increased so did their influence.

1. A Phoenician warship, depicted on a relief from the Assyrian palace at Nineveh. At different times the Phoenicians became either allies or enemies of the Assyrians.

⭐ In about 1250 BC the Assyrian king wrote to the Hittite king requesting a supply of iron. His request was met – with a single dagger blade.

Their reliance on sea trade encouraged the Phoenicians to make advances in ship construction and navigation, and they became skilled in naval warfare (▷ pp. 166–7). Phoenician traders may have sailed as far as Britain in search of tin for bronze making, and another Phoenician expedition is reported to have circumnavigated Africa. Phoenician metal smiths were also among the first to take up the new technology of iron making.

The Phoenician cities in the Levant gradually lost their independence, becoming tribute-paying subjects of the Assyrians before being absorbed into a succession of other eastern empires. The western colonies, however, prospered as independent settlements. One of the most successful of these colonies was Carthage, which was to challenge the might of Rome (▷ p. 160).

Israel

At about the same time as Phoenician shipping began to re-establish trade contacts across the Mediterranean, the kingdom of Israel emerged in the southern hill country of the Levant. The Jewish story of the emigration of Hebrew slaves from Egypt, as related in the Book of Exodus, may contain some elements of historical truth – the Egyptians did capture some slaves in the Levant – but most historians agree that the Israelites originated as a confederation of local hill tribes. Attempts to move into the lowlands brought them into conflict with other settled groups, such as the Philistines.

King David (who ruled around 950 BC) established a capital in the walled city of Jerusalem, where his successor, Solomon, built the first temple. The story of the queen of Sheba demonstrates the importance of long-distance contacts at this time, even to newly emerging states such as Israel. Sheba (present-day Yemen) was the main source of

1. This detail on the 'Black Obelisk' of the 9th-century BC Assyrian king Shalmaneser III shows the Israelite king Jehu prostrating himself at the feet of the Assyrian emperor, to whom he has brought tribute.

2. The simple temple at Jerusalem built by king Solomon was destroyed by the Babylonians but rebuilt under Persian rule. King Herod later rebuilt it on a grand scale but it was destroyed by the Romans in AD 70.

Westward expansion

The destruction of the Mycenaean empire had created a trade vacuum in the Mediterranean. Phoenician traders gradually extended their range westwards until they eventually reached the Atlantic coast of Spain around 800 BC. A series of Phoenician colonies, in Sicily, the Balearic islands and North Africa, including several on the Atlantic coast, were established along this great east–west trade route, which brought the urbanized civilization of the Levant into direct contact with the emerging cultures of southern Europe.

frankincense, which was transported north to the Levant by caravan. An alliance between Sheba and Israel would have cemented both ends of this valuable trade route.

Political differences caused Israel to disintegrate, and the divided kingdoms of Israel and Judah were easy prey to the Assyrians, who were content to exact annual tribute. The Neo-Babylonian empire (▷ p. 55) was not so tolerant, however, and the temple was destroyed and the Jews marched into captivity in Babylon by King Nebuchadnezzar. After their release by the Persian emperor, Cyrus, in 538 BC the Jews were permitted to return to the southern Levant and rebuild the temple in Jerusalem. **2**

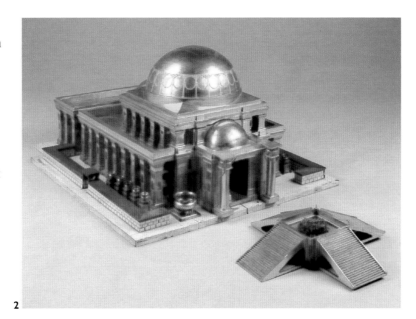

 ## THE SEA PEOPLES

One of the most important features of the disruptions in the Mediterranean around 1200 BC was the presence of seaborne warriors known as the Sea Peoples (illustrated in this Egyptian relief). In Hittite, Ugaritic and Egyptian records they are described as groups of distinctively armed and dressed warriors who raided and plundered civilized ships and cities. The king of Ugarit on the Syrian coast wrote to the king of Cyprus that enemy ships had set fire to his towns and done great damage to his countryside.

According to the Egyptians, the Sea Peoples were composed of several different groups who 'gathered in their islands' before launching their raids. Some of these groups have been associated by scholars with particular areas of the Mediterranean. The Shardana have been located on the island of Sardinia, and the Shekelesh on Sicily. The Pelset, who have been identified as the Philistines (a group who settled in the Levant), may have counted Mycenaean Greeks among their numbers.

What remains less clear, however, is when particular groups first became associated with these areas – before, during or after the general upheaval. Undoubtedly, many of the Sea Peoples found themselves stranded far from home – some as slaves or mercenaries in Egypt, others more comfortably in one of the increasingly cosmopolitan city-ports of the Levant. The scattering of peoples across the Mediterranean during the years around 1200 BC had a major impact on the cultures that were to develop in the aftermath of the disruptions.

ALPHABETS AND DEVELOPED WRITING

Writing was well established in the Middle East by 2000 BC (▷ pp. 56–7). In Egypt and the lands it controlled, Egyptian hieroglyphic and hieratic scripts were used, while elsewhere cuneiform (wedge-shaped writing) scripts were employed to write Akkadian, the international diplomatic and commercial language of the time, or local languages. These scripts were by now far from their pictographic beginnings, and had become sophisticated systems that made it possible to write anything. Both systems used a variety of signs. Some stood for whole words or part of words, while many others were syllabic, with some representing a single consonant.

1. This early example of an alphabetic inscription comes from the Greek city of Ephesus in Asia Minor and dates from the 6th century BC. The text deals with omens taken from the pattern of birds' flight.

2. Tablets written in the Linear B script found at Pylos shed light on many aspects of life in this Mycenaean palace. They also give details of the organization of naval defences and census data on the kingdom's population.

New writing systems

Several new writing systems appeared over subsequent centuries, using the principle of syllabic signs to create syllabic scripts suited to local languages. In the Aegean, for instance, the Minoan civilization devised the Linear A script to write their (still unknown) language, and this was taken over and adapted (becoming Linear B) by the Mycenaeans, who spoke, and wrote, an early form of Greek.

From syllable to letter

The Egyptian script showed the consonants but not the accompanying vowel sounds, which could be worked out from the context. Egyptian single-consonant signs represented the sound of the first consonant of the pictured object. For example, a mouth, ri, stood for the consonant 'r' combined with any vowel. Around 1700 BC, perhaps as the result of a brilliant individual's idea, Semitic-speaking people from the Levant began using some Egyptian single-consonant signs to write their own language, giving these signs the sound of the first consonant in their own word for the object depicted. For instance, the Egyptian sign for house, 'bet' in Semitic, became 'b'. Like the Egyptian script, this new script – the very first alphabet – had signs only for consonants, with the vowels filled in mentally by the reader.

The alphabet was a revolutionary idea because it reduced the number of signs that had to be used, from a few hundred to only a handful – there were 22 letters in the first alphabet, in contrast to about 600 signs used to write cuneiform. The earliest surviving alphabetic inscriptions come from Sinai where slaves or subject workers from the Levant toiled in the Egyptian turquoise mines. These inscriptions name the Canaanite goddess Ba'alat – who was perhaps being clandestinely invoked by these unfortunates in a secret alphabetic 'code'.

A few centuries later a similar experiment was made in the northern Levant, using cuneiform instead of Egyptian signs as the basis. Although briefly successful in its own area, the cuneiform alphabet did not take off, perhaps because, being adapted for writing on clay, it was unattractive in other regions where parchment, papyrus or other writing media were used. The first alphabet, on the other hand, was ancestral to virtually all the scripts used in the world today, those of eastern Asia being the most notable exception.

Adding vowels

From the original Levantine alphabet came those used by the Phoenicians, Israelites and Aramaeans in the Middle East, as well as the Arabian, Ethiopian and Arabic scripts. Contact with the West by 500 BC introduced Middle Eastern scripts to India, where a system suited to the Indian languages was devised. This was Brahmi, which was ancestral to virtually all Indian scripts. Although inspired by an alphabetic script, these scripts are syllabic, representing vowels by varying the form of the basic consonant sign.

By the 8th century BC the Greeks had adopted alphabetic writing from the Phoenicians. They now made another momentous innovation – they took signs from the original alphabet that were not needed in Greek and made them represent vowels. This was because in Greek, an Indo-European language, it was not easy to supply vowel sounds from context, as it was in Semitic languages. The Greeks also devised new signs for sounds absent from Semitic, such as 'ph'. From these beginnings come not

2

only the Latin alphabet used in Europe and much of the modern world, but also the Russian Cyrillic alphabet, the ancient Etruscan alphabet and the runes used by the Vikings in the Middle Ages.

TOPIC LINKS

2.6 Zone of Conflict
p.95 Minoan Life
p.97 Seaborne Enterprise
p.101 Metal Brokers

3.2 The Athenian Role Model
p.119 The Ancient Greeks

3.3 The Land of the Buddha
p.133 The Mauryas

3.4 The Great Han
p.153 Emerging Kingdoms

A WIDENING WORLD

As civilization spread beyond its core areas, the number of civilized states multiplied and international trade became increasingly important. Contacts made through trade permitted the further spread of accumulated wisdom, and new technologies, such as iron making and easily learned alphabets.

This process was by no means always peaceful. Trade routes often turned into invasion routes, and control of important sea lanes became vital. For the first time, naval warfare became an important factor in politics.

Flourishing long-distance trade permitted more than just the exchange of goods – art styles, belief systems, even whole cultures could be exported. In Europe, India and China great empires were established that endured for centuries. Within them, society became increasingly standardized as local cultures were swamped by the dominant imperial culture.

Previous page. The era of the great empires saw the emergence of several world religions. Christianity became widespread following the conversion of the Roman emperor Constantine.

TENTACLES OF TRADE

All of the earliest civilizations had engaged in foreign trade, but they were rarely dependent upon it. Their power base lay in fertile agricultural heartlands, which provided the staples of urban life. Trade beyond their frontiers (for luxury goods or raw materials) often took the form of official military expeditions. Only after about 2000 BC, around the enclosed waters of the eastern Mediterranean, did a different pattern emerge, and international trade became a central part of the Minoan and Mycenaean economies (▷ pp. 95–100).

This trading tradition was continued when the Mediterranean region began to recover after 1000 BC, following a period of disrup-

tion. New empires developed – such as those of Athens, Carthage and Rome – that were substantially dependent on seaborne trade. Advances in shipbuilding and navigation meant that it was no longer necessary for states to be based around an agricultural heartland. Growing cities could be fed on imported foodstuffs, thus freeing their inhabitants to participate in more interesting and profitable activities.

Elsewhere, Indian traders, who had already mastered the monsoons, continued their trade with Arabia and began extending their range across the Malay Archipelago (modern Southeast Asia). After about 100 BC Greek and Roman sailors also learned the secrets of sailing back and forth across the Indian

⭐ Leap years, originally proposed by Egyptian astronomers in 238 BC, were introduced by Julius Caesar when he reformed the Roman calendar in 45 BC.

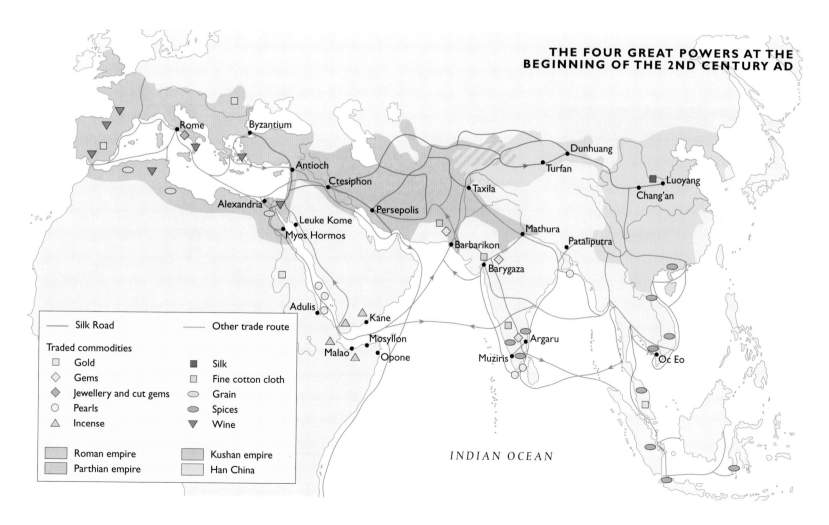

THE FOUR GREAT POWERS AT THE BEGINNING OF THE 2ND CENTURY AD

Rome · Byzantium · Antioch · Ctesiphon · Alexandria · Leuke Kome · Myos Hormos · Persepolis · Taxila · Turfan · Dunhuang · Chang'an · Luoyang · Mathura · Barbarikon · Barygaza · Pataliputra · Adulis · Kane · Mosyllon · Malao · Opone · Muziris · Argaru · Oc Eo

INDIAN OCEAN

— Silk Road   — Other trade route

Traded commodities
- ☐ Gold
- ◇ Gems
- ◆ Jewellery and cut gems
- ○ Pearls
- △ Incense
- ■ Silk
- ☐ Fine cotton cloth
- ⬭ Grain
- ⬭ Spices
- ▽ Wine

Roman empire
Parthian empire
Kushan empire
Han China

⭐ In AD 552 enterprising traders managed to smuggle silkworms to the West, breaking the Chinese monopoly on silk production.

Ocean on the changing monsoon winds, and traded with India directly. China expanded westwards in about 120 BC (and again in AD 90) to secure the land route, known as the Silk Road, that stretched across Asia to the Levant. Contacts between China and its neighbours became so close that Korea and Japan adopted many elements of Chinese culture (writing, administration and art) as a package in the centuries after AD 300.

As trade became more complex and sophisticated, regional trade routes became linked to form a 'world' system of trade, with goods travelling many thousands of kilometres from their source to their eventual destination. In about 100 AD four great empires – Chinese, Kushan, Parthian and Roman – controlled interlinking trade routes that ran right across Eurasia from the Pacific to the Atlantic oceans. The volume of trade was sufficient that it was not unknown for a wealthy Roman citizen in London (for example) to wear clothes made of Chinese silk and to eat food flavoured with Indian spices.

The value of the trade between Rome and the East was enormous, but it was not a balanced trading system. In general, exotic goods (such as silk, spices and gems) travelled from east to west, and huge quantities of gold and silver coins were sent eastwards to pay for them. This trade imbalance was apparent at the time, and some Roman commentators blamed the citizens' taste for exotic luxuries for bankrupting the empire.

Individuals in society

This growing internationalism was most apparent in the confined waters of the Mediterranean with its many islands and

1. Amphorae (large jars), used by the Romans and their contemporaries to transport wine, oil, grain and other goods, have been found in wrecked ships.

2. Trading towns grew up in oases across Central Asia, linking the empires of the west with Han China. Irrigation ensured their agricultural prosperity.

peninsulas. By AD 100 the Mediterranean
had become a 'Roman lake', completely
surrounded by the Roman empire, and was
referred to by the Romans as 'mare nostrum' –
'our sea'. Although the many nations and
cultures surrounding the sea maintained their
separate character to some degree, they
became linked by the laws, coinage, customs
and language of the Roman empire. In the
Mediterranean region the increase in trade had
been matched by the increasing importance of
the individual in society. As society became
more complex and cosmopolitan it also
became more 'open' in terms of economic and
political activity, and philosophy.

Previously, international trade had been
mainly a state activity, carried out between
rulers and their representatives. In the lands
of Greece and Rome, although trade was still
regulated by the state, it was largely carried

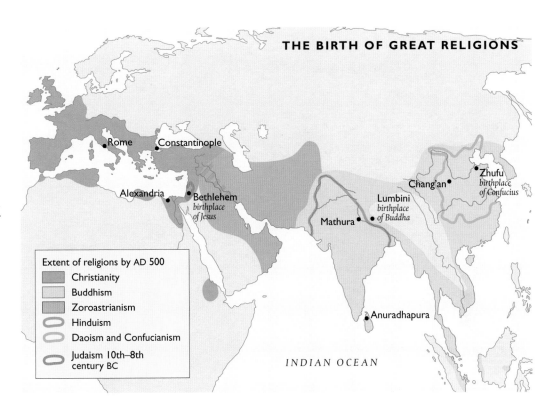

THE BIRTH OF GREAT RELIGIONS

Extent of religions by AD 500
- Christianity
- Buddhism
- Zoroastrianism
- Hinduism
- Daoism and Confucianism
- Judaism 10th–8th century BC

Rome · Constantinople
Alexandria · Bethlehem *birthplace of Jesus*
Mathura · Lumbini *birthplace of Buddha*
Chang'an · Zhufu *birthplace of Confucius*
Anuradhapura
INDIAN OCEAN

THE PERIPLUS

The *Periplus of the Erythraean Sea* – a mariners' coastal guide to the
Indian Ocean – was written by a Greek sea captain shortly before AD
100. The book describes the voyage of a merchant ship from Egypt, south
through the Red Sea and along the east coast of Africa, then across the
ocean to India. It gives details of more than 20 Indian Ocean ports that
were regularly visited by Greek shipping. The book also lists the major
commodities handled by each port, and helpfully mentions which of the
ports are 'official' trading centres, and which are 'unauthorized'.

According to the *Periplus*, in addition to spices and gems, the many
commodities that could be loaded at Indian ports included cotton cloth,
dyes, Chinese iron, tortoiseshell, mother-of-pearl and circus animals.
These goods were mostly purchased with money, but Rome also
exported copper, tin, glassware, carved gems and coral as payment.

The author of the *Periplus* also recounts what he has learned of the
world beyond the limits of his own voyaging, and he was very aware
that he was familiar with only a small part of a much larger trade network which extended overland to China and by sea around the Bay of
Bengal on the east coast of India and thence into Southeast Asia.

1. Buddhism spread to the East, becoming established in China (where this Buddha was carved at Yungang), Korea and Japan.

2. A Sasanian coin depicting a Zoroastrian fire altar. Zoroastrianism was the official religion of Persian empires from around 500 BC.

During the reign of the emperor Domitian (AD 81–96) the mint in Rome produced up to 32 million silver coins each year.

out by private individuals such as manufacturers, merchants and ship owners. Although wealth was still mainly associated with the acquisition of large estates, the growth in trade and the introduction of coinage (▷ pp. 116–17) enabled some individuals who were not landowners to amass private fortunes, some modest and some immense.

The development of an economic middle class – between the aristocratic landowners and the landless poor – brought about a transformation in the way in which societies were governed, and in a sense created politics. The traditional ruling class (king and large landowners) had to make room for the aspirations of middle classes. Property qualifications for participation in government were progressively lowered. The larger numbers of people involved in decision making encouraged the

development of rival groups vying for support – in other words, politics.

The increasing political importance of the individual was mirrored in philosophy. As individuals travelled along the international routes and saw more of the world, they began to develop their own ideas about 'the way of the world', and to share these ideas with others. Around the crowded sea lanes of Eurasia there developed networks of men (and a few women) of ideas – travellers, teachers, authors, mathematicians and scientists, students of nature and of humanity – who circulated and exchanged philosophies and speculations. Although still primitive by today's standards of material comfort, this was in some ways the beginning of the modern world – with goods, money and ideas being freely exchanged.

THE BIRTH OF GREAT RELIGIONS

During this period several of the world's great religions – including Buddhism, Confucianism and Christianity – were founded by inspired teachers.

In India, Buddhism was established by the teachings of Siddhartha (Gautama; 563–483 BC), a Nepalese aristocrat who gave up his riches for a life of holy poverty. The Buddhist belief that a personal 'nirvana' could be achieved offered a hopeful alternative to the Hindu hereditary caste system that operated throughout India. At about the same time the teacher Mahavira (599–527 BC) founded Jainism, which also rejected Hindu teachings and the caste system.

In China, the turmoil and hardships of the eastern Zhou and Warring States periods produced a widespread desire for calm and order. The teachings of Confucius (Kongfuzi, 551–479 BC) became extremely popular. He emphasized respect for ancestors and obedience to authority, and encouraged people to concentrate on an orderly family life. Confucianism was later adopted as the official philosophy of the Chinese empire. The teacher Lao Zi (lived around 500 BC), whose works form the basis of Daoism, took a more mystical approach, but placed a similar emphasis on personal goals and strategies for survival.

In Palestine, then part of the Roman empire, the teachings of Jesus (c. 4 BC – c. AD 30) formed the basis of Christianity. In some respects, this was the most radical of all the new religions – it not only rejected traditional Jewish beliefs, but also refused to acknowledge the official Roman religions. As a result, its believers were persecuted for centuries before it became properly established.

These religions are all very different, yet some common features can be identified.

Although they are each rooted in the long-established religious traditions of their region, they each represent a definite break with tradition and the beginning of a new approach. These religions all recognize the sanctity of life, and their moral codes are generally non-violent and encourage correct behaviour between people. In general, there was a trend towards emphasizing a person's own spiritual relationship with the deity, and a marked shift from the collective to the individual. In this respect, these new religions may be seen as another result of long-term civilizing processes – such as urbanism and trade – producing a more human-orientated world.

Routes of faith

Exotic goods and precious metals were not the only commodities to be transported along the trade routes of the ancient world – faith also travelled. Two of the new religions, Buddhism and Christianity, spread far from their places of origin.

From northern India, Buddhism spread along the trade routes across the Himalaya, first becoming established at Silk Road cities such as Khotan, and from there into western China and Tibet. The religion was sufficiently well established in China by AD 500 for it to be part of the cultural package exported to Japan, where, as Zen, it developed its own distinctive characteristics. From southern India, Buddhism diffused across maritime Southeast Asia along with merchant cargoes.

The early Greek-speaking Christians used Roman trade routes to exchange letters, and to spread their faith to cities all around the eastern Mediterranean. During periods of Roman religious toleration, Christians were able to travel freely to all parts of the empire, although they were not exempt from local persecution. When Christianity was made one of the official religions of the Roman empire in about AD 335, there were already many believers scattered, from Hadrian's Wall to the Persian Gulf.

Christianity also spread eastwards along trade routes, and St Thomas is said to have travelled to Madras in southern India in about AD 45. After doctrinal disputes in the 4th century AD some heretic Christians migrated along the Silk Road, establishing churches in Central Asia, and eventually in China.

3. Christianity became an official religion of the Roman empire in the 4th century AD. Clandestine Christian signs, such as the 'Chi-Rho' (seen here behind the head of Jesus), could now be used in openly Christian art.

COINAGE AND MEDIA OF EXCHANGE

Trading is made easier and more efficient when it is conducted through a medium of exchange, rather than by the direct exchange of goods. There are two requirements for a medium of exchange: portability and mutually acknowledged value – it must be equally acceptable to all parties. Prehistoric peoples and the early civilizations used a variety of rare and precious materials for this purpose, including feathers, cocoa beans, high-quality stone, and metals. Inland peoples sometimes used seashells imported from the coast.

The value of metals
In the Old World, metals became the most widely accepted medium of exchange. The precious metals – gold and silver – were weighed out each time on balances. Silver used in this way is known as 'hacksilver'. Copper, bronze, and later iron, were also traded by weight, but were also sometimes made into useful objects such as knives, axes and hoes.

First strike
Coinage was invented in the second half of the 7th century BC when Greek kings in Asia Minor began issuing uniformly weighted lumps of electrum (gold and silver alloy) as a convenient way of making payments. By around 600 BC, these first coins were stamped with the king's name or symbol to authenticate the purity of the metal. Instead of being weighed, which required accurate balances and weights, coins could simply be counted.

For traders the advantages of coinage were obvious, and by 500 BC dozens of Greek cities were issuing their own silver coins of precise weight and marked with an identifying design. Soon afterwards, Indian rulers began issuing silver coins marked with a series of small punch marks. By about 200 BC coinage had spread to continental western Europe, where Greek and Roman coins were extensively imitated.

In China coinage evolved independently from metal tools used as a medium of exchange. Bronze 'token' tools were in use as money by about 500 BC and in about 220 BC the first emperor issued standardized circular bronze coins with a square hole in the middle. Chinese coins were cast in moulds, and this method of production was used until the end of the 19th century.

Common currency
Within the Greek world coinage quickly became extremely sophisticated. Coins were struck between a pair of dies, producing coins with a design on either side. The designs themselves were made increasingly complex, often by highly skilled artists, to prevent counterfeiters making forgeries from inferior quality silver. Coinage was also adopted by ordinary city dwellers. Because weekly and daily shopping involved much

Punch

Upper die

Lower die

Anvil

1. Several techniques were used to produce coins. Some were cast in moulds, while others were just discs or bars of metal on which official symbols were punched. Greek and Roman moneyers used a pair of dies to strike a design on both sides of a metal disc.

smaller sums than international trade, silver coins were made in increasingly smaller sizes. The dramatist Aristophanes jokes about people keeping them in their mouths because they were too small for purses or pockets. This problem was solved in the Greek cities of southern Italy by the introduction of a bronze coinage for small denominations.

This was a daring innovation. Unlike those of silver and gold, bronze coins usually had a higher value than the actual metal content.

2. Early Chinese coins like these were cast in moulds in the shape of miniature spades and knives.

3. Gold staters depicting a lion and a bull, issued by King Croesus of Lydia, were some of the earliest coins minted.

4. Since coins circulated widely, they were an important vehicle for official propaganda and information. This Roman coin, issued by the emperor Nero, announced the opening of a new harbour at Rome's port of Ostia.

◆◇ TOPIC LINKS

2.4 The Middle Realm
p.75 Other Changes

3.2 The Athenian Role Model
p.126 Prosperity and Power

3.3 The Land of the Buddha
p.133 The Mauryas
p.136 Indo-Greeks and Foreign
Dynasties

3.4 The Great Han
p.151 Developing States in
Southeast Asia

3.6 The Might of Rome
p.176 Barbarian Attacks

The risk of forgeries was considerable, but these coins only circulated within their particular area and were not used in trade, so the dangers of large-scale fraud were reduced. City authorities, however, kept a close eye on what was changing hands in the marketplace. After the conquests of Alexander the Great, who issued coins of progressively smaller denominations in gold, silver and bronze, coinage systems using these three metals became widespread in western Asia and the Mediterranean region. Alexander also introduced the custom of placing the ruler's portrait on one side of a coin.

The Romans adopted and refined the Greek system of coinage. By AD 300, the whole Roman empire used a unified coinage, with regularly changing designs that carried a propaganda message, usually about the strength and abilities of the emperor. Each coin was struck with a special mark that identified the city and mint where it was made.

THE ATHENIAN ROLE MODEL

Around 800 BC Greece began to emerge from the 'Dark Ages' that had followed the collapse of Mycenaean civilization some four centuries before. This renewal of Greek culture was based around numerous independent city-states, the earliest of which grew from isolated remnants of Mycenaean civilization.

The Greeks founded many other cities around the Mediterranean, and this brought them into conflict with the expanding Persian empire. The Greeks emerged from this conflict into a brief 'golden age' in which art, architecture and literature achieved a state of near-perfection. Athens became the cultural and political centre of Greece, not least through its adoption of democracy.

This golden age was brought to an end by the rise of Macedonian power. Under Alexander the Great, the Macedonians invaded and conquered the whole of the Persian empire, and extended Greek rule to the borders of India and China.

THE ANCIENT GREEKS

When long-distance trade around the Mediterranean started again after about 1000 BC, the scattered Greek-speaking communities were drawn into the trading networks and became reconnected with each other. This process was cemented around 800 BC when the Greeks adopted the Phoenician alphabet to write their own language (▷ pp. 110–11).

As general prosperity increased, some of the Greek cities (such as Athens, Corinth and Rhodes) became centres for the manufacture of high-quality decorated pottery. Others, most notably Phocaea in Asia Minor (Asiatic Turkey), became trading states in their own right, challenging the Phoenician monopoly of the seas. For reasons of commercial strategy, and because many communities were becoming overpopulated, Greeks began colonizing the Mediterranean coastline. Between 750 and 600 BC Greek city-states founded dozens of daughter cities.

Initially the Greek colonists settled around the Aegean, in northern Greece and Asia Minor. By 600 BC, however, they had established trading centres at Al Mina in the Levant and Naucratis in Egypt, and colonies around the Black Sea and in Spain, France, Italy and Sicily, until there were pockets of the Greek world all around the northern and eastern shores of the Mediterranean. As well as trading and language, the Greeks also shared a common religion, which, from 776 BC, had been celebrated by sacred games at Olympia in southwestern Greece. Other Greek

GREATER GREECE

Area of Greek settlement

1. Greek statues in the 6th century BC were strongly influenced by the formal art styles of ancient Egypt.

2. This bronze helmet, of so-called 'Corinthian' style, was part of the armour of a hoplite citizen-soldier.

religious centres grew up around certain temples, oracles and sanctuaries, such as the sacred island of Delos.

Inter-city rivalries

Like their mother cities, Greek colonies were intended to be largely self-sufficient parts of the trading network. Farmland around the city provided most of the necessities of life, and the city might also specialize in some exportable commodity, for example producing grain for the homeland, raising horses or making wine. Obtaining metals and ores, either by mining or by trading with non-Greeks, might also provide the basis for a city's success.

The majority of Greek city-states were small, with populations (including those who lived in the countryside) of 5,000–15,000 people, and few exceeded 25,000 inhabitants. Most cities were no more than large market towns, with one or two public buildings and temples, although some, such as Athens, grew much larger.

The early city-states were ruled by dynasties of kings, although power often passed to groups of aristocratic landowners, who collected taxes, administered justice and conducted relations with other cities. Disputes between city-states were often settled by warfare, and each city had its own army. Greek warfare developed into a very formal affair conducted by elaborate rules. Battles were fought between regiments of hoplites – part-time citizen soldiers who provided their own armour and weapons.

Most wars were caused by boundary disputes or failed dynastic alliances, and there were few wars of conquest. One notable exception was the city of Sparta, which had a particularly militaristic regime – only soldiers could be citizens and all citizens had to be soldiers. Around 600 BC Sparta conquered neighbouring settlements in southwestern Greece, forcing their inhabitants to become a servile workforce, known as the helots, who greatly outnumbered their Spartan masters.

Despite their shared culture (language, religion, trade and warfare), Greeks at this time had no sense of political unity – more one of rivalry. A citizen's loyalties were to his city (only men could be citizens in Greek civilization) and he had no need of any wider allegiance. After 600 BC, however, this perception was to be changed by encounters with rival civilizations.

In the west the inhabitants of Greek colonies became increasingly involved in conflicts with Phoenicians and the native inhabitants of Italy and Spain. For the first time Greeks found themselves fighting alongside each other against a common enemy. These troubles in the west, however, paled into insignificance in comparison to the gathering threat from the east.

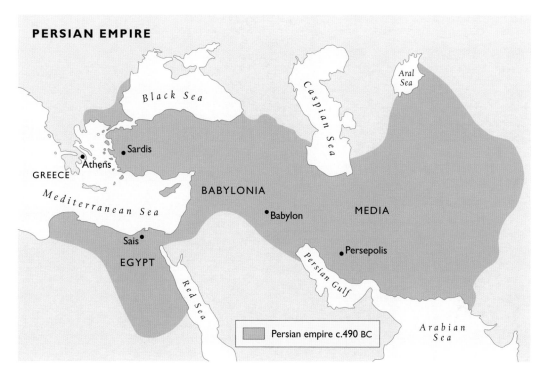

PERSIAN EMPIRE

Persian empire c.490 BC

THE PERSIAN EMPIRE

Since the mid-9th century BC, western Iran had been occupied by two peoples, the Medes and the Persians. During the 7th century BC Persians became subject to the Medes, who also expanded westward at the expense of the Assyrian empire. In 550 BC the Persian king Cyrus II led a revolt against the Medes and took control of Iran. Within 15 years he had conquered the whole of Asia Minor (including all the Greek city-states in the region known as Ionia), Bactria (Afghanistan) and the whole of the Levant and Mesopotamia. This great Persian state is also known as the Achaemenid empire, after the dynasty to which Cyrus belonged. His son, Cambyses II, conquered Egypt and Nubia, and later Sind and Punjab (Pakistan and northwest India) were added to the empire. In 513 BC another Achaemenid, Darius I, invaded southeastern Europe and took nominal control over northern Greece.

A 'Suez Canal' connecting the Mediterranean and the Red Sea was completed by the Persian emperor Darius I in about 500 BC.

1. The elaborate ceremonial of the Persian court is preserved in carved stone sculptures at the palace of Persepolis. The king is shown standing or sitting on a throne, attended by distinctively costumed officials – here, Darius receives a Mede and two Persians.

2. Reliefs at Persepolis show people from the diverse regions of the Persian empire bearing local offerings as tribute.

3. Realism characterized Greek art from the 5th century, as seen in this sophisticated cast bronze statue of a charioteer from Delphi.

Under the Achaemenids Iran underwent an economic and artistic renaissance as irrigation canals were cleared and repaired, and temples and palaces were remodelled to Persian taste. A magnificent new capital was established at Persepolis, with great stairways flanked by the carved figures of the subject peoples of the empire bringing tribute to the 'great king'.

The vast Persian empire, which stretched from the Himalaya to the Mediterranean, was efficiently administered by satraps – local governors who collected taxes and supervised public works. A widespread network of official spies and messengers ('the king's ears and

eyes') kept the palace fully informed. A 'Royal Road' was constructed, linking the capital to the distant frontiers, so that troops could be sent rapidly to deal with any threat to security. The Achaemenids adopted Zoroastrianism as their official religion, although they tolerated the various religions of their diverse subject peoples. Zoroastrianism was revived as the state religion by the later Sasanian empire. The religion's founder, Zoroaster, may have lived in eastern Iran in the 10th century BC. He taught that every individual's strivings for good had a part to play in the overall defeat of evil.

Revolt and retaliation

In 499 BC the Greek cities of Ionia rebelled against Persian rule and, with help from one or two mainland Greek cities, attacked and burned the satrap's city of Sardis. The Persians counterattacked and quickly regained control of Ionia, destroying many of the Greek cities. In 490 BC Darius I launched an invasion of mainland Greece to punish the city-states that had supported the rebellion and those that afterwards had violently refused to submit to Persian rule, notably Athens and Sparta. The Persian forces of around 20,000 men landed at Marathon just north of Athens, and were defeated by a mainly Athenian army of only 9000 men. Darius was forced to retreat.

In 480 BC Darius's successor Xerxes launched a second invasion of Greece with a huge army gathered from all over the empire. On land the Greeks could not face such a force, and retreated. After the defeat of a Spartan rearguard at Thermopylae, the city of Athens was looted and its temples burned. At sea the Greeks had more success and, led by the Athenians, decisively defeated the Persians at the naval battle of Salamis and prevented any Persian advance.

The following year the combined Greek armies defeated the Persians at the battle of Plataea and drove them from Greece. The threat was ended, although Ionia remained under occupation. Persian power in the Mediterranean region was declining and a new 'Greek' power was rising. The Achaemenid empire was also beset by revolts elsewhere – in Babylon and Egypt – and, although the dynasty survived for another century and a half, it never regained its former glory.

2

3

4

4. The riches of the Persian empire and the skill of its craftsmen are illustrated in this head-ornament in the form of a stylized griffin.

THE GOLDEN AGE OF ATHENS

At the end of the Persian wars the inhabitants of Athens were in triumphal mood. Their city had led the defence of Greece, and they had a powerful navy and a thriving economy based on trade and manufacture. What followed can only be described as a cultural explosion. Many of the ideas expressed in Athens – in architecture, literature, art, science and politics – have been handed down over the centuries and are still part of contemporary Western civilization.

The most visible signs of this new mood were the public-works schemes that rebuilt the damage caused by the Persians. The finest was the Parthenon temple in the centre of Athens. Gathering so many skilled craftworkers – such as masons, sculptors, architects and painters – into one place provided a major a boost to other forms of artistic expression, and Athens became a leading producer of high-quality painted pots, which were widely traded and copied.

Annual competitions were held for the best works of music, poetry and drama, and entries were performed in public. Those works that have survived – great tragedies and sophisticated comedies – formed the basis for much of later Western theatre. Athens also became a centre for learning and intellectual debate, and schools and colleges were established, attended by students from all over the Aegean.

Two schools of philosophy were established in the city – the Academy and the Lyceum – by Plato (427–347 BC) and Aristotle (384–322 BC) respectively. The works of these two thinkers, translated and retranslated over the centuries, still form the basis for much of Western philosophy.

1

ATHENS VERSUS SPARTA

Resistance to the Persian invasions (▷ p. 122–3) had a profound effect on Greek society. The Greek 'public' was extremely aware of the magnitude of its achievement – by defeating Persia the Greeks had preserved their own civilization. During the celebrations of their collective victory, some may have felt a sense of nationhood for the first time.

With the outside threat lifted, however, Greek unity quickly disintegrated. Two states emerged from the wars as rivals for the leadership of Greece – Sparta and Athens – each with their own allies and supporters.

During the Peloponnesian Wars that developed out of this rivalry (▷ p. 126), the propaganda war was fought just as fiercely as the battles on land and at sea. In propaganda terms, Athens was the victor, portraying itself as the modern, liberal centre of Greek freedom and achievement, and demonizing Sparta as old-fashioned, reactionary and oppressive. Although this Athenian view contained some truth, it was largely just propaganda. Athens's treatment of rebellious allies could easily match Sparta for brutal repression – in 427 BC, for example, Athens voted to massacre all the male inhabitants of the city of Mytilene.

1. Chief among the new buildings in Athens was the magnificent Parthenon temple built atop the Acropolis – the rocky citadel in the city's centre.

2. Drama gave the Greeks an opportunity to explore the human condition and the nature of the gods, as well as to air social and political views.

1. Pieces of broken pottery (ostraka) were re-used for a wide variety of purposes, from shopping lists to ballot slips. This example may have been used to vote for the exile of an unpopular politician, whose name has been scratched on it.

1

The idea that matter is composed of individual tiny 'atoms' was first proposed by the Greek philosopher Democritus in about 425 BC.

Open democracy

These cultural achievements were paralleled by political developments. Following a series of reforms that can be traced back to the 6th century BC, Athens had by 450 BC established the world's first urban democracy. Decisions, such as how much money to spend on refurbishing the navy, were made by the majority vote of an assembly composed of all citizens (about 25 per cent of the adult population – the rest being women, slaves and foreigners). For the first time, political issues were debated in front of the voters. One result of this new democracy was that it placed great emphasis on a politician's powers of persuasion, rather than other facets of his political abilities.

Despite their cultural sophistication, most Athenians lived in modest houses with few luxuries or rich furnishings. Thanks to the mild climate of Greece, most activities took place in the open air. The centre of Athenian life was the Agora (market place) at the foot of the Acropolis. As well as being the commercial centre for shopping, trading and banking, the buildings around the Agora housed the city's administration, courts and mint. Public notice boards kept citizens informed of the latest debates and decisions.

Prosperity and power

Athens could afford fine temples because the city had sources of wealth in addition to the profits and taxes on trade and manufacturing. South of the city were rich deposits of silver ore that were mined by contractors using slave labour. Most of the silver was made into coins that rapidly became accepted as an international currency.

The important part played by Athens in defeating the Persians was rewarded with leadership of the Delian League of Greek city-states. Athens soon seized control of the league's communal treasury, and established what was in effect an Athenian empire, with other Greek states and cities paying tribute. By now significant rivalry was developing between Athens and Sparta, formerly allied against the Persians. Both cities had made vital military contributions to victory, and both had a moral claim to leadership – they had made sacrifices in the name of Greece. Ordered to resist to the last man, the Spartan contingent at Thermopylae had done just that, and with their lives they had bought enough time for the Athenians to evacuate their city and watch it burn.

In 461 BC Sparta attacked Athens and began the first of the Peloponnesian Wars (named after the peninsula in the south of Greece where Sparta was situated). These conflicts raged intermittently across the Greek world from Asia Minor to Sicily, and ended in 404 BC when Athens, depopulated by plague, finally surrendered. Athenian political power, but not its cultural influence, was ended. Mainland Greece became dominated by a struggle between Sparta and Thebes, until the independence of the city-states was swept away by Philip of Macedon.

THE CONQUESTS OF ALEXANDER

In the far north of Greece was the mountainous kingdom of Macedonia – regarded as an uncivilized place by the urban populations further south. After the Persians were expelled from mainland Greece the increasingly powerful Macedonian kings wanted to play a more active part in Greek affairs. In 338 BC King Philip II of Macedon won the battle of Chaeronea and united Greece under his leadership. As a sign of his commitment to Greek ideas, Philip hired Aristotle, the greatest thinker of his time, as personal tutor to his son Alexander. In 336 BC Philip was assassinated, and Alexander, aged just 20, became king of Macedonia and the whole of Greece.

Alexander wanted revenge against the Persians for the sack of Athens, and in 334 BC he invaded Asia Minor and defeated a Persian army at Issus. He continued south into the Levant and captured Egypt, before turning north to attack Mesopotamia and Iran. In 331 BC he defeated the Persian king, Darius III, at Gaugamela, and continued through Iran into Afghanistan almost to the borders of present-day China, and then southwards into north-west India, where he defeated the local ruler.

After ten years of campaigning he and his men were thousands of kilometres from their homeland and had conquered most of the world as it was known to the Greeks. Alexander's empire was now greater even than that of the Persians. Alexander returned to Babylon, where he died of fever in 323 BC.

During his short rule Alexander tried to bring together the cultures of Greece and Persia – for example by promoting ethnically mixed marriages – but the effects were mainly one-sided. Although Greek rulers in Asia may have adopted eastern titles and regalia, most of the cultural exchange was in the opposite direction. Greek ideas, especially about art and philosophy, spread far and wide and had an enduring influence.

☆ In the 6th century BC Greek engineers building an aqueduct on the island of Samos tunnelled straight through 1 km (2700 feet) of solid rock.

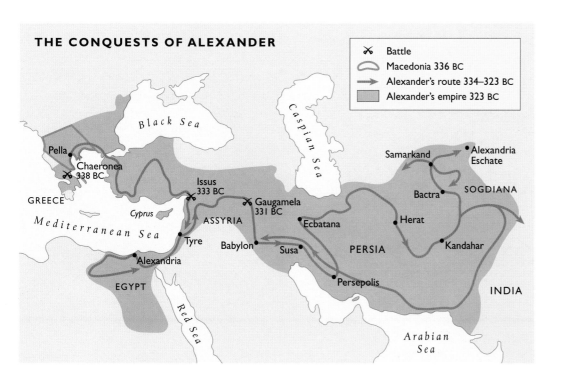

THE CONQUESTS OF ALEXANDER

⚔ Battle
⌒ Macedonia 336 BC
→ Alexander's route 334–323 BC
▮ Alexander's empire 323 BC

Black Sea

Caspian Sea

Pella
Chaeronea 338 BC
GREECE
Issus 333 BC
Cyprus
Mediterranean Sea
ASSYRIA
Gaugamela 331 BC
Ecbatana
Tyre
Babylon
Alexandria
Susa
EGYPT
Red Sea
PERSIA
Persepolis
Herat
Kandahar
Samarkand
Alexandria Eschate
Bactra
SOGDIANA
INDIA
Arabian Sea

The Hellenistic world

Alexander reputedly bequeathed his empire 'to the strongest'. It did not survive him, but was fought over and soon divided between his leading generals. Ptolemy took Egypt and his dynasty ruled there for 300 years until the last of his line, Queen Cleopatra VII, became entangled with the Romans.

Seleucus took all the Asian possessions, but his successors – the Seleucid dynasty – failed to keep them intact. India was lost to the Mauryans in 303 BC, and Bactria and Parthia were established as independent states around 250 BC. The Parthians gradually wrested control of Iran from the Seleucids, whose power began to crumble around 190 BC. In about 141 BC Mithridates I extended the Parthian empire into Mesopotamia and founded a new capital, Ctesiphon, opposite the old Seleucid capital of Seleucia-on-the-Tigris. By the time the Romans became interested in Asia the Seleucids ruled only parts of the Levant and Asia Minor.

Antigonus, Lysimachus and Cassander, the rulers who succeeded Alexander in Greece, Macedon and Anatolia, were even less successful, and by 275 BC their successors had lost control even of the rest of Greece.

Although Greek political power gradually declined after Alexander, Greek cultural influence was immense, and this era is often described as the Hellenistic period (the Greeks called themselves Hellenes). From northern India to southern Spain a version of mid-5th-century BC Athenian taste became the accepted style of art and architecture.

This was an age of tremendous cultural and scientific development. Alexandria, founded by Alexander and capital of Ptolemaic Egypt, became a leading centre. It was famous not only for its lighthouse, the Pharos, but also for its great library, which housed several hundred thousand volumes, and the Museum, where scholars, scientists, philosophers and writers gathered to exchange ideas.

Greek influence was particularly strong in Italy, where the colonies in the south had been largely untroubled by Persian wars and Macedonian conquests. They had, however, been embroiled in their own struggles – first with Carthaginians and Etruscans, which ended with an uneasy truce, and then with the Romans, who proved to be unstoppable.

2

1. (opposite) Alexander, probably the greatest general the world has ever known, began his conquest of the Persian empire at the age of 21 and was only 32 when he died. Had his army not prevented him, he would have invaded China.

2. This coin, issued by Alexander, shows him on horseback attacking the Indian king Poros, who is riding on a war elephant. Elephants were actually of very limited use in warfare.

 ## PHILOSOPHY AND LOGIC

The ancient Greeks were a religious people, respecting the gods, whom they thought of as superhuman beings with human emotions and foibles. But they also had what has been described as a 'spirit' of scepticism about such matters. In much of the Greek world individuals began to develop their own ideas about various fundamental philosophical questions – about the natural world, the nature of reality itself, and about the source and nature of human knowledge, morality and aesthetic sense.

A central problem for the early philosophers was how to determine the truth of a statement or argument. This was especially relevant to a people experimenting with democracy. Arguments made by demagogues to sway the citizen assembly might be persuasive, but were they truthful? The same problem faced jurors listening to lawyers, and students listening to a teacher. Greek philosophers tested the truth of complex arguments by breaking the argument down into a series of simple steps, each of which could be tested separately. If any step failed the truth test, or the conclusion could be shown not to follow from the previous steps, then the whole argument was wrong. This process is known as logic. One of the greatest achievements of the Greek philosophers was to try to apply mathematical standards of proof to non-mathematical arguments.

SLAVERY

Slavery was widespread throughout the ancient world, and was seen as part of the natural order of things. Slaves were a significant but 'invisible' segment of the population of early civilizations. In Athens – the birthplace of democracy and individual liberty – about a fifth of the population were slaves.

The institution of slavery – in which people are treated as property – probably arose early on as a humane, and more profitable, alternative to the wholesale slaughter of captured enemies. High-status prisoners might be ransomed back to the losing side, but ordinary soldiers and non-combatants became involuntary members of the victor's labour force.

The value of people

Slavery was not essential to the development of civilization, but as societies grew in size and complexity, slave labour became of increasing economic importance. In Egypt and Mesopotamia all captive slaves were initially the property of the state, although some might be allocated to individual temples. These slaves were organized into labour gangs or workshops that produced pottery or clothing.

The earliest-known law codes, from the Mesopotamian city of Ur around 2100 BC, show that slavery was well established, with some slaves being owned by individuals. The laws also allowed for the freeing of slaves and for marriage between slaves and free citizens. By this time 'debt slavery' had developed, whereby impoverished individuals contracted to become slaves as a means of staying alive. In times of famine, children were often given as slaves to temples for the same reason.

From being a by-product of warfare, the acquisition of slaves became one of its aims. The wealth of the Mycenaeans, for example, was largely based on trade in high-quality textiles produced in workshops staffed by slave women, some of whom may have been captured in pirate raids. An Egyptian pharaoh of the same period boasted of acquiring nearly 100,000 captives in a single raid on Palestine.

The conquests of the Roman empire produced enough captives to spread slave ownership to all but the poorest levels of society. Slaves were widely bought and sold across the empire, and were also acquired at the frontiers. Roman traders boasted of being able to purchase a Celtic slave for a flagon of wine.

Slave life

The conditions of slaves varied enormously, both in legal status and in bodily comfort. Initially laws tended to protect slaves as valuable property, rather than allow them any personal rights, but generally they were fed and treated like productive farm animals. Slavery was usually for life and often had

1. Slaves were one of Britain's exports to the rest of the Roman world, exchanged for wine and luxury tableware. Linked neckrings secured the slaves during transportation.

3

2. When the Assyrians defeated an enemy town, they usually marched off its women, children, and sometimes men, into slavery.

3. Roman slaves had a reasonable chance of saving up to purchase their freedom or of being granted it in their master's will.

hereditary status, although most societies had mechanisms whereby slaves could be freed. The complete abolition of slavery was attempted only once, in China under the usurper Wang Mang (ruled AD 9–23), and his reform did not outlive him.

Perhaps the worst conditions of slavery were in Mesoamerica (Mexico and Central America), where religious tradition demanded a constant stream of human sacrifices. High-status prisoners could expect to be tortured and sacrificed on an appropriate occasion. Ordinary captives were used for slave labour on construction projects, but might be chosen for sacrifice at any time. In the Americas generally, slaves had no legal status or rights,

and appear to have been kept separate from the rest of the population, although noble captives might receive special privileges.

Elsewhere, a slave's life was a matter of luck and talent. For a slave to be sent to work in the Laurion silver mines near Athens was a death sentence, as was being sent to a Roman gladiator school. On the other hand, a slave who was a competent pot painter or weaver might have a fairly long and comfortable life. Household slaves, such as cooks and maids, probably had an easier life than manual workers, but abuse was rampant and even institutionalized. Under Roman law, evidence from slaves was only allowable in court if it had been extracted under torture.

◆ TOPIC LINKS

2.2 The Lands Between the Rivers
p.48 Sumerian Cities

2.6 Zone of Conflict
p.97 Seaborne Enterprise
p.104 Israel
p.105 The Sea Peoples

3.2 The Athenian Role Model
p.126 Prosperity and Power

3.5 Mediterranean Conflicts
p.160 The Carthaginians
p.161 The Rise of Rome
p.162 International Influence
p.163 Military Power

3.6 The Might of Rome
p.170 Roman Society
p.171 The Eternal City

4.4 Flowery Wars and Conquerors
p.225 Pochteca Merchants

Between 500 BC and 500 AD many aspects of classical Indian culture crystallized. The focus shifted from the Indus valley to the lands of the Ganges, which remained thereafter the heartland of Indian civilization. Although around 500 BC there was a reaction against the developing caste system – resulting in the birth of Buddhism and other sects – caste became through time the backbone of India's social organization. Caste – which dictated everybody's rank and occupation according to their birth – provided continuity and stability through the ebb and flow of dynasties, empires and foreign invaders. The greater part of the land was united under the Maurya dynasty in the 3rd to 1st centuries BC, and again under the Guptas from the 4th century AD. At other times smaller kingdoms and principalities divided up the subcontinent. Buddhism provided a major encouragement to native industry and spread widely as a consequence of international trade.

THE MAURYAS

As the Indus cities disappeared around 1800 BC (▷ p. 67), horse-riding Indo-Aryan nomads, keeping cattle and worshipping warlike gods, infiltrated the northwest and swelled the ranks of the rice farmers who were beginning to penetrate the forests of the Ganges valley and that of its great tributary, the Yamuna.

The pioneer settlers established villages that soon grew large enough to come into conflict with each other. Indian epic poetry glorifies one of these conflicts as the great Mahabharata War between the rulers of two neighbouring kingdoms, into which all other kingdoms of north India were reputedly drawn. Several hundred years later, historical kingdoms of greater size, centred on walled towns, were still fighting for dominance of the rich Ganges lands. The rulers of many of these small states (there were traditionally 16 in the 5th century BC) began minting coins marked with signs symbolizing their state and themselves. At the same time, writing recommenced with the development of the Brahmi script, which was adapted from a script from western Asia. Gradually the centrally located state of Magadha gained the upper hand. In 321 BC a new dynasty came to power in Magadha – the Mauryas, whose founder, Chandragupta Maurya, unified the whole of northern India.

Buddhist realms

The 6th century BC was a time not only of physical conflict but also of religious upheaval. Dissatisfaction with the rigidly structured caste system and other aspects of traditional Hindu religion brought about the emergence of a number of breakaway reform movements, including Buddhism and Jainism. The Buddha ('the enlightened one') was born as Prince

Siddhartha (563–483 BC) in a Himalayan republic, but renounced the world to search for a way to end human suffering. Gaining enlightenment through meditation, he devoted the rest of his long life to preaching the Middle Way between the extremes of indulgence and asceticism. By following this path through life, an individual could shed human desires and eventually attain the perfect peace of Nirvana, unity with the Absolute.

These reforming religions, and particularly Buddhism, strongly influenced the third Mauryan emperor, Ashoka (reigned 272–232 BC). Appalled by the suffering caused by the wars that had brought most of India under Mauryan rule, Ashoka renounced violence and organized his realms along enlightened lines, setting out his political philosophy in edicts that he caused to be carved all over his empire. He also set up beautifully polished

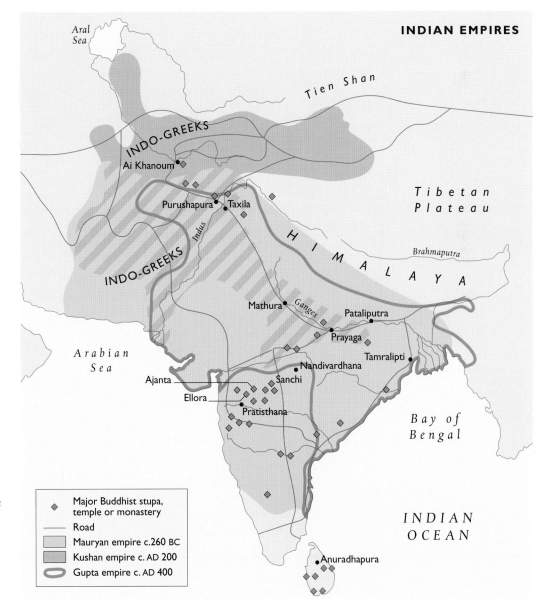

sandstone pillars at places that had been important in the life of the Buddha. The animals and other Buddhist symbols on the capitals of these pillars are superb artistic achievements.

Under Ashoka, India prospered. He sponsored many land-clearance and reclamation projects and set up hospitals for people and animals. His administrative system was efficient and prosperous, although things fell apart under his successors, bringing Mauryan rule to a close by 180 BC. Thereafter the empire fragmented into smaller kingdoms and republics, some ruled by native dynasties, such as the Shungas in the Ganges heartland and the Satavahanas in the Deccan. Other regions came under the sway of foreigners: in the northwest, kingdoms were carved out by the Shakas – nomads from Central Asia – and by the Indo-Greek descendants of the armies of Alexander the Great (▷ p. 136).

Trade and religion

Ashoka sponsored a number of Buddhist missions to foreign lands, most notably to Sri Lanka, where Buddhism still flourishes. When the Buddha died, his cremated remains had been shared between eight of the major kingdoms of the time, who interred them in eight stupas (dome-shaped funerary structures). According to tradition Ashoka had these mounds opened and the relics re-deposited in 84,000 stupas across his lands, each stupa becoming a focus for Buddhist devotions (▷ p. 140). Ashoka's patronage was not confined to Buddhism: he also caused cave shelters to be carved for the Ajivika sect.

Initially Buddhist monks led a nomadic existence, travelling and preaching, but as time passed the temporary shelters they occupied during the rainy season developed into large monastic establishments, growing wealthy through the patronage of lay devotees – kings, princes and merchants. Monasteries along the main highways provided both accommodation and a pool of knowledge and expertise for travelling merchants. As trade moved further afield, monasteries and merchant towns developed side by side at oases along the route through Central Asia to China, and Buddhist and Hindu merchants spread their respective religions among the emerging kingdoms of Southeast Asia.

Urban life

Cities well placed for trade became particularly prosperous. One such city was Taxila in the north, which lay on the crossroads between the east–west Silk Road and the Grand Trunk Road into India. The latter led to the Mauryan capital Pataliputra (modern

1. The emperor Ashoka had pillars erected at major places associated with the life of the Buddha. These were surmounted by capitals with Buddhist symbols. That at Vaishali, shown here, had a lion, one of the Four Noble Beasts.

2. (opposite) Scenes from Buddha's life are depicted on the gateways of the Great Stupa at Sanchi. Here the demon, Mara, vainly assails the Buddha with his demon followers and alluring daughters to prevent him from attaining enlightenment.

Patna), at the heart of the empire, and finally reached Tamralipti (modern Tamluk), a thriving port in the Ganges delta. In such cities magnificent halls and substantial mansions stood alongside Buddhist stupas, monasteries and shrines, together with parks, gardens, pools and canals. Taxila boasted a university, as well as shrines of a variety of religions to serve the needs of its cosmopolitan population. Many industries prospered, such as iron working and textile weaving – Indian cotton cloth was a highly sought-after commodity in many distant lands. Domestic architecture flourished, and the towns often had sophisticated drainage systems to carry off waste water.

Craft production was organized by guilds in the cities, linked by caste relationships with other guild members throughout the land. This provided considerable social cohesion, even in times of political disintegration. Roads were constructed and maintained by the Mauryas and their successors. One such road ran southwards through the Deccan – the vast plateau of central-southern India – and on into the far south, home of several small Dravidian kingdoms whose culture was little touched by the invasions that periodically swept the north. It was from here, a land of seafarers, that trading expeditions to Southeast Asia began to be undertaken.

INDO-GREEKS AND FOREIGN DYNASTIES

The vast Seleucid empire stretching from the Levant to northwest India had been established by one of the successors of Alexander the Great (▷ p. 129). It soon started to disintegrate, and in about 250 BC the governor of Bactria (northern Afghanistan) broke away from the empire and established an independent kingdom. Bactria was well situated – on both the main north–south and east–west routes – to profit from trade, and the rulers issued large silver coins in the Greek style. Despite being made at the very edges of the

 SRI LANKA

Sri Lanka was traditionally colonized in the 5th century BC by northern Indians, who subdued the native population and founded a kingdom where towns rapidly developed and rice farming prospered. Farming on most of the island relied on a sophisticated network of canals, dams and reservoirs with complex sluice gates, fully developed by the 3rd century BC.

The Mauryan emperor Ashoka sent a Buddhist mission to Sri Lanka in 246 BC under his own son, Mahinda. The religion was enthusiastically taken up by the king, Devanampiya Tissa (reigned 247–207 BC), who donated a large park in the centre of the capital, Anuradhapura, for the construction of a Buddhist monastery and a stupa, Thuparama, to enshrine the Buddha's collarbone and begging bowl, pious gifts from Ashoka. Over the years many other shrines and monasteries were established, such as the Ruvanveli dagoba (stupa), illustrated right. Under Dutthagamani (reigned 101–77 BC) – who freed the island from southern Indian invaders – the Great Stupa was constructed, while another shrine surrounded the sacred Bodhi tree, grown from a cutting taken from the tree under which the Buddha gained enlightenment.

Canals kept Anuradhapura well supplied with water – large reservoirs met irrigation and other needs, and small bathing pools were dotted around the city, which was full of gardens. Many-storeyed wooden palaces and pavilions supported on stone pillars were decorated with silver and jewels. Buildings were enhanced by beautifully sculpted stones depicting Buddhist themes, and figures of benevolent spirits guarded their entrances.

Greek world, these coins bear some of the finest portraits achieved by either Greek or Roman artists. The Bactrians also maintained Alexander's military traditions, and their prowess in war gained the respect of the Chinese, who visited the region in search of good horses.

The collapse of Mauryan power in India allowed the Bactrians to expand southwards, and they established control over much of the Indus valley region, which was divided into a number of kingdoms. Although ruled by Greek kings, these new states did not impose their own culture on the native populations. The rulers issued bilingual coins, inscribed with both Greek and Indian scripts, and tolerated the local religions. One of them, Menander (ruled c.155–130 BC) may have converted to Buddhism, and certainly used Buddhist imagery on his coins. These Indo-Greek states were the last outpost of Greek culture in Central and southern Asia, and they lasted less than 200 years. By AD 40, first the Bactrians, then the Indo-Greeks, had been overrun by successive waves of invaders from the steppes.

Nomad rulers

The first nomad group to move into India were the Shakas. The Shakas were cousins to the Scythian peoples who lived around the northern shore of the Black Sea, and are consequently sometimes known as the Indo-Scythians. In about 90 BC they captured the important northwestern city of Taxila, which became their capital. Already familiar with Greek culture through trade contacts, the Shakas made few innovations, and the lives of ordinary people were little affected by the change in rule. Shaka control was soon threatened by a warrior group who migrated from eastern Iran, perhaps as the result of a dynastic dispute within the Parthian empire

1

2

1. The art styles of the Classical world clearly influenced the Buddhist art of Gandhara (north-west India and Pakistan), a cultural crossroads where many traditions met and interacted.

2. A coin of one of the later Kushan kings, Vasudeva I (2nd century AD).

⭐ Free hospitals for the poor, cripples, orphans and widows were a feature of Gupta towns. Medical texts describe treatments for people and elephants.

1. Hinduism saw a major revival under the Guptas, and Buddhist art now began to give place to sculptures of Hindu deities, particularly Shiva and Vishnu, seen here in an eight-armed form. **1**

(▷ p. 129). Known as the Indo-Parthians, they established their own kingdom in southern Afghanistan and the region west of the Indus. One of their kings, Gondophares, is reported to have received the Christian apostle St Thomas at his court, employing him to build a palace.

Neither the Shakas nor the Indo-Parthians were able to supplant the Greeks completely, and small Indo-Greek kingdoms continued to exist in the western foothills of the Himalaya. They were all swept away, however, by the next wave of invaders, the Yuezhi, a loose confederation of nomad tribes. Forced to migrate from their homeland near the north-western borders of China, the Yuezhi reached Bactria in about 130 BC and quickly conquered the Greek cities.

As the Yuezhi continued southwards into India, one of the tribes in the confederation, the Kushan, established dominance over the other Yuezhi tribes. By about AD 40 the Kushans had completed the conquest of most of the other 'foreign' kingdoms in northern India and controlled an empire that stretched from the Aral Sea to the Ganges, only a small region on the northwestern coast of India remaining under Shaka rule.

The Kushan empire grew rich through its control of overland trade, especially the Silk Road – during the Kushan period the trade between Rome and China along this route was at its height. In Central Asia the Kushans constructed canals to irrigate the Oxus valley, and in India they proved tolerant and enlightened rulers – King Kanishka (c.AD 120) organized an international Buddhist conference. Although a great patron of Buddhism, Kanishka also erected a statue of himself as a divine emperor in the Kushan dynastic shrine at Mat in the Ganges region. In the mid-3rd century AD the northern Kushan territories were lost to the Sasanians (successors to the Parthians in Iran) and their control of India collapsed.

THE GUPTAS

An obscure dynasty from the middle reaches of the Ganges, the Guptas rose to power in the early 4th century AD, rapidly bringing under their control the numerous kingdoms that had emerged or expanded after the collapse of the Kushans. The Gupta empire almost rivalled that of the Mauryas in extent, but its organization was far looser. Where the Mauryas had centralized their administration, with governors and viceroys appointed from the centre to control outlying areas, the Guptas operated a feudal system in which provincial nobles and large landowners enjoyed considerable local autonomy but paid taxes and services to the emperor. At a lower level, villages were also virtually autonomous, with the same obligations to their local landlord, and the castes and guilds exercised local authority.

Caste played an increasingly important role in the organization of life, with every member of a community having an occupation determined by the caste they were born into, a set of rights and duties within the community and a network of kinsfolk across the land. Most craft activities were organized by guilds. Often these were made up of people of the same caste practising the same craft and having wide-ranging affiliations, but some guilds existed to provide all the skills required in a complex operation, such as the construction of shrines and palaces, where stonemasons, carpenters, sculptors, painters and textile manufacturers might be required, as well as architects.

The greatest Gupta emperor was Chandragupta II (reigned c.AD 375–415), whose reign is often considered India's golden age. Under his rule the economy prospered, with considerable overseas trade promoted by the Guptas' control over ports on the western seaboard. Arts and crafts flourished, including music and the manufacture of cotton textiles that were highly prized by overseas trading partners. Technology and intellectual life also prospered, and major developments in mathematics, medicine and astronomy were achieved. After Chandragupta II, Gupta rule began to decline, and in the late 5th century the empire fell to the Huns. These 'White Huns' (or Hephthalites) who invaded India were one branch of a warlike horse-riding

A GREEK CITY IN CENTRAL ASIA

Greek architects refined the planning and construction of new cities to a fine art. The greatest of the Hellenistic city builders was Alexander the Great, and among the many cities he founded during his campaigns was Ai Khanoum, built to settle some of the veterans from his army.

Located in northern Bactria (Afghanistan), Ai Khanoum was built on a small fertile plain near the eastern end of the natural 'corridor' formed by the Oxus river (the Amu Darya). Across the steppes to the west was the great trade centre of Merv in Iran, and to the north, reached through mountain passes, were the cities of Samarkand and Tashkent. Although quite small, with perhaps no more than 7000 inhabitants, Ai Khanoum had all the amenities of a city in mainland Greece – temples, colonnades, a theatre and a huge public gymnasium. The palace library contained numerous papyrus scrolls with works by Aristotle and other Greek writers. The philosophers of Ai Khanoum seem to have engaged in lively dialogue with their Indian counterparts. Some of the scrolls discovered by archaeologists contain carefully prepared counter-arguments to aspects of Buddhist philosophy.

Greek culture flourished at Ai Khanoum for about 200 years, until the invasion of the Yuezhi (see left), who attacked the city in about 130 BC. After this the city was abandoned by its Greek inhabitants.

★ As well as practising Buddhism, the Kushan rulers erected dynastic shrines, in which the objects of worship were portraits of themselves as divine kings.

people from Mongolia and northern China who menaced Europe and western Asia at much the same time (▷ p. 177).

Religion

Although Buddhism had become the main religion of merchants and many others throughout India and adjacent regions, with Jainism and other sects also having many adherents, Hindu traditions continued alongside the newer religions. For example, in the southern Indian kingdom of the Ikshvakus, the rulers worshipped Hindu deities such as Kartikeya while their wives and sisters were

1

Buddhists. With the rise of the Guptas, Hinduism underwent a revival and Buddhism gradually declined. This was partly because many of the aspects of the revived Hinduism were similar to those of Buddhism, so the latter was gradually assimilated. For example, the new Hindu practices of meditation and devotion to a personal deity both found parallels in Buddhist practice with its reverence for the Buddha and Buddhist saints. Another new aspect was the growing importance of goddesses, drawn in from earlier folk religion. This was echoed in Buddhism by the introduction of female deities as counterparts to the Buddhist saints. The blood sacrifices of the Aryans who had invaded India some 2000 years before were now largely (but not completely) replaced by offerings of fruit and flowers. The notion of rebirth, central to Hinduism, continued to grow in importance, reinforcing the growing rigidity of the caste system, which viewed an individual's station in this life as a reflection of his or her achievements and failures in former incarnations.

Stupas

Stupas were sacred mounds built to house relics of the Buddha and of Buddhist saints. They became places of veneration, where people worshipped by making offerings of fruit and flowers and by walking round in a clockwise direction. The first stupas were simple hemispherical mounds, but rapidly more elaborate forms developed, with the mound raised on a drum and surmounted with umbrellas (a royal status symbol). Although the traditional figure of 84,000 may be an exaggeration, many stupas were erected by the Mauryan emperor Ashoka (▷ p. 134).

Decorations were carved on the massive stone railings around the stupa and on the elaborate gateways. Later, decorated slabs were also attached to the stupa. These depicted scenes from the life of the Buddha and his former incarnations, providing a wealth of educational detail for the illiterate. Motifs from folk art were woven into the decoration – for instance tree spirits adorn the gateways of the early stupa at Sanchi, one of India's greatest monuments. Particular panels were often the gift of pious individuals, not only princes but also successful merchants and artisans, while craft guilds also donated panels.

Rock-cut architecture

Some of the most remarkable surviving examples of early Indian architecture are in the form of temples and monasteries cut into the soft rock of the Deccan. Although most of these structures were Buddhist, there were also Jain and Hindu examples, notably those at Udayagiri and Ellora. Caves hewn into the side of cliffs mimicked free-standing wooden architecture in every detail, down to individual nails. The temples took the form of pillared halls housing a stupa or, later, a statue of the Buddha, with an intricately carved facade in the shape of a horseshoe, with windows and balconies.

Alongside the temples were rock-cut monasteries, consisting of a central courtyard for meetings and other communal activities, surrounded by the cells of individual monks. Within the complex would be many other structures such as a refectory and water-storage tanks, as well as guest houses where visitors could lodge. Within the large complex at Ajanta, steps led up and down the cliff face, linking the many monasteries and temples and allowing the monks to descend to the river running round the foot of the valley. Most rock-cut monasteries and shrines were beautifully decorated with carvings, and at Ajanta these were supplemented by exquisite paintings depicting the Buddha and scenes from his former lives.

2

1. The Guptas encouraged the establishment and growth of great Buddhist monasteries that were centres of learning, like universities. Chinese pilgrims, such as Fa Xian (5th century AD), studied in the monastery at Nalanda.

2. The façade of the rock-cut Buddhist temple at Karle in Maharashtra is partially obscured by a broken gateway and a decorated pillar. The horseshoe-shaped main arch originally held a wooden screen, now gone.

Overleaf. A fight to the death between pairs of Roman gladiators, armed in various ways, was a lavish and costly spectacle – gladiators took years to train and fights usually ended when one of the opponents was seriously wounded.

RECREATION: SACRED AND SECULAR

Since early times, people have played games of skill or chance and competed physically and mentally to pass their leisure hours or to honour the gods. Music and dancing have also played an important part in both social and religious life worldwide, and dancing is a favourite subject of rock art in many lands.

Drummers and pipers appear on Indian stupas, and conch-shell trumpets survive from earlier Indus times. Similar trumpets were used in religious ceremonies in the Americas. The diversity and sophistication of ancient musical instruments is clear from panpipes, bells, zithers and other instruments found in many places.

1. Greek pottery often shows scenes from the gymnasium, such as boxing, wrestling, running and throwing the discus. This example depicts a youth performing the long jump under the watchful eye of his trainer. Weights held in his hands help to propel him further.

2. Board games and attractive gaming pieces have been found in cities and towns of the Indus civilization. Such amusements were to become extremely popular in later India.

Games of skill and chance

Many of the pebbles and pieces of clay found in early settlements are likely to have been gaming pieces, though we cannot identify them as such. However, board games were certainly being played by around 2500 BC, when several beautifully made gaming boards were buried in the royal graves at Ur in Mesopotamia (▷ p. 49). These consisted of an arrangement of squares decorated with a mosaic of shell, lapis lazuli and red limestone, and shell counters in black and white.

The Egyptians played *senet*, moving their pieces along a board of 30 squares arranged in three rows, with some lucky or unlucky squares. A handsome ebony *senet* board inlaid with gold, ivory and silver was one of the offerings in Tutankhamun's tomb. To determine the moves, the players threw a bundle of 'throw-sticks'. The Indus peoples, on the other hand, used six-faced dice in their games of chance, along with beautiful bone and ivory counters decorated with birds. Board games like snakes and ladders, draughts and parcheesi (similar to ludo) became extremely popular in ancient India. Gaming boards were often carved in public places so that people could easily play. One legendary Indian king, Yudhisthira, was such a keen player that he gambled away not only his clothes but also his wife and his kingdom.

Such games were an amusement, sharpening people's wits, but they often had a symbolic or ritual significance too. Games of chance might be used to predict the future. The Egyptian *senet* (which means 'passing') symbolized the hazardous passage of the soul from the world of the living to the underworld.

Sport: religion, war and entertainment

Physical contests could also relate to religious matters. The Mesoamerican ritual ball game, for example, often ended in the losers being sacrificed (▷ p. 197). Funerary games were held by many societies; for example, the games at the funeral of the legendary Mycenaean hero, Patroclus, included a chariot race, a boxing match, a wrestling contest, a foot race, an archery contest and an armed combat in which the victor was the first to draw blood. Prizes for these games included metal vessels, parade armour and slave women.

The Greeks continued this tradition of sporting contests, holding religious festivals such as the Olympic Games, which included many such events. The prize was an olive wreath, but successful competitors also had the glory of winning. This reflected honour on their native city too, and during the year young men devoted much of their time to exercising in the gymnasium in all the sports in the hope of being chosen to represent their city.

Sporting activities helped to keep men fit, and also in training for war. The ancient Chinese spent much time shooting at targets or hunting game with bows and arrows. Hunting was the pastime of the nobility in many cultures, from the Moche of South America, out after deer with their dogs, to the ancient Korean lords pursuing tigers from horseback.

Some sports were exceedingly dangerous, such as bull-leaping, an activity with a strong religious significance, best known from Minoan Crete but also practised by hunter-gatherers in ancient India. Generally few women took part in sporting activities, but the bull leapers of Minoan Crete were of

both sexes, and in Sparta all girls participated in gymnastics and athletics.

The Romans provided chariot races for public entertainment, and also gladiatorial contests involving men against men or against wild beasts, such as panthers and bears. On rare occasions they would even flood the amphitheatre and stage a mock naval battle. A successful and skilful gladiator often had a popular following, rather like footballers today. When Pompeii was destroyed by the eruption of Vesuvius, a wealthy woman was paying her heroes a visit and died in their barracks.

3. A painting in the tomb of Nefertari, wife of Ramses II, shows the queen playing *senet*, a popular Egyptian board game. Two opposed players moved their own pieces along the track and each tried to block the opponent's progress.

◆ TOPIC LINKS

2.2 The Lands Between the Rivers
p.49 Royal Graves at Ur

3.3 The Land of the Buddha
p.139 A Greek City in Asia

3.4 The Great Han
p.148 Daily Life
p.119 The Ancient Greeks
p.124 The Golden Age of Athens

3.6 The Might of Rome
p.173 Bread and Circuses

4.2 Builders of Mounds and Pyramids
p.197 The Sacred Ball Game

3.4 THE GREAT HAN

The mighty Han dynasty that came to power in northern China in 202 BC was to rule for over 400 years. The Han extended their empire into southern China, northern Korea, Manchuria and the lands along the Silk Road in Central Asia. Beyond these regions China also influenced the cultural development of its neighbours in southern Korea, Japan and Southeast Asia, while even the untamed nomads on its northern border valued Chinese products such as silks and bronze mirrors. Silk was a major export to the West, from where the Chinese imported luxuries such as Roman glassware.

It was also a time of great prosperity within China. Trained civil servants ran an efficient administration, and agriculture and technology saw many advances. The high standards of craftsmanship in the well-run industries can be seen particularly in the exquisite textiles and objects of jade, bronze and lacquer buried with the wealthy élite.

QIN UNIFICATION AND THE HAN DYNASTY

For almost three centuries before the Han came to power, northern China had been plunged into disunity by the 'Warring States'. In the 4th century BC the small state of Qin was reorganized along efficient though ruthless lines. It began to defeat and take over the neighbouring states, and by 221 BC had swallowed them all up. Its king, Zheng, took the title Shihuangdi – 'First Emperor'.

Shihuangdi reformed and systematized the administration, standardized the currency and weights and measures, built roads and canals and encouraged agriculture. But his rule was harsh and repressive. He destroyed all records of happier former times, ruthlessly suppressed opposition and caused the deaths of tens of thousands of his subjects, whom he recruited as forced labour for his building projects. Shihuangdi died in 210 BC and revolts rapidly tore the empire apart. From this a new leader, Liu Bang (Emperor Gaozu), emerged victorious in 202 BC, founding the Han dynasty. This endured, apart from a short period under the usurper Wang Mang (reigned AD 9–23), until AD 220.

The Han empire

The Han took over and improved upon the efficient administrative system created by Shihuangdi. They instituted a professional civil service, entrance to whose ranks was by examination. Officials were posted to areas far from their homes, to avoid corruption. To finance public building and military campaigns, iron and salt production were made state monopolies in 117 BC. Salt was mined as brine from deposits deep underground. Once brought to the surface, salt was produced by evaporating the brine in iron pots heated by burning natural gas.

Canals and dykes were built to improve irrigation, and new or improved agricultural tools (such as the iron plough and the wheelbarrow) increased productivity by the peasants – who made up the vast majority of the Han population. Nevertheless, a prolonged period of drought in the early years AD caused great suffering and loss of life. Peasants were required, as in former times, to undertake conscript labour on public works, and also had to perform military service in the immense armies used against the Han's neighbours.

The Han empire at its height extended some 1600 km (1000 miles) from north to south and east to west, with a population of 57 million people. Much of this expansion took place under early rulers and particularly Wudi (reigned 141–87 BC), their conquests reaching as far as Manchuria and central Korea in the north and northern Vietnam in the south. The Han also came to control a strip of land along the Silk Road as far west as Ferghana (in modern Uzbekistan).

Chinese culture influenced the way of life in these areas, and many Chinese features persisted long after Chinese rule had ended. In the final years of the Han dynasty weak emperors and civil disturbances allowed three strong lords to carve up authority between them and form three separate kingdoms. Although the political situation fluctuated, it was not until AD 581 that China was once again united, under the Sui dynasty.

Despite the political upheavals, however, the cultural pattern set by the Han endured, forming the basis for the traditional way of life consciously adhered to by the later

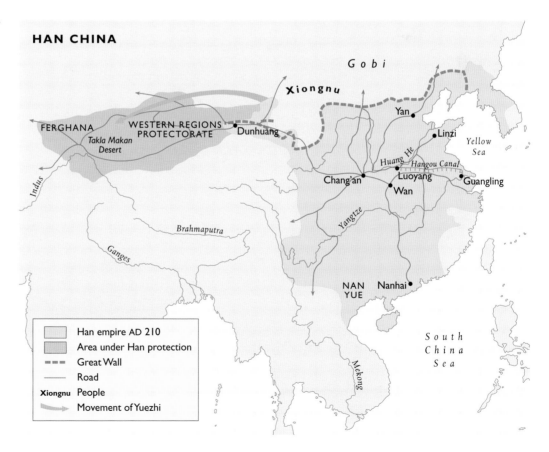

HAN CHINA

	Han empire AD 210
	Area under Han protection
- - -	Great Wall
——	Road
Xiongnu	People
⟹	Movement of Yuezhi

tiled roofs. In the large public rooms of such a mansion the master of the house would receive guests with good food and drink, while musicians, dancers, acrobats and jugglers entertained them. The women of the household would attend to domestic duties like weaving silk, while the children amused themselves with such pastimes as board games. Hunting was a popular sport of the nobility, particularly shooting wild birds with bows and arrows.

The early Han capital, Chang'an, was one of the largest cities in the world at the time, housing a quarter of a million people. Many of its buildings were royal palaces, resplendently painted in red and gold. Wide streets built in a regular grid were designed to accommodate processions. Within its walls nine markets flourished, where peasants might sell their produce, craftsmen their wares and hungry shoppers could pick up a snack at cooked-meat stalls. Outside the massive walls and moat that defended the city was a pleasure park in which the emperor could hunt. Later the city of Luoyang, further east, replaced Chang'an as the capital – this city had been the capital long before, under the eastern Zhou.

1. A Han brick shows brine being extracted from deep underground and carried to cauldrons where it was boiled to extract the salt.

2. Another brick from a wealthy individual's tomb depicts him relaxing in his home, entertained by musicians, dancers and jugglers.

Chinese, whether rulers, scholars or peasants. Although ancient practices such as ancestor worship endured, it was the Han who consciously crystallized the Chinese tradition of an ordered hierarchical society run by efficient public servants. This administrative system was accompanied by major invest-ments in public works such as canals and roads, and the encouragement of scholarship and craftsmanship. From this time on, China saw itself as a single, culturally unified state rather a collection of separate, rival polities – and this remained the ideal even in periods of political dissolution.

Daily life

The majority of Han Chinese were farmers. Some were substantial landowners who enjoyed a very comfortable lifestyle, others were peasants who owned enough land to support themselves, and some were poor landless labourers, employed by the wealthy. Peasants lived in simple thatched mud-brick huts, but wealthy landowners and nobles might live in substantial houses, several storeys high, made of wood and plaster with

Tombs

Many of the most splendid Han objects that survive come from tombs. The Chinese thought it necessary to provide their wealthy dead with everything that they might require in the other world. The practice of sacrificing servants to accompany the dead had by now given way to the provision of models of people such as servants and musicians. Some other important items were also provided as miniature models in terracotta or bronze, such as houses and horse-drawn chariots, though often the real objects were buried. The tombs of the 2nd-century BC prince and princess of Zhongshan, Liu Sheng and Dou

Wan, were constructed in the form of houses, with stables (complete with sacrificed horses and chariots) and storerooms flanking the entrance, a public hall with tented pavilions in the centre and a private chamber at the rear. Jade had long had associations with the spirit world and with immortality, and this pair were buried in complete suits of jade plaques fastened together with gold wire, which they believed (wrongly) would preserve their bodies.

Lady Dai

One of the most splendid Han burials not looted in the past was that of the elderly widow of the marquis of Dai. Somewhat overweight, she had died around the age of 50 of a heart attack shortly after eating a melon. Her body was perfectly preserved – owing to the careful oxygen-free conditions of burial – and was wrapped in many brocade robes and buried inside a nest of lacquer coffins. The innermost one was covered by a wonderful silk banner depicting her journey to the spirit world, where people were judged by the Celestial Being on the basis of meticulous records of their lives kept by divine civil servants.

Lady Dai's wooden tomb chamber was filled with both her everyday necessities and her precious possessions – beautiful sets of tableware made of red lacquer, her silk slippers, bales of fine silk cloth, musical instruments and many other objects. Boxes contained food such as cooked game and fish, cereals and fruit. Wooden models of musicians provided music for eternity. The mound that covered her burial also housed the tombs of her husband and younger son. In the young man's tomb a library was buried, containing thirty volumes including the classic works of Confucianism and Daoism. His tomb also yielded several maps, the oldest known from China.

NEIGHBOURS OF THE HAN

Korea and Japan were strongly influenced by their powerful neighbour, China. Rice cultivation spread from China into Korea around 1500–1000 BC, and later bronze metallurgy was also transmitted to Korea. From there both had spread into Japan by about 500 BC. Although the Japanese had lived in villages for thousands of years, supported by hunting game and gathering shellfish and plant foods, the change to agriculture was revolutionary, promoting rapid population growth. As the population grew, so did competition and conflict between communities, marked by the appearance of fortified settlements.

Han China seized control of the northern part of the Korean peninsula in 108 BC, and was not driven out until AD 313. Even in the areas beyond direct Han rule, Chinese influence was strong. In the early centuries AD three kingdoms emerged in Korea: Koguryo in the north, closely linked to northern China, Paeche in the southwest, in close contact with both Japan and southern China, and Shilla in the southeast. Between the southern kingdoms lay the region of Kaya, a zone of independent city-states, important for its abundant iron ores and its manufacture of stoneware pottery. The three kingdoms buried their royal dead in impressive mounded tombs, laying them to rest with elaborate gold funerary offerings. Sometimes the tombs were painted with beautiful scenes of aristocratic and royal life. Conflict between the kingdoms culminated in AD 668 with the triumph of Shilla, supported by Chinese armies.

In Japan a closely related state developed, known as Yamato. This gradually extended its power over the islands, with the exception of Hokkaido in the far north. The Yamato also built mounded royal tombs, constructed in the shape of a keyhole and often surrounded

A wooden wagon made by steppe nomads around 500 BC was constructed using more than 12,000 carefully worked mortise-and-tenon joints.

3

3. The great burial mounds of the Japanese élite were generally surrounded by earthen- ware 'haniwa' figures of buildings, ships, animals and people, like this warrior.

by a moat. Massive terracotta statues of tomb guardians (*haniwa*), in the form of warriors, horsemen or animals, were placed around the periphery of these tombs.

Buddhism was introduced to both Korea (in AD 366) and Japan (in AD 550) from China. Missionaries and merchants from India had established Buddhist monastic communities and spread the ideas of Buddhism through Central Asia, reaching China in the 1st century AD. By the 5th century AD Chinese pilgrims were making pious expeditions to India to visit Buddhist holy places and to acquire relics and copies of holy books.

Central Asia and the Silk Road

The nomads of Mongolia were a continual thorn in China's side. During the reign of the martial emperor, Wudi (reigned 141–87 BC), the ferocious Xiongnu nomads drove their

rivals, the Yuezhi, westwards – where in time they gave rise to the Kushan empire (▷ p. 138). Wudi hoped to make common cause with the Yuezhi against the Xiongnu and in 139 BC sent one of his generals, Zhang Qian, to find them. Thirteen years and many hair-raising adventures later, Zhang Qian returned – without an alliance, as the Yuezhi were now comfortably settled in the west. But Zhang Qian did bring back information that led directly to the development of the Silk Road trade route through Central Asia, a route that eventually reached the eastern Mediterranean.

In subsequent years the Han succeeded in gaining control over the 'Western Provinces', keeping the nomads at bay and establishing military outposts in the oases around the formidable Taklamakhan Desert. Silk from China was traded westwards, along with furs from the nomads, while the highly prized noble horses of Ferghana were traded east to

China, along with glassware and other Roman luxury goods, Indian spices and cotton textiles, and Arabian incense.

The Xiongnu were difficult to deal with. The Great Wall and garrisoned outposts through Central Asia kept them at bay for some of the time. Their mobility and general lack of settled homes made it almost impossible to defeat them in battle or subdue them in defeat. However, the nomads were interested in Chinese luxury goods and it was often possible to bribe them to keep the peace, sending them what amounted to tribute, such as silken robes, bronze mirrors and fine vessels and even, on occasion, Chinese princesses as wives, to flatter their vanity. In AD 48 the Han succeeded in dividing the Xiongnu – the southern branch settled in Chinese lands and became a useful buffer against the predations of the still untamed northern branch.

1. The fortress at Jiayuguan near the Jade Gate was built by the Han and marked the western end of the Great Wall.

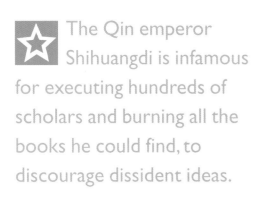

The Qin emperor Shihuangdi is infamous for executing hundreds of scholars and burning all the books he could find, to discourage dissident ideas.

DEVELOPING STATES IN SOUTHEAST ASIA

The Malay peninsula was a rich source of tin, a rare but much prized commodity needed for bronze making. Other regions of Southeast Asia also had abundant sources of metal ores – copper, gold, silver and lead. Within the region there developed a trade in metal ores and other prized raw materials and manufactured luxuries such as Dong Son drums (▷ p. 76), and by 400 BC trade networks extended as far as southern India and the Ganges delta. The lands of Southeast Asia were known to the Indians as Suvarnadvipa – the Land of Gold.

In 111 BC the Han conquered southern China as far as the Gulf of Tonkin. Their agri-cultural and irrigation skills promoted a great increase in agricultural prosperity in the region. Lach Truong, at the mouth of the Red River, developed into a major international port, linking China with the developing kingdoms of Southeast Asia and bringing them into the international trade network that linked this area with India and thence with the Roman world. Roman glass, cut and engraved gemstones and gold coins, Chinese silk and Indian textiles and beads, were avidly snapped up by princes of Southeast Asia in return for spices and metal ores.

China became a more active participant in this trade network after AD 220 when the Han empire fell and northern China was overrun by barbarians. The long-established land trade route across Central Asia was now

2. The importance of seaborne trade between India and Southeast Asia is reflected in the popularity of ships in the art of both regions. This vessel, fitted with a tripod mast and outrigger, was typical of those sailing in the 8th century AD.

 THE FIRST EMPEROR'S TOMB

Zheng (Shihuangdi), king of Qin and later 'First Emperor' of China (▷ p.147), began work on his tomb in 246 BC. This employed 700,000 men throughout his reign. His cruelty made him exceedingly unpopular – at least one attempt was made on his life and he lived in terror of assassination. He died before he reached 50, and some say he was poisoned.

His tomb at Mount Li is said to have been constructed as a vast model of the world in miniature, its ceiling mapping the heavens in jewels, while through the land below, complete with model buildings, mercury flowed perpetually along the Yangtze and Yellow rivers into the ocean. The emperor's copper coffin was surrounded by a vast treasury – safeguarded from grave robbers by traps such as automatically firing crossbows.

No one knows if looters ever did penetrate the emperor's tomb, but in 1974 his army was discovered: more than 8,000 life-size terracotta soldiers (illustrated right), buried in battle formation with horses and chariots in three pits within the vast tomb complex. Originally the soldiers were painted and were furnished with real weapons – but these were stolen during the civil war that brought about the collapse of the Qin empire. Remarkably, although constructed of pieces cast in moulds, all the soldiers have individually sculpted details of face and uniform, distinguishing their ranks, from humble infantryman to general.

unusable and the Chinese rulers fled south, establishing a kingdom in southern China.

Emerging kingdoms

Chiefdoms had been developing in many parts of Southeast Asia during the last few centuries BC. The graves of the chiefs were rich in luxury goods, of which the decorated Dong Son bronze drums were the most prestigious. By the early centuries AD kingdoms were beginning to emerge – territories that ebbed and flowed with the strength and power of the individual rulers. They operated from stronghold towns with impressive public buildings surrounded by moats, such as Oc Eo in Cambodia and U-Thong in Thailand, centres not only of political power but also of craft production. Efficient networks of irrigation canals ensured high agricultural productivity. These petty kingdoms laid the foundations for the more powerful realms that were to emerge from around the 5th century AD – Funan in Cambodia, Dvaravati in Thailand, Srivijaya in Sumatra and Java, Linyi in Vietnam and Sriksetra in Burma.

Although the Chinese had some impact in the region, it was to India that these Southeast Asian kingdoms turned for cultural models. Merchants from southern and eastern India had been accompanied on their voyages by Buddhist and Hindu missionaries, and both religions were widely adopted by the kings of Southeast Asia. Among the earliest and most impressive public buildings in the moated towns were Buddhist stupas and monasteries. The Indian Brahmi script and Sanskrit language were adopted for inscriptions, and many kings took Indian names and used seals with Brahmi inscriptions for official purposes.

The symbolism on early coins in the region reflects that of the Indian originals on which they were modelled. Indian legal institutions and political ideas were also widely adopted, native rulers enhancing their own status by flaunting their adoption of these prestigious trappings. In subsequent centuries, warfare between kingdoms often altered the political boundaries, and thus Buddhism and Hinduism ebbed and flowed in importance with the states that practised them. By AD 1100 much of the region had been united under the rule of the great kingdom of Angkor, which emerged around AD 800.

 THE GREAT WALL

1. (opposite) The Great Wall runs 2700 km (1678 miles) from east to west. It reached its present form under the Ming dynasty (14th–17th century AD).

During the wars of the 5th–3rd centuries BC, many states had built stretches of wall along their borders to defend themselves against rival states and the nomads of the north. When Shihuangdi unified China, he had various stretches amalgamated and extended as a massive earthen rampart that ran the entire length of China's northern borders, defending it against the Xiongnu nomads. Half a million conscript labourers were involved in the enormous undertaking, and very many lost their lives there. Later emperors maintained and extended the Great Wall. Forts and towers were constructed at key places along the wall, and fire beacons made it possible for alarms to be signalled.

In the cold, dry environment of the desert regions through which the Great Wall passed, many documents – written on strips of wood, bark or silk – have survived. These include not only official documents from the routine military organization of the frontier, but also poetry and letters – the personal writings of homesick soldiers in these lonely outposts.

The Great Wall as we know it today was constructed in the 14th to 16th centuries AD, replacing the earlier ramparts of solid beaten earth with a stronger wall of stone – but with the same purpose, to keep out the warlike and hard-to-defeat nomads of the north.

MATHEMATICS AND MEASUREMENT

Counting, measuring and calculating became important skills as cities developed and people's lives became more regimented and organized. Mathematics played its part in every field of life – assessing taxes, weighing goods, calculating workers' rations, or constructing siege works, irrigation channels or pyramids.

Each region developed its own system of recording numbers. Some were simple, but those of the Chinese, Babylonians, Indians and Maya made possible complex calculations such as square roots and quadratic equations, and gave rise to sophisticated mathematical concepts.

1

Counting

The simplest way to record numbers is to make marks and blocks of marks to represent individual units – like our tallies of four strokes crossed by the fifth. Many cultures began like this, using symbols to represent larger numbers. For example, the Egyptians used strokes for units and had special symbols for 10s, 100s, 1000s and so on. Numbers were therefore expressed as so many units plus so many tens plus so many hundreds and so on. Such systems are fine for recording numbers but not easy to use for calculations, particularly multiplication and division.

The idea of nothing

A pair of brilliant inventions made things much easier: place value and zero. The Babylonians began to use the first of these ideas and may have used the second. Unlike the decimal (base-10) system we are familiar with, the Babylonians counted in batches of 60. We still retain the Babylonian system in our reckoning of time (60 seconds to the minute, 60 minutes to the hour) and geometry (dividing a circle into 6 x 60 degrees).

The Babylonians began to use the place-value system, with a limited number of symbols whose significance depended on their position. So in Babylonian notation,

2

'11' represented $(1 \times 60) + (1 \times 1) = 61$ – the same principle that underlies our decimal place-value system. However, the Babylonians did not at first have a zero, which made it impossible to distinguish between '11' = 61 and '11' = $(1 \times 3600) + (1 \times 60)$ or '11' = $(1 \times 1) + (1 \times 1/60)$.

Later the Babylonians found ways to indicate that some columns were empty – the idea of zero. The credit for inventing the idea of zero, though, goes jointly to two quite separate cultures, the early Indians of the Ganges valley and the Classic Maya of Mesoamerica. Our decimal system is based on the notation that was first used by the Indians and which spread via the Arab world into medieval Europe. The Maya had a particu-

1. This Roman inscription includes the letters 'XX', a numeral in the Roman counting system which was largely cumulative. 'I' stood for one, II was two, V was five and IV four, while VI meant six. X was 10, so XX was 20. Other numerals were L for 50, C for 100 and M for 1000.

2. Practical calculations like these Old Babylonian geometrical problems were an important part of a scribe's training in Mesopotamia.

3. A set of 17 bronze weights in the shape of lions, from the Assyrian city of Nimrud, range in weight from about 50 g to a massive 20 kg

Chinese frequently used mathematics in surveying and engineering. The Maya were particularly interested in the passing of time, so they constructed elaborate calendars (▷ pp. 206–7). Egyptian texts are frequently concerned with working out the quantity of grain needed to produce beer and bread for temple employees. Mesopotamian school exercises include similar practical problems, dealing with the rations for the workers needed to dig a canal of a stated length, or the volume of earth required to construct siege ramps. Compound interest was calculated on loans and investments, in trading and other enterprises. The division of inherited property was another widespread ancient concern.

Commerce required the use of weights, for measuring both the quantity of goods for sale or official issue and the amounts of silver or other valuables given in exchange. The Indus civilization employed a series of cubical graduated stone weights, and these were also used by their trading partners in the Persian Gulf. Mesopotamian weights were often in the shape of ducks and other animals, while later Greek, Roman and Chinese weights took a variety of ornamental forms.

larly elegant system, using only three signs: dots, used for 1 to 4, bars used to represent up to three 5s, and a shell for 0. With these they could represent any number in their base-20 counting system.

The Chinese adopted a different approach, based on the decimal system. They used a counting board divided into boxes. Each of these represented a power of 10 (units, tens, hundreds and so on) and within each, an arrangement of rods in different patterns allowed the numbers 0 (empty) to 9 to be represented.

Maths at work

Ancient texts give us a glimpse of how mathematics served different cultures. The

3

◈ TOPIC LINKS

2.1 Prelude to Civilization
p.43 Uruk

2.2 The Lands Between the Rivers
p.54 Control and Collapse

3.1 The Widening World
p.112 Individuals in Society

3.2 The Athenian Role Model
p.129 Philosophy and Logic

3.3 The Land of the Buddha
p.139 The Guptas

4.4 Flowery Wars and Conquerors
p.224 The Inca

MEDITERRANEAN CONFLICTS

Phoenician and later Greek metal prospectors and traders exploited the western Mediterranean from about 1000 BC. When the eastern end came under Assyrian control around 750 BC, the western zone grew considerably in importance. By this time, contacts through trade and colonization had stimulated some local peoples, such as the Etruscans, to adopt the habits of urban living.

Two broad areas of influence developed: Phoenician in the southern Mediterranean and Atlantic Spain, and Greek along the northern shores. Most of Italy, however, lay outside either Phoenician or Greek control, remaining a flash point until a new power emerged in the region.

The Romans, once a minor subject people of the Etruscans, established control of central Italy, and through centuries of near-constant warfare created an empire that by 30 BC stretched right around the Mediterranean and into western Europe, linking east and west as never before.

THE ETRUSCANS

The Etruscans were farmers in central Italy who had inherited excellent bronze-working skills from their ancestors, and were quick to take up the new technology of iron working soon after 900 BC. Within a century they were in regular contact with Phoenician traders, and some Etruscans grew rich exporting metals mined on the island of Elba. After about 750 BC Greek merchants also began to trade luxury items for metals.

As their prosperity increased the Etruscans began transforming their settlements into small cities, often situated on hills. Cities such as Chiusi, Caere and Populonia grew in size and shared in the development of Etruscan civilization, but they remained politically independent. Even in times of war there was never an Etruscan state, only a temporary league of cities.

Etruscan culture developed from a mixture of native traditions and elements imported from the eastern Mediterranean. Greek pottery (from Athens and southern Italy) was especially admired. The Etruscans modified the Greek alphabet to write their own language, but no Etruscan literature survives. They buried their dead in elaborate cemeteries (often carved out of rock) outside their cities, with highly decorated and lavishly equipped tombs.

The Etruscans seem to have been a very superstitious people, and their religion placed great emphasis on the interpretation of natural signs and omens, such as the behaviour of flocks of birds. Etruscan priests were also trained in 'reading' the internal organs of sacrificed animals in order to understand 'messages' from the gods. The organs were divided into sections, each related to a different god, whose omens could be read from the appearance of that section. These modes of divination were later adopted by the Romans.

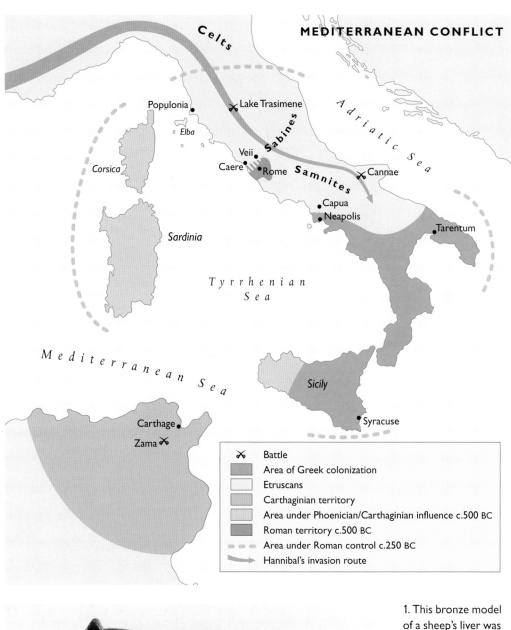

MEDITERRANEAN CONFLICT

Celts

Adriatic Sea

Populonia

Elba

Lake Trasimene

Sabines

Veii

Corsica

Caere • Rome

Samnites

Cannae

Capua

Neapolis

Sardinia

Tarentum

Tyrrhenian Sea

Mediterranean Sea

Sicily

Carthage

Syracuse

Zama

✕	Battle
	Area of Greek colonization
	Etruscans
	Carthaginian territory
	Area under Phoenician/Carthaginian influence c.500 BC
	Roman territory c.500 BC
	Area under Roman control c.250 BC
	Hannibal's invasion route

1. This bronze model of a sheep's liver was designed to guide Etruscan soothsayers in reading omens from the livers of sacrificed animals. It is divided into 28 parts, each inscribed with the name of a god.

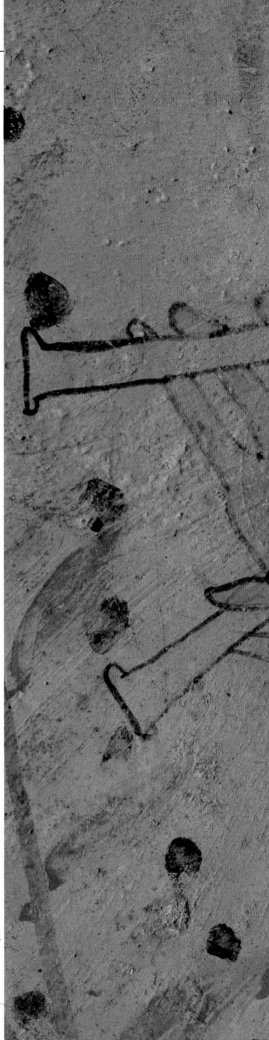

Conflict with neighbours

Around 600 BC competition for trade encouraged the Etruscans to expand beyond central Italy. In the north they established the city of Felsina to gain direct access to the trade across the Alps into central Europe. In the south they took over many native settlements, including the Latin-speaking village of Rome, which they began transforming into a city ruled by an Etruscan dynasty of kings.

Their attempts to expand geographically brought the Etruscans into conflict with their neighbours. In about 540 BC they allied with the Carthaginians to defeat a Greek fleet off the coast of Corsica. In 519 BC the city of Rome expelled the last of its Etruscan kings and established a republic governed by a form of Greek-inspired democracy. Rome then began carving out its own state from the lands of the Etruscans and other Italian peoples.

Around 400 BC Italy was invaded by Celtic peoples from across the Alps, and many Etruscan cities were conquered. Those that survived were soon afterwards conquered by Rome. Their Etruscan populations became Roman citizens, and their distinctive culture for the most part disappeared.

1. The Etruscans often had themselves modelled on their sarcophagi. The depiction of women in Etruscan art indicates that they enjoyed greater equality with men than in many other societies.

2. Etruscan tombs were sometimes exuberantly painted with scenes of the banquets, music-making and dancing that accompanied their funerals. Other paintings show them in their daily lives, at work and at play.

1. The goddess Tanit was the Carthaginian equivalent of the Phoenician mother-goddess Astarte. Worshipped alongside the god Baal Hammon, Tanit was extremely popular among the Carthaginians from the 5th century BC.

THE CARTHAGINIANS

When the Phoenician home cities in the Levant were captured by the Assyrians in about 750 BC, the western colonies remained independent. Under the leadership of the city of Carthage (near present-day Tunis), they were the first to develop trading links with the Etruscans and with the emerging kingdom of Tartessos in southwestern Spain. When the Greeks began expanding westwards from Italy around 600 BC, the Carthaginians retaliated by establishing colonies on the western coast of Sicily, and the island soon became the main battleground in the struggle between rival colonial powers. Both sides won victories and burned the other's cities, but neither could win decisively. Further west, the Carthaginians strengthened their position in Spain, but could not prevent the establishment of some new Greek colonies.

Having fought the Greeks to a stalemate, the Carthaginian trading empire flourished. Spain was an extremely rich source of metals and the Carthaginians controlled most of its Mediterranean coastline, although they never subdued the inhabitants of the interior. From the great port of Gades (Cádiz) on the Atlantic coast, Carthaginian traders and explorers sailed north to Britain and south to Africa in search of further metal sources.

But the Carthaginians were no match for Rome. In three great wars (the First, Second and Third Punic Wars), Rome first curtailed Carthaginian power, then annexed its empire, and then obliterated the entire civilization. After the final Roman victory in 146 BC, the city of Carthage was razed to the ground, its inhabitants enslaved and its farmland covered with salt so that nothing would grow. The site remained deserted until it was later refounded as a Roman colony.

 HANNIBAL

Hannibal was the greatest of all Carthaginian generals. In 218 BC he led an army, including 37 war elephants, from Spain, through France, across the Alps into Italy – one of the most famous military exploits in history.

Once in Italy, Hannibal proved almost unbeatable. In 217 BC he ambushed a Roman army at Lake Trasimene, killed more than half and captured the rest. He destroyed two more Roman armies at Cannae in 217 BC. These defeats created shock and panic among Roman citizens. Many southern Italian cities defected, although central Italy stayed loyal.

Hannibal remained in Italy for the next 14 years but was unable to attack Rome. He failed to capture a port through which to obtain reinforcements from Spain until 212 BC, when the Carthaginian armies in Spain were fully committed against a Roman counter-invasion.

In 203 BC Hannibal was recalled to command the last-ditch defence of Carthage, but in 202 BC he was defeated at Zama and forced to conclude peace on crippling Roman terms. Hannibal remained an enemy of Rome, and planned a further invasion of Italy. Captured by allies of Rome in about 183 BC, he committed suicide rather than be handed over to the Romans.

THE RISE OF ROME

In 519 BC, when Rome expelled the last of its Etruscan kings, the population of the entire Roman city-state was about 25,000. To the north were Etruscan cities, to the south Greek cities, and to the east native peoples such as the Samnites and Sabines. Within 250 years Rome had established control of nearly all of the Italian peninsula. Only the far north, occupied by invading Celts, was outside Roman domination.

Rome expanded through a combination of astute diplomacy and military strength. Initially the Romans had to fight for survival against native rivals in central Italy. Some cities were captured, their inhabitants enslaved and their lands added to the Roman state. Many others chose to make a formal alliance with Rome and were treated tolerantly but lost some of their autonomy.

In 396 BC the Romans moved against the Etruscans and captured the nearby city of Veii. Seven years later Rome itself was sacked by Celtic raiders, but soon recovered. The Greek cities in southern Italy now began to take the power of Rome seriously. Neapolis (Naples) was the first to ally with Rome, in 327 BC, and others soon followed this lead. Rome also began to establish its own colonies in the south. In 312 BC the Via Appia (Appian Way) was constructed between Rome and Capua. This was the first of the Roman military roads, which were intended mainly for the rapid movement of troops. Eventually, a network of military roads linked all parts of the empire.

Government and citizens

Etruscan rule had left Romans with a strong distaste for kingship, and they established a republic with an elected Senate that appointed

⭐ The largest Greek bronze vessel yet discovered was found in the grave of a Celtic princess buried in about 530 BC at Vix in central France.

2. Some of the finest Greek temples were built in the Greek colonies in southern Italy and Sicily. Many colonies became far more powerful than their founding cities.

3. This bronze wolf is a fine example of Etruscan metalwork. The two children, added 2000 years later, illustrate the legend of Romulus and Remus, who supposedly founded Rome.

★ In 212 BC the Greek scientist Archimedes devised and built giant war catapults to defend the Sicilian city of Syracuse from Roman attack.

two consuls as heads of state and military commanders. All free males were citizens with voting rights, and were divided into two classes on the basis of wealth – patricians (land-owning aristocrats) and plebs (plebeians – the rest). Only patricians could stand for office as consuls, senators or magistrates. Over time, a series of reforms moderated the power of the patricians. An intermediate social class, the equites, was introduced to allow for the aspirations of those who were not born into the aristocracy. Special magistrates (tribunes) were appointed to safeguard the rights of the plebs, and had the power of veto over any legislation proposed in the Senate.

Citizens of Rome enjoyed voting rights and the protection of rigorously enforced laws. In return they owed a duty of military service. The armies of early Rome were a citizen militia, called up in times of war and crisis,

that soon became accustomed to victory. The inhabitants of allied cities, although their basic civic rights were largely respected, were treated as second-class citizens. They were allowed to maintain their independence, but were expected to follow Roman policy and fight alongside Roman troops.

International influence

Roman involvement in southern Italy and Sicily led to war with Carthage in 264 BC. Although Rome had no previous experience of shipbuilding or fighting at sea, it quickly built and equipped a fleet and defeated the Carthaginians, who were forced to cede Sicily, Corsica and Sardinia to Rome, which then appointed its first overseas governors.

After Hannibal's failed invasion of Italy in 218 BC, Rome counter-attacked in Spain and

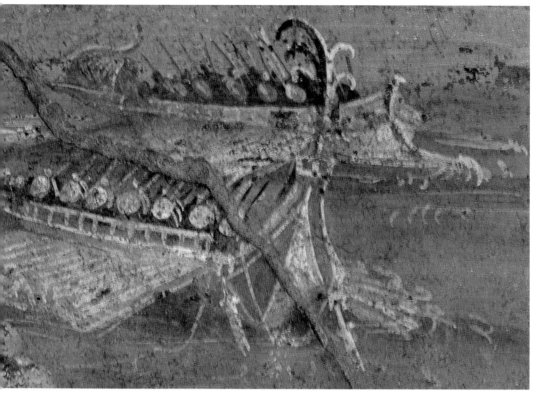

1. This glass pendant is a vivid portrait of a bearded Carthaginian. The Phoenicians were pioneers in the manufacture of glass.

2. Roman warships were equipped with beaks, which they used to ram the enemy. During the First Punic War, Carthage had mastery of the seas until the Romans used a captured Carthaginian warship as a model to build their own navy.

captured the important city of New Carthage (Cartagena). Roman troops then crossed to Africa and defeated the Carthaginians at the battle of Zama. Carthage was forced to give up its overseas territory, and Rome inherited the Carthaginian empire in Spain. By about 160 BC Rome had consolidated its control of Spain and driven the Celts from northern Italy. Rome was now a major international power, with influence far beyond its frontiers. When the Seleucid king invaded Egypt in 168 BC, against the wishes of Rome, he was publicly humiliated and forced to withdraw by the threats of an unarmed Roman envoy.

During the Second Punic War Macedon had allied with Carthage. Rome defeated the Macedonians in 196 BC, but had proclaimed the liberty and independence of Greece under nominal Roman control. When the Third Punic War broke out Macedon rebelled against Roman rule, and was joined by many Greeks. The revolt was ruthlessly crushed, and in 146 BC the Greek city of Corinth was totally destroyed and depopulated, like Carthage, as an example to others.

Greece then became incorporated into the growing Roman empire. From the earliest days, Rome had been influenced by Greek thought, for example in its form of government. The conquest of Greece brought a flood of Greek artworks and slaves into Rome. Greek culture became extremely fashionable, and Roman playwrights and architects began imitating Greek originals.

In 133 BC Rome got a foothold in Asia when the last king of Pergamum in Asia Minor bequeathed his kingdom to Rome. Later, the king of Pontus did the same. The need to defend these new territories led Rome to annex Syria, the last remnant of the Seleucid empire (▷ p. 129), in 67 BC and to capture Jerusalem. Further expansion in the east was blocked by the Parthians, who had taken control of Iran and Mesopotamia and were fiercely opposed to further Roman expansion (▷ p. 129). With their nomadic background, the Parthians were superlative mounted warriors. Their great nobles went into battle as armoured heavy cavalry, supported by the swift light cavalry of lesser nobles armed with the powerful reflex bow. A Roman expedition against Parthia in 53 BC was almost annihilated at Carrhae in the Mesopotamian desert.

Military power

Centuries of warfare had transformed the Roman army from a citizen militia into an extremely efficient fighting machine. The most important reforms had been instituted by a prominent general, Gaius Marius, in about 100 BC. Marius began recruiting poor, landless citizens to create a completely professional army made up of paid volunteers. He organized the army into legions of 6000 men divided into centuries of 100 men under the command of a centurion, who was the equivalent of a sergeant.

The army's officers, however, continued to be ambitious young aristocrats who saw military service as the first step to a political career. Successful generals were granted the great honour of leading a triumphal procession through the streets of Rome to receive the praises of the citizens, and were often elected to the Senate. The practice of allowing soldiers to take part in politics was, however,

to prove disastrous for the Roman republic.

In 91 BC Rome's Italian allies rebelled because their citizens, who fought for Rome, wanted the same political rights as Roman citizens. The revolt, known as the Social War, was crushed by a general named Sulla, who hunted down and exterminated its chief supporters and their families. During the war Sulla briefly suspended democratic govern-

★ Ptolemy IV, who ruled Egypt around 220 BC, built a warship 125 m (410 feet) long that had a crew of 4000 rowers and nearly 3000 soldiers – but it was too big for active service.

1

ment in Rome and made himself dictator. This was to prove a dangerous precedent.

Another general who became extremely powerful was Pompey. He put down the slave rebellion led by Spartacus in 70 BC and went on to conquer Syria. Although in theory under the orders of the Senate, Pompey became in effect an independent ruler in the eastern Mediterranean. Pompey's great military and political rival was Julius Caesar. Between 58 and 50 BC Caesar added central and northern Gaul (France, Belgium and parts of the Netherlands and Germany) to the empire and became very popular in Rome. The rivalry between Pompey and Caesar erupted into a civil war for control of the whole empire. Caesar made himself dictator

in Rome, and defeated Pompey's army in Greece in 46 BC. Pompey was murdered when he sought refuge in Egypt.

Caesar's brief rule as dictator ended when he was assassinated in 44 BC by conspirators who claimed to be acting in the name of republican liberty. His supporters were rallied by two more politician-generals – Octavian, who claimed to be Caesar's heir, and Mark Antony – and the assassins were pursued and eventually defeated in Greece. Octavian and Antony then split the empire between them, but conflict was inevitable. Antony took refuge with the Egyptian queen, Cleopatra, and their combined forces were defeated at the battle of Actium in 31 BC. Octavian was now in sole charge of the Roman empire.

2

THE CELTS

North of the Alps, Celtic languages were spoken across large parts of central and western Europe. Since about 600 BC Celtic chieftains had been trading with Greek and Etruscan merchants for luxury goods, such as wine and decorative metalwork. Under these influences, Celtic craft-workers developed their own distinctive (La Tène) art style.

About 400 BC, probably as a result of population pressures within the tribally organized Celtic society, large numbers of Celts migrated south-wards and eastwards. Several tribes invaded northern Italy and established control of the fertile Po valley region. Others followed the Danube into southeastern Europe, where they established small king-doms, and raided Greece and the Black Sea coast. One group of Celts crossed to Asia Minor, where they founded the kingdom of Galatia. By about 200 BC most of these new territories had been lost, as native rulers regained control. In the west, however, Celtic society continued to flourish and the first towns (*oppida*) were built.

Having driven the Celts from Italy, the Romans gradually invaded the Celtic lands, defeating the Celtiberians in the interior of Spain, the Gauls in France and then the Britons. Despite the Celts' famed prowess as warriors, and the bravery of their leaders – such as Vercingetorix in Gaul and Boudicca in Britain – by AD 70 all of Celtic Europe was under Roman occupation, except the remotest corners of the British Isles.

1. This sculpture of a marriage ceremony shows wealthy Romans in typical dress – a length of cloth draped over a tunic to form a toga.

2. This 6th-century BC gold tablet bears an inscription written in the Punic script used by the Phoenicians and Carthaginians. Punic script was derived from the very first alphabet, which was invented by the ancestors of the Phoenicians.

SHIPS AND NAVIGATION

The sailors who transported cargoes around the Roman world were heirs to a seafaring tradition that was already many thousands of years old. By 50,000 BC people had arrived in Australia, and the only way they could have got there was by crossing at least 60 km (36 miles) of open sea. By 6000 BC peoples around the Mediterranean were able to build ships to carry themselves and their cattle hundreds of kilometres to colonize islands such as Crete. In South America coastal peoples were using balsa rafts for trading expeditions by about 3000 BC.

Shipbuilding

The construction of the earliest craft depended on the materials available – early designs included hollowed-out logs, craft made of bamboo, balsa or bundles of reeds, or leather stretched over basketwork frames. In many cases these ancient designs have survived to the present day. The outrigger, an ancient Southeast Asian invention that prevents canoes rolling over at sea, is still used in both traditional and modern craft.

The earliest-known ships to be made of wooden planks were built by the Egyptians around 2800 BC – before their adoption of metalworking. Hundreds of wooden planks were carefully shaped and drilled, before being 'sewn' together with cord to make ships up to 50 m (165 feet) long. The hulls were waterproofed either with naturally occurring pitch or tree resin. Egyptian ships were mainly used on the Nile river, but they also sailed along the coast to Syria to obtain good-quality timber for building more ships.

The introduction of bronze – and later iron – nails enabled ships to become larger and more seaworthy, but the basic design of sea-going vessels remained unchanged. A long slender hull was fitted with a mast that carried a simple linen or leather sail to take advantage of favourable winds. Ships also carried sufficient oars and rowers to make progress on windless days, and were steered by one or two large oars at the stern.

Trade and war

As international trade increased in importance, so did shipping. The Minoan and later Mycenaean civilizations (▷ pp. 95–8) traded and communicated by sea. Mycenaean ships were probably state-controlled and were used both for cargo and for naval patrols. Later, by the time of the Greeks and Romans, these two functions became separated and most merchant ships were owned and operated by groups of private individuals.

Naval ships became increasingly specialized for speed and strength, because the main tactic in naval warfare was ramming enemy ships. The Phoenicians (▷ p. 103) developed this technique, adding a second tier of rowers for additional power and fitting a sharp metal spike at the prow, so that their ships were in

1. Evidence of ancient Egyptian shipbuilding skill came from two pits alongside Khufu's pyramid at Giza. Each pit contained a dismantled 40m-long wooden boat.

2. An early Egyptian pot, made around 4000 BC, depicts a sailing ship and its crew. Some of the crew are aloft, furling or unfurling a square sail.

3

effect giant, bronze-tipped missiles. The Greeks, especially the Athenians, perfected this design, and constructed triremes 30 m (100 feet) in length with three tiers of rowers.

Merchant ships, which were much less concerned with speed and relied entirely on sail, grew even larger. Many Roman ships could carry up to 500 tonnes of cargo (equivalent to more than 5000 passengers). These slow, clumsy ships were especially important to populations – like that of Rome – that depended on imported foodstuffs.

Navigation

The earliest mariners generally stayed within sight of land, with ships halting at a safe anchorage or beach each night. In the Pacific the Polynesians used crude maps to assist their long-distance island hopping (▷ p. 19). Made from woven sticks and shells, these maps showed the position of islands and strong surface currents.

4

The Phoenicians are generally credited with discovering how to sail at night, by using the positions of certain stars as a guide, and used this knowledge to develop an extensive maritime empire after 1000 BC. A form of magnetic compass was used by overland explorers in China from about 100 BC, but the magnetic-needle compass did not come into widespread use by Chinese sailors for at least another thousand years.

3. A full-sized replica of a Greek trireme, of the type used by the ancient Athenian navy. It was propelled by three tiers of oarsmen.

4. South American pottery, particularly that of the Moche, depicts reed boats like these modern examples on Lake Titicaca in Peru.

◆ TOPIC LINKS

1.1 Taking Over the World
p.12 Modern Humans
p.19 Pacific Voyagers

2.3 The Indus and its Neighbours
p.63 The Gift of the Rivers
p.66 Persian Gulf Trade

2.6 Zone of Conflict
p.95 The Fall of the Palaces
p.97 Seaborne Enterprise
p.103 The Phoenicians
p.104 Westward Expansion

3.1 A Widening World
p.111 Tentacles of Trade
p.113 The Periplus

3.5 Mediterranean Conflicts
p.162 International Influence

During the 1st century BC, the Roman world had been ravaged by civil wars. These came to an end when one man, Octavian, emerged victorious. Augustus, as he became known, was the first of a succession of emperors who were to rule the empire for the next five centuries.

The Roman empire proved remarkably resilient, surviving periods of internal collapse and constant military threats along its northern and eastern borders. Within the empire a standardized form of Roman culture – itself largely Hellenistic – was established and maintained. In many respects, the Roman empire provided the physical and intellectual infrastructure – such as roads, towns, language, religion and philosophy – upon which modern Europe was founded.

When the western Roman empire was overrun after 500 years, the invaders were already familiar with the Roman way of life, which they adopted in the politically independent states they established.

IMPERIAL SYSTEM

When Octavian came to power Rome was still in theory a republic. By the end of his rule Rome, which already ruled a territorial empire, had acquired the political system to match. In 27 BC Octavian became known as Augustus, and this name together with that of Caesar became the formal titles of all future Roman emperors. Over the following two decades he gathered all the major republican titles and appointments – such as consul, tribune of the plebs, pontifex maximus (chief priest) – to the person of the emperor, and the Senate was reduced to at best a powerless debating chamber. He designated certain parts of the empire, such as Egypt, as the personal possessions of the emperor. This not only gave him a huge income from tax revenues, it also gave him control of one of Rome's major sources of wheat.

Augustus established a hereditary dynasty and was succeeded by his adopted son Tiberius in AD 14, but the hereditary system did not last long. In AD 68 civil war broke out and there were five emperors in just 18 months. The hereditary principle was abandoned in the AD 90s, when emperors began adopting their successors to ensure a peaceful transfer of power. But it was resumed in the early 3rd century and again in the 4th century.

Many emperors sought to follow the example of responsible and law-abiding government set by Augustus, and they tried to rule the empire to the best of their abilities. A few, such as Hadrian – who spent most of his reign travelling around the empire instigating local reforms and public works – were outstanding administrators. Some emperors, however, notably Gaius (Caligula) and Nero, ruled on personal whim for personal pleasure, and openly flouted Roman law and custom. The reigns of such tyrants invariably ended in violent overthrow.

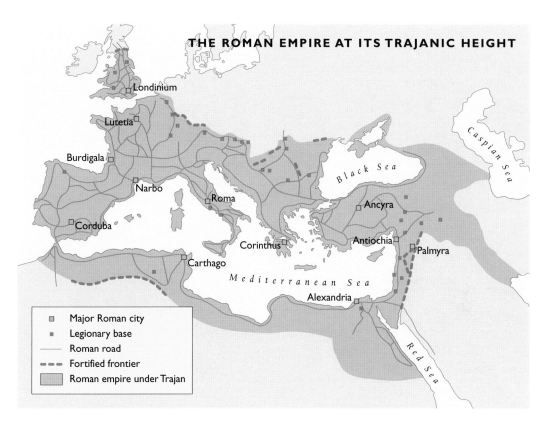

THE ROMAN EMPIRE AT ITS TRAJANIC HEIGHT

- ▪ Major Roman city
- ▪ Legionary base
- —— Roman road
- – – – Fortified frontier
- ▨ Roman empire under Trajan

Expansion of empire

The empire continued to expand, and Rome was almost constantly at war – it was a remarkable event when, in AD 64, the emperor Nero was able to announce that there was a state of peace throughout the empire.

Western Germany had been subdued under Caesar. In 12 BC Augustus began an attempt to annex eastern Germany, a source of periodic raids. The region was abandoned in AD 9 after the total destruction of three entire legions in an ambush by a confederacy of Germanic warriors led by Arminius, a German aristocrat who had formerly served in the Roman army. A fortified frontier was established along the Rhine and the Danube. Over the centuries this was to prove one of the worst trouble spots in the empire.

Caesar conducted two raids on Britain in 55 and 54 BC, establishing mixed relations with the tribes of southeast England. The emperor Claudius undertook the full-scale invasion of Britain in AD 43. Like Hannibal, he included war elephants in his army. Under Agricola the Romans campaigned in northern Scotland in the 80s, though no permanent territorial gains were made.

The Levant had come under Roman rule in the 60s BC but in AD 66 the Jews revolted against Roman rule. By AD 73 Vespasian and his son Titus had ruthlessly put down the rising, destroying Jerusalem, including the Temple. A second rising in AD 132–5 was suppressed by Hadrian.

The empire reached its maximum extent in AD 116 after Trajan's campaigns in the east. He added Dacia (Romania), establishing a frontier beyond the Danube, and forced the Parthians out of northern Mesopotamia. This new Middle Eastern frontier could not be sustained, and Roman troops soon withdrew from Mesopotamia.

The northern frontier of the empire was established in AD 122 when Hadrian ordered the construction of a wall across Britain, marking the limits of Roman control. However, for a brief period in the mid-2nd century the empire extended into lowland Scotland, with the frontier (the Antonine Wall) across the Forth–Clyde isthmus.

The next 60 years or so is often referred to as Rome's 'golden age', when each emperor nominated an able successor and commerce, industry and agriculture all flourished.

ROMAN SOCIETY

For the inhabitants of the eastern part of the empire – which had been under Greek control for centuries – Roman rule meant little more than a change in government. Roman culture was sufficiently Hellenized that ordinary people's lives were not greatly affected. In the west, where Greek influence had been minimal, Roman control meant a major transformation of society.

Rome had evolved from a settlement of farmers, and agriculture remained the mainstay of the Roman economy and Roman culture. New colonies were founded by a ritual ploughing of their boundaries, and the life of the citizen-farmer, master of his own

 POMPEII

Pompeii was a small Roman town of about 20,000 people, situated south of Rome on the Bay of Naples. In AD 79 the nearby volcano, Vesuvius, erupted explosively, burying Pompeii beneath several metres of volcanic ash, and engulfing the nearby town of Herculaneum in a mud slide. Most of the inhabitants fled as the eruption began, but some delayed, attempting to collect their belongings. In Pompeii some of these citizens were caught in the open and entombed by the ash where they fell.

Excavations at Pompeii have revealed the life of a prosperous Roman town in almost perfectly preserved detail. The streets were narrow, lined with shops, taverns and fast-food counters. Stepping stones were provided for crossing the streets (illustrated right), which must have been almost ankle-deep in dirt, rubbish, waste water and animal droppings from carts and wagons. Inside the houses of the wealthy, rooms were decorated with brightly painted frescoes. Many of the frescoes are in the form of fake windows opening onto landscapes and gardens, but some portray scenes from religious ritual or mythology. Floors were often decorated with mosaics made of tesserae – small coloured cubes of stone.

Pompeii had all the amenities of Roman civilization – public baths, a theatre, and an amphitheatre for contests between gladiators, during which passions ran high. One fresco in the town depicts a riot that broke out between rival groups of supporters at one contest in AD 59.

small household, was idealized by poets such as Virgil (70–19 BC). By this time the realities of Roman agriculture were far from the idealized smallholdings celebrated by poets. In Italy, farming had become big business, dominated by huge ranches and estates that were mainly worked by slave labour.

In the rest of western Europe the native peoples still followed the traditional pattern of farming, with fields clustered around small villages and only very few large settlements with more than 1000 inhabitants. The Romans encouraged the development of an additional network of towns and villas.

The urban network developed as an extension of the Roman road system, which was initially designed to allow the legions to move rapidly to a threatened frontier. Many of the new towns grew up around military garrisons, and also served as local centres of government. In each province one town was selected as the capital and residence of the Roman governor, with public buildings that echoed the originals in Rome.

Outside the towns throughout western Europe, hundreds of villas were built. They were often the homes of wealthy natives who aspired to the Roman lifestyle. Villa estates were not only expected to produce the food to feed the family and the workforce, but were also intended to make a profit for their owners. On many villa estates, innovations such as animal- and water-driven mills, and improved ploughs and farming techniques, helped to improve productivity.

As well as these technological innovations, native aristocrats were also encouraged to adopt other elements of Roman culture, such as food, fashion, manners, language and religion. The diffusion of these ideas is called Romanization, and many of the features of Roman everyday life, such as the calendar, major trunk roads and codified laws, have survived to the present day. Modern French,

Spanish, Italian and Romanian have all evolved from Latin, and are closely related. The process of Romanization was cemented in 212, when the emperor Caracalla extended Roman citizenship to all non-slave subjects of the empire. An inhabitant of London or Paris was now just as much a Roman as an inhabitant of the mother city itself.

The Eternal City

The city of Rome grew up around a group of seven low hills overlooking the Tiber. The site was easy to defend, and avoided the marshy ground near the river. At the heart of the city

1. Trajan's column was carved to commemorate the emperor's successful campaigns against the Dacians in south-east Europe. Scenes include not only battles but also aspects of the daily lives of the soldiers.

In the ruins of Pompeii at least one house has been found with a mosaic panel warning 'Beware of the dog'.

was the Capitoline Hill, on which stood Rome's most important temple (first built around 600 BC), which was dedicated to Jupiter – the Roman equivalent of Zeus, the father of the Greek gods. Nearby was the Forum, which, like the Agora in Athens, was the main focus for politics and commerce. The Senate met in a building just off the Forum, and it was here that Julius Caesar was stabbed to death. The Forum was redesigned and rebuilt several times. Trajan added another forum, which included the Roman equivalent of a shopping mall.

To the east of the Forum, overlooking the Circus Maximus racetrack, was the site of the imperial palaces. The largest of these, the Golden House, was built by Nero, who was accused of setting fire to the city to clear a space for his palace. Later emperors occupied smaller but no less magnificent palaces.

Over the centuries the Romans erected innumerable statues, arches, columns and other monuments to the achievements of consuls, generals and emperors. The most prestigious sites for these were in the Forum and along the main streets of the city centre. Some emperors, including Trajan, Caracalla and Diocletian, opted for more practical monuments in the form of public baths, where ordinary Romans washed, exercised and gossiped.

At the beginning of the 3rd century AD Rome was the largest city in the world, with a population of more than 1 million. A small, wealthy minority lived in elegant houses, with running water piped in from the city's aqueducts, and large retinues of slave servants. Many people, however, lived in apartment buildings, often known as *insulae* because each one occupied a complete block in the street layout. Insulae could be up to seven storeys high and contained a variety of accommodation. Typically, the street level housed shops, taverns and craftworkers, with grand apartments on the first floor, and smaller ones above. In the poorer districts of the city, insulae quickly became overcrowded and insanitary slums, with hundreds of families depending on a single public water fountain.

Bread and circuses

Many of the city's poor – bankrupt farmers, injured war veterans, the unemployed, widows and orphans – were kept alive by a daily ration of grain (usually in the form of bread), to which all poor citizens were

1. (opposite) This model shows the heart of ancient Rome, with the Circus Maximus, scene of chariot races, in the foreground and the massive arena of the Colosseum in the distance. Between them lay the Forum, with many temples.

2. A network of tunnels, where animals and people could be kept until required, lay under the Colosseum amphitheatre in Rome. Many tiers of seats rose up above this level to accommodate the packed audiences.

2

entitled. For the most part, this state subsidy was sufficient to keep a lid on the social pressures within the city. However, when roused by a reduction in the ration or by an inflammatory demagogue, Rome's poor could become transformed into the Roman mob – an extremely potent political force, easily incited to murder and destruction.

The rest of the city's inhabitants, including the imperial household, greatly feared the mob and its violence, and the authorities attempted to divert the energies of the poor with a series of games and other 'sporting' attractions. Rome's public games originated in the Greek style, as sacred contests to honour the gods. By imperial times, however, the games had turned into gladiator shows – extravagant and bloodthirsty displays of public butchery, each one involving the deaths of hundreds of animals and human beings. After AD 70 the games were staged in the Colosseum, which seated 70,000 spectators, comfortably shaded from the sun.

The other main attraction was chariot racing at the Circus Maximus, between four permanently established teams – red, green, blue and yellow. Chariot racing backfired on the authorities, when the fanatical supporters of the various teams became yet another factor in the volatile politics of the mob.

1. Hadrian's Wall, which runs from coast to coast across northern England, is the best-known surviving example of a fortified Roman frontier.

2. In the later empire, chariot racing (shown on this coin) became as popular and as partisan a sport as modern football and several serious riots started among rival supporters.

3. The Parthians were noted for their ability to shoot backwards from a moving horse.

4. Provincial Roman towns were created to encourage native civic development. They contained public buildings such as a forum, bath-houses and temples, like this one at Nemausus (Nimes), dedicated to Rome and Augustus.

IMPERIAL POWER AND DECLINE

The Roman empire – a spider's web with Rome at its centre – was maintained by the vigilance of the legions along its frontiers, thousands of kilometres distant from Rome. Stationed beyond the zone of towns and villas, the legions were the farthest outposts of the Roman world. Along Hadrian's Wall soldiers patrolled day and night in case of raids by Picts and Britons. Along the Rhine frontier a constant watch was kept for attacks by Germanic tribes. In the east legionaries might find themselves defending a desert oasis or wadi against Parthian and later Sasanian warriors from Persia.

The legions not only protected and preserved the empire: in many respects they *were* the empire. Each legion was an entirely self-sufficient island of Roman culture. In addition to all its military and engineering skills, a legion might also, for example, run a factory making its own roofing tiles. With their veterans settled nearby, the legions were often the most 'Roman' element in a particular region or area. Collectively, with their uniform level of Roman culture, the legions formed what almost amounted to a state within a state. Considering the long-standing links between emperors and legions, it was inevitable that the legions should sometimes play a leading role in deciding who was to be emperor.

The 'golden age' of the 2nd century AD did not last long. After around AD 230 the empire experienced a period of political and territorial turmoil, and almost collapsed completely. The eastern frontiers were breached by the Sasanians, who captured the emperor Valerian, and in Syria Queen Zenobia proclaimed the independence of her kingdom of Palmyra. In the west usurpers briefly established a separate Gallic empire in France, Spain, western Germany and Britain.

Having perfected the technique of glass-blowing around 50 BC, the Romans began making panes of glass to put in the windows of their houses.

The title of Roman emperor became a prize to be taken by whoever commanded the most troops – or paid the biggest bribes. Some of these soldier-emperors established short-lived dynasties of their own, but none lasted for long. Between AD 235 and 286 there were no fewer than 28 official Roman emperors, including some who never even visited Rome, and many more short-lived local usurpers in various parts of the empire.

Late empire and schism

Order was gradually restored, the frontiers stabilized and the empire brought under unified control once more, but it was obvious that the old system could not continue. In AD 286 the emperor Diocletian instituted a system known as the tetrarchy, with two joint emperors responsible for east and west, each with a designated deputy and successor. Diocletian also attempted other reforms: for example, in 301 he introduced price controls to deal with the empire's inflation problem, largely caused by huge governmental expenditure on the army and currency devaluation, as well as the outflow of precious metals to pay for oriental luxuries.

Diocletian's attempt to restore stability failed. After he retired in AD 305 the tetrarchy collapsed into civil war, and in 324 Constantine, the son of Diocletian's co-emperor, emerged in sole control of the empire. Constantine divided the empire into two regions – east and west – and in 330 established Constantinople (the ancient Greek city of Byzantium; now Istanbul in Turkey) as the new capital of the east. Shortly before he died in 337 Constantine proclaimed Christianity to be the new religion of the empire, and the first churches with official approval were built soon afterwards.

The two halves of the empire remained united under Constantine's dynasty and its successors until they separated in 395. The eastern Roman empire endured as the Byzantine empire until it was conquered by the Turks in 1453. The western empire, however, was overrun by 'barbarian' hordes during the 5th century AD.

Barbarian attacks

To the east of the Roman frontier in Europe, the Germanic tribes remained very loosely organized, and the Romans became adept at exploiting rivalries between tribes to keep them divided. During the 3rd century AD this system broke down and several groups crossed the Rhine–Danube frontier and were permitted to settle within the empire. Other groups moved around the Roman frontier at this time – a large group of Goths, for example, migrated from southern Scandinavia to the Black Sea region, where they became known as the Ostrogoths (eastern Goths). The threat that was eventually to destroy the western Roman empire came, however, from much farther to the east.

In about AD 350 the nomadic Huns were driven from northern China, from where they migrated westwards across the steppes, initially settling in southern Russia. The arrival of the Huns displaced other peoples, who in turn displaced the Visigoths (western Goths), who burst through the Roman frontier and defeated the armies of the emperor Valens in 378. Within 30 years many other Germanic tribes had also invaded the western empire. The Burgundians and the Franks occupied France and Germany, while the Vandals settled in Spain, and later occupied North Africa. In 410 the Goths sacked the city of Rome itself, and only withdrew after receiving a massive bribe of gold coins.

The Huns became a far greater menace when, in 434, Attila was elected their leader.

1. Trajan had a distinguished military career before and after being made emperor. The empire reached its maximum extent in his reign (AD 98–117).

2. Like many other barbarian groups, the Vandals, who overran North Africa in the 5th century AD, rapidly adopted the trappings of civilization. Here a Vandal nobleman rides away from the villa he has seized from its Roman owner.

2

He united the Huns and other barbarian groups, and led them against the empire. By 450 his army had reached central France and northern Italy, and only Attila's death in 453 prevented further Hun conquests. But Attila's campaigns had fatally disrupted the western empire. Rome was captured by Germanic mercenaries in 476 and the last western emperor overthrown. The empire in the west ceased to exist, and the former Roman territories were divided into a number of Germanic kingdoms. In Europe the fall of the Roman empire marks the end of the ancient world, and the beginning of the medieval period.

☆ Roman craftsmen created mosaics to order. One popular design depicted an unswept floor covered with food debris, such as discarded bones.

CIVIL ENGINEERING

The Romans are often regarded as supreme among the ancient world's civil engineers. But their achievements were by no means unique. Because the laws of physics are universal, the same engineering solution has often been independently 'discovered' by different peoples around the world.

Monumental pyramids, for example, were built by ancient peoples in Egypt, Mesopotamia and the Americas. The pyramid shape is the most stable and enduring form for a monument built from the bottom up. This principle, which we can now prove with mathematics, was discovered by ancient engineers through a process of trial and error.

2

1. Water control was vital for the Sri Lankans, who built complex irrigation works, like these reservoirs in the hilltop fortress of Sigiriya.

2. The pyramid of Zoser, the first Egyptian pyramid ever built, had tiered steps rather than the smooth profile of later pyramids.

Public works

Aside from monuments to gods and rulers, the civil engineers of the ancient world were mainly concerned with devising solutions to pressing problems, such as how to deliver drinking water to a growing city, or how to transport water through a desert, or how to link the distant parts of a mountain realm.

The citizens of Rome drank and bathed in water taken not from the sewage-polluted Tiber, but delivered by a series of aqueducts that brought fresh water from distant sources. The Marcia Aqueduct, for example, built in 114 BC, carried about 1 million litres (225,000 gallons) of water an hour from a source nearly 100 km (60 miles) from the city. These aqueducts required extremely careful planning and design so that the water was always flowing gently downhill. By sealing the top of an aqueduct, so forming a pipe, Roman engineers were even able to make water flow uphill over short distances, using the principle of the siphon.

In ancient Iran, oases and desert towns were supplied with water by qanats (subterranean aqueducts) running beneath the desert floor. By keeping the water underground, losses to evaporation were kept to a minimum. Qanats were dug and maintained through a series of vertical shafts, and the tunnels had to maintain a constant downward slope just like aqueducts above ground. A very similar system was built and maintained by the Nazca people (▷ pp. 212–13) of the Peruvian coastal desert.

In the Andes mountains the Incas constructed a road system that ran the entire length of their empire (▷ p. 225). Valleys were often crossed by swooping suspension bridges made of wood and rope. Some of these bridges, repaired and renewed countless times, are said to be still in use today.

The arching problem

Other problems faced by ancient engineers were smaller in scale, but no less important. The arch is a strong, useful and attractive structure, but it is difficult to make a good one.

It is fairly easy to make an arch from mud or mud brick, because the material will bend somewhat into shape, but the resulting structure will not be very strong, because

1

3

mud brick is not very strong. Strength requires stone, which will not bend at all.

The first attempts at stone arches were corbelled roofs. In such roofs, stones are piled up in slightly overlapping rows to make a step-sided inverted-V shape. Later, as people's skills in stone working and mathematics improved, they were able to construct the keystone arch, in which a series of carefully shaped stones are locked securely in place by a central keystone. These arches could also be made of baked brick. Without keystone arches, made of stone and brick, the Romans could not have built the elegant, multi-layered viaducts along which many of their aqueducts flowed. Any other design would have been too massive to be practical.

Through increasingly precise control over design and materials some ancient civilizations were able to construct arches that are still impressive today. Mastery of the arch eventually led to the construction of domed roofs, and the largest of these – the Pantheon in Rome, 44 m (145 feet) in diameter – was constructed in about AD 120, using a relatively new material: concrete.

3. The Romans were superb civil engineers. Their skills in bridge-building and in transporting water over long distances were combined in this masterpiece, the 270-m (890-feet) long Pont du Gard aqueduct in southern France.

TOPIC LINKS

2.3 The Indus and its Neighbours
p.60 The Indus Cities

2.5 The Gift of the Nile
p.85 Building a State

3.2 The Athenian Role Model
p.129 Hellenistic World

3.4 The Great Han
p.153 The Great Wall

3.6 The Might of Rome
p.171 The Eternal City

4.4 Flowery Wars and Conquerors
p.225 Inca Builders

EMPIRES OF THE NEW WORLD

THE CONTINENT AWAKES

The first civilizations of the Americas emerged around 1200 BC in the Andes region of South America and in Mesoamerica. In North America towns started to appear after AD 800. Despite many differences, these areas shared several significant features. Religion played a central role, uniting people from diverse regions and prompting the construction of massive ceremonial complexes, often featuring magnificent pyramids. Religion encouraged warfare, to acquire captives for ritual sacrifice. It also stimulated trade, to obtain items such as shells needed for ritual purposes.

Underlying the prosperity of the ancient American civilizations were various sophisticated agricultural practices. Skilled artisans produced superb pottery and textiles. However, the arrival of Europeans from the 15th century – bringing superior weapons, new diseases and a way of life at odds with the locally balanced systems – cut short the flowering of these indigenous cultures.

Previous page. Beautiful polychrome textiles made of cotton or wool were among the most distinctive products of the Andean civilizations. Many, like this example from the Paracas culture, featured deities in the form of birds or animals.

THE EARLY AMERICANS

The rich and diverse lands of the Americas were rapidly settled after 12,000 BC (▷ p. 18). In many regions the hunter-gatherer way of life established by the first settlers endured until recent times. In others – notably Mesoamerica and the Andes – people began to transplant and tend locally available plants, and also to exchange useful plants between regions. This led to the development of agriculture from around 7000 BC onwards. The first colonists probably already kept domestic dogs; no new animals were domesticated in Mesoamerica, but llamas and guinea pigs were kept in the Andes, and turkeys in parts of what is now the USA.

North America

The early inhabitants of North America were big game hunters, their quarry mammoths, which became extinct within a few millennia. Their descendants in the Great Plains turned to hunting bison, while in other regions hunter-gatherers developed a lifestyle geared to the local ecology, from the hunters of caribou and sea mammals in the icy far north to the resourceful groups who wrung a living from the Great Basin desert of the southwest, and the prosperous salmon fishers of the Pacific coast.

Mesoamerica

Farming developed in Mesoamerica over a long period. Groups who lived mainly by hunting and gathering found it profitable to sow, transplant and weed their preferred food plants to increase the length of time they could stay in one place during the year. They traded with their neighbours to obtain commodities that were not locally available – these included not only prized luxury materials such as

NEW WORLD STATES AND CHIEFDOMS

PUEBLOS

MISSISSIPPIANS

ATLANTIC OCEAN

HIGHLAND MESOAMERICAN STATES

MAYA

SOUTH AMERICAN CHIEFDOMS

PACIFIC OCEAN

ANDEAN STATES

States
Chiefdoms

seashells and obsidian (a sharp-edged volcanic glass) but also plants and seeds native to other areas. This early agriculture did not yield enough food to support communities all the year round, so hunting and gathering continued. One of the plants that was widely cultivated was maize. At first the cobs were tiny and not very useful, but natural genetic mutations – probably enhanced by human selection – caused the cobs to increase progressively in size, until around 2000 BC maize yields were high enough to support completely sedentary communities.

South America

Agriculture had begun in the Andes region of South America by 6500 BC. The Andes present an unusual situation: as the slopes of the mountains rise very steeply, they provide great ecological diversity within a short horizontal distance. This natural diversity encouraged the development of different ways of life: fishing on the coast in the cold, immensely rich Pacific waters; hunting and

1. Agricultural terraces constructed on the steep slopes of the Andes were among the many innovative technological achievements that enabled ancient farmers to exploit the region more efficiently than many of their modern successors.

BLOOD SACRIFICE

According to Mesoamerican beliefs, the gods had created humanity from their own blood. Blood sacrifices in their turn nourished the gods, and created a pathway for communication with the other world. Blood was also ritually significant in South America – for instance, captives' blood was drunk by Moche priest-kings during religious ceremonies.

Wars were conducted primarily to acquire victims for sacrifice. Many South American peoples, such as the Nazca, practised cults involving trophy heads. The Aztecs offered up huge sacrifices, cutting the heart from the living breasts of their victims. But it was an honour to be sacrificed, offering one's blood to ensure the continuation of the world, so many victims went proudly and willingly to their deaths.

Personal bloodletting was important in Mesoamerica. It was the duty of priests and rulers to offer their own blood to open a path to the spirit world. They pierced various parts of their body with stingray spines or obsidian knives, or drew cords with cactus spines through their tongues.

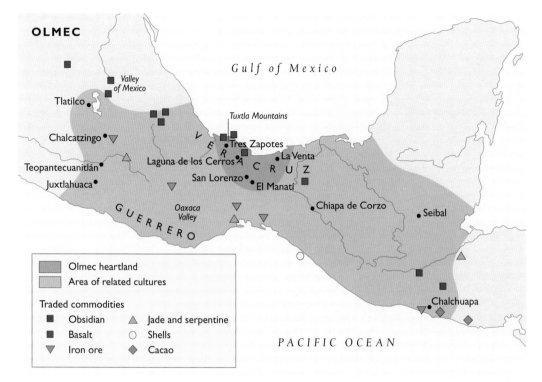

OLMEC

Gulf of Mexico

Valley
of Mexico

Tlatilco

Chalcatzingo

Teopantecuanitlán

Juxtlahuaca

Tuxtla Mountains

V
E
R
A
C
R
U
Z

Tres Zapotes

Laguna de los Cerros

San Lorenzo

El Manatí

La Venta

Chiapa de Corzo

Seibal

G U E R R E R O

*Oaxaca
Valley*

Chalchuapa

PACIFIC OCEAN

Olmec heartland
Area of related cultures

Traded commodities
■ Obsidian   ▲ Jade and serpentine
■ Basalt   ○ Shells
▼ Iron ore   ◆ Cacao

The first rubber balls were made by the Olmec 3000 years ago to use in a ritual ball game. In this game the losing team was often executed.

irrigated cultivation of cotton and other crops in the lowland valleys; cultivation of potatoes and cereals, such as quinoa, in higher regions; and herding llamas in the highest pastures. People came not only to trade foodstuffs between regions, but also to travel up and down themselves in order to exploit cultivated plots and grazing grounds in the various zones – a vertical economy. Llamas were used as pack animals to transport food and other commodities between the regions, while their relatives, the alpaca and the wild vicuña provided wool for textiles. Farming communities also developed in areas to the north, relying on maize by 2000 BC. In the Amazon basin, cultivation of chillis and beans probably began before 6500 BC, and manioc (a poisonous plant with a starch-rich root) was being grown by 1000 BC. Later the more easily prepared and nutritious maize was also cultivated in the region, where fishing and hunting were always important.

THE OLMEC AND THEIR PREDECESSORS

The villages that developed in Mesoamerica after 2000 BC traded widely. From the coasts came stingray spines used in ritual bloodletting ceremonies and conch shells for trumpets. Iron ore from the Pacific coast and the Oaxaca valley in southern Mexico was cut and polished to make mirrors, which were worn either as badges of office or as ornaments by the élite. Jade and obsidian were similarly sought after – both for the prestige they endowed and for their ritual significance – and were widely traded.

Around 1200 BC the Olmec culture emerged in the Veracruz region on the coast of the Gulf of Mexico. This well-watered area was particularly favourable to farming without irrigation, and populations here rose more rapidly than in other Mesoamerican regions. Many features that appeared first in

this area – the Olmec heartland – became widely disseminated throughout Mesoamerica. People disagree how this happened. Some believe that the Olmec (the people of Veracruz) conquered other regions and imposed their way of life. Others suggest the Olmec set fashions that were widely adopted by the élite of Mesoamerican societies. Most likely is the suggestion that the Olmec were more organized than the people of other regions. They were no longer content for exotic but ritually essential materials to trickle through to them via haphazard and unreliable exchange networks, but instead made expeditions to the source areas to obtain what they wanted. The inhabitants of these areas interacted with the Olmec in various ways, but frequently they became caught up in the belief system that underlay the Olmec way of life. For a time the Olmec approach was adopted by other developing regions, but subsequently

Bitter manioc is a staple food in the Amazon Basin. It must be peeled, grated and squeezed to remove its poison before it is safe to cook and eat.

2. Olmec figurines of slit-eyed infants are generally referred to as 'were-jaguars', the supposed offspring of a human and a jaguar. This unusually naturalistic example is made of typical white Olmec pottery.

1. (opposite) The colossal heads that were an impressive feature of Olmec ceremonial centres such as San Lorenzo and La Venta are probably portraits of individual rulers, who are shown wearing a helmet for the ritual ball game.

many different local versions emerged. Nevertheless, all were manifestations of a similar way of life that had been developing all over Mesoamerica for centuries. Many features that first crystallized in Olmec culture continued as the underpinning of Mesoamerican civilizations.

A religious society

The religious side of Olmec culture was paramount, as it was to subsequent cultures. Many later gods, such as Quetzalcoatl, the Feathered Serpent, have their counterparts in Olmec iconography. Dangerous animals, such as jaguars and sharks, feature prominently. The most characteristic Olmec figurines depict slit-eyed babies, often with cleft skulls and fangs (known as 'were-jaguars', by analogy to the werewolves of European folklore). These may represent the mythical offspring of a human woman and a male jaguar. Many were made of greenstone (jade or serpentine), a material that may have symbolized water, and

which could only be obtained from a few areas. The Olmec established a trading outpost at Teopantecuanitlán in southwestern Mexico to control the supply of local greenstone. The 'were-jaguar' figurines were frequently deposited in élite burials and in ritual caches at the Olmec ceremonial centres. Similar figures made of white pottery using a distinctive Veracruz kaolin clay were popular in centres all over Mesoamerica, and show how widespread was the political and religious influence of the Olmec.

The best known examples of Olmec art are the colossal heads carved from basalt – another sacred material, representing fire – brought from the Tuxtla mountains and set up at the ceremonial centres at San Lorenzo and La Venta. These appear to be portraits as each is different, and it has been suggested that they depict rulers. Most of the heads are depicted wearing a helmet – this was probably worn when taking part in the sacred ball game (▷ p. 197), which began in Olmec times.

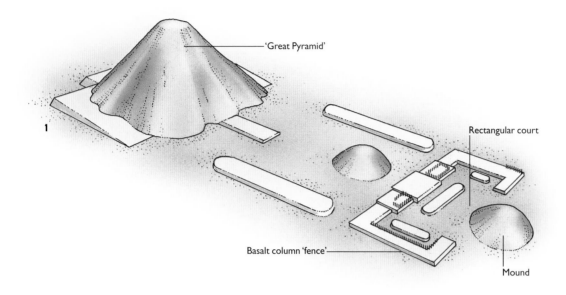

'Great Pyramid'

Rectangular court

Basalt column 'fence'

Mound

1

Olmec ceremonial centres

Ballcourts were a feature of Olmec ceremonial centres, which were probably the main religious focus of the whole area and major places of pilgrimage. That at San Lorenzo was in use between 1200 and 900 BC, when it was deliberately and carefully destroyed and a new one constructed at La Venta, which was in use until about 400 BC. Plazas and pyramids or mounds were the main features of these ceremonial centres, which were laid out in accordance with astronomical patterns. One mound at La Venta mimics the form of a volcano: there were many active volcanoes in Mesoamerica, and they were revered by the people of the region.

Within these ceremonial centres were other sacred monuments, including ponds, stelae (upright stone slabs) and so-called 'altars' decorated with figures carved in relief. La Venta also had mosaic floors depicting the face of a were-jaguar (▷ p. 187). Votive caches of jade figurines, jade axes and other prized objects were placed within pits, which were periodically opened and the contents inspected.

Other Olmec sacred places included a pool at El Manati in Veracruz in which wooden figurines, pots and new-born babies were ritually deposited. Olmec carvings show a

1. At the heart of La Venta was an artificial mound shaped like a volcano, facing onto a large plaza with other religious structures.

2. Ballcourts were already in use in Olmec times. Here teams played a ritual game using hips and shoulders to hit a rubber ball.

2

number of sacrifices of adults, and there seems also to be evidence of ritual cannibalism. Human sacrifices and personal offerings of one's own blood were ritual practices that were to characterize most later Mesoamerican cultures.

Dominance and development

The Olmec ceremonial centres were set apart as religious sites, but the area immediately around them housed thousands of people whose labour was required to construct the monuments. Major settlements developed in many other regions too. Some were trading outposts set up by the Olmec. Among these were Chalcatzingo, which controlled an important trade route into southwestern Mexico, and Chalchuapa in the south (in present-day San Salvador), an area from which the Olmec obtained cacao as well as iron ore for mirrors. Monumental architecture and carvings in the Olmec style were characteristic of these outposts, which often had workshops for working locally obtained raw materials. Other settlements, like Tlatilco in the Valley of Mexico (around present-day Mexico City), were indigenous settlements with some Olmec features. In particular, the graves of the emerging ruling class in such settlements contained many imported Olmec objects or imitations of them – notably white pottery figurines and incised Olmec pottery.

By 900 or 800 BC many of these settlements, such as Tlatilco or San José Mogote in the Oaxaca valley, were beginning to break away from Olmec dominance and to display their own versions of sacred art and architecture. New settlements also appeared that show no Olmec features. Although Olmec culture endured for many more centuries, by 500 BC other regions were becoming more important, particularly the Valley of Mexico and the Oaxaca valley.

3

3. A carefully arranged ritual deposit of six long polished stone axes and 16 'were-jaguar' stone figurines was found at La Venta. They had been placed in a pit dug into red sand and infilled with white sand.

A second pit dug down to the level of the top of the deposit seems to have intended to check up on the deposit at a later stage. Such votive caches were a common feature of La Venta.

Domestic dogs were raised by the peoples of the Americas for hunting, and sometimes to draw sleds or carry packs, but mostly to be eaten as food.

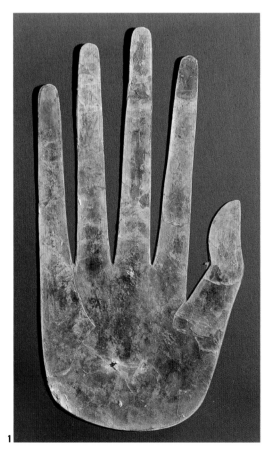

1

THE WOODLANDERS OF NORTH AMERICA

The woodlands of eastern North America were home to many communities who lived by hunting deer, waterbirds and other game, catching fishing and gathering seeds, nuts and other plants. These peoples moved with the seasons when necessary, but inhabited settled villages for part of the year. From around 2000 BC they also began to cultivate some local plants such as sunflowers. Despite intense territorial disputes between groups, well-developed exchange networks existed throughout the region, serving the demand for exotic materials that were significant as indicators of individuals' status in the community. Trade items included small objects made of cold-hammered native copper from the Great Lakes region. Many of these were deposited with their owners in the large cemeteries that were an important social and religious focus of the communities of the eastern woodlands.

Certain points in the trade network may well have had a particular significance, and it is possible that this lies behind the enigmatic and impressive earthworks that were erected in the lower Mississippi valley between 1700 and 700 BC. Best known of these is Poverty Point, an arrangement of banks in six concentric hexagons. An alternative explanation is that these earthworks may have had an astronomical function.

The moundbuilders

From around 500 BC many groups began to erect funerary mounds. In the fierce competition for land, these mounds were probably seen as a way of marking and making explicit a group's ownership of its territory. Mounds were erected over a burial or group of burials, and more burials were added later, with more earth being piled on the original mound. Burials took a variety of forms: sometimes the complete body was buried, sometimes only cremated bones collected in a dish, while in some cases the burials consisted of wrapped bundles of bones from which the flesh had decayed.

Not all the mounds covered burials. Some took the form of geometric figures or the shapes of animals. The most famous is the great Serpent Mound in Ohio, which is nearly 400 m (1300 feet) long. By 200 BC more elaborate treatment was accorded to the dead, who were placed with their possessions in special charnel houses (buildings for housing the dead) where ceremonies were periodically held, or stored in communal crypts. Some unusual burials were furnished with false noses made of copper, or other additions to their appearance: one man, who was perhaps a shaman, wore a wolf's palate in his mouth. Important individuals were not only accompanied by a wealth of exotic ornaments and tools, but were also placed in log tombs within the charnel house. Eventually the community would dismantle or burn down the charnel house and construct a massive mound over the dead.

Interregional trade was by now highly developed, circulating prestige materials such as bear claws and obsidian from the Rocky Mountains, and shells and sharks' teeth from the southern coast. Many communities specialized in producing luxury goods from their local materials, such as animal silhouettes cut from sheets of mica from the southern Appalachians, ornaments made from Great Lakes copper, and beautifully decorated tobacco pipes of Minnesota pipestone (catlinite). For reasons that are not yet understood, this interregional trade came to an end around AD 400, at the same time as the peoples of the region stopped building mounds.

2

1. Hands cut out of thin
mica sheets were
among the beautiful
objects made by the
moundbuilders of
North America from
materials which they
traded over vast
distances. This example
was placed as a grave
offering in a burial.

2. The great Serpent
Mound snakes its way
across the Ohio land-
scape. Some of the
magnificent earthworks
built in this region 2000
years ago take geo-
metric or animal forms,
while others are burial
mounds, like the one in
the serpent's mouth.

TEMPLES

Most societies had their sacred places where people could worship or consult their gods. Often these were natural places – in the Andes of South America the Inca offered sacrifices of children in high mountain sites of religious significance, while the Minoans of Crete built peak sanctuaries. Other natural features might also be sacred. The Celts, for example, worshipped in groves in their woods, and made offerings, including human sacrifices, in rivers and lakes. Such places were also venerated in the Americas: precious objects and people were thrown into sacred wells and lakes.

2

1

1. This pyramidal temple from El Tajín in the Veracruz region of Mesoamerica contains 365 niches, symbolizing the days of the year.

2. This painting from the town of Herculaneum shows a ceremony in honour of the Egyptian goddess Isis, whose cult was popular among the Romans.

Towards the underworld

Caves often had a sacred significance, in some cases being seen as the womb of the earth. The Minoans and Mycenaeans venerated a cave in Crete thought to be the home of the infant god Zeus. But caves might have grimmer associations. The Pyramid of the Sun at Teotihuacán (▷ p.196) in Mesoamerica was built over a cave thought to give access to the underworld. A deep painted and inscribed Maya cave with many burials was recently found at Naj Tunich in Guatemala – a shrine and a gateway to the spirit world. The Greeks and Romans built an extraordinary underground complex by the lake at Cumae in central Italy, which they believed was an entrance to the underworld. The complex was designed to terrify and inspire awe in those who came to consult the spirits of their ancestors. The labyrinthine passages, with their strange noises, within the early South American temple at Chavín de Huántar (▷ p.211) served a similar purpose, confusing and frightening those who approached the oracle at its heart.

Worship and ritual

The form of ancient shrines related to the way in which worship was conducted, and also to the beliefs of their builders. Perhaps the most holy place of the Indus people was the Great Bath complex at Mohenjo Daro (▷ p.67). Here, as in later Indian religious practices, the worshipper might have been purified by bathing, but might also have performed the ritual of walking round the holy place three times in a clockwise direction – a form of worship common in later Buddhist and Hindu practice.

Some temples were designed to admit worshippers, who could participate in the ritual that was being performed. Christian churches, for example, took this form. In many cultures, however, the worshipper observed from the outside, and only the priests had access to the interior of the shrine. In some cases the rituals that took place in the temple were seen only by the priests and perhaps the king, and were shrouded in mystery for the common person.

3

In others they were openly performed with thousands looking on – as, for example, the great human sacrifices in which Aztec priests cut the hearts out of their living victims. Like most Mesoamerican cultures, the Aztecs built their shrines on the tops of great pyramids, flinging the bodies of their dead victims down the pyramid steps.

Reaching to the stars

Such raised shrines were found in many societies. Different forms of pyramid were constructed by the various cultures of Mesoamerica: those of the highland civilizations had alternate sloping and vertical sections, while the tall and elegant pyramids of the Maya were built in steps. Further south, among the cultures of the Andes, pyramidal mounds of mud bricks not only supported shrines on their

summits but also housed the tombs of kings, a practice also followed in Mesoamerica.

On the other side of the world, the ziggurats constructed by the people of Mesopotamia (▷ p. 48) led up sacred stairs to a shrine that reached towards the heavens. Mesopotamian shrines followed a widespread pattern of outer temple and inner sanctum. Surrounding these was a temple complex in which the priesthood lived and administered many aspects of Mesopotamian life. Temple complexes in many cultures included not only the residential palaces or simple cells of the priesthood, but also storerooms in which offerings were kept, and workshops where temple employees made goods for temple use or for the religious authorities to use in trade. Finally, there would be the archives in which the temple records were stored.

3. Delphi was one of the most sacred places in ancient Greece, where Apollo delivered prophecies through his priestess. Many Greek cities built shrines here, and treasuries in which to place their offerings to the god.

BUILDERS OF MOUNDS AND PYRAMIDS

Religion was central to human existence in Mesoamerica. The actions of the gods determined events on earth, and many human activities focused on sustaining the gods. Religious ceremonies in the great ballcourts and magnificent temples often involved the letting of human blood. The demand for materials rich in ritual significance and power – such as obsidian and jade, seashells and incense – spurred the development of long-distance trade. Everyday commodities, such as salt and hard stone for grindstones, also circulated along these routes.

Three great civilizations – the empires of Teotihuacán and Monte Albán, and the city-states of the Classic Maya – developed after 500 BC. By AD 900 they had declined, their place later being taken by other warlike states, such as the Toltec. This later period saw trade reaching as far as the American southwest, where Pueblo towns were beginning to flourish. At the same time, city-states were also emerging in the Mississippi region.

MONTE ALBÁN AND TEOTIHUACÁN

The Olmecs set the scene for Mesoamerican civilization, but by 500 BC other groups were overtaking them. In the highlands, irrigation agriculture now supported larger and more complex communities, with leaders who organized trade, craft production and public building programmes. Religion was the driving force, as it was to remain throughout Mesoamerican history. Rulers were either priests themselves or played an important role in ritual life.

In the Oaxaca valley of southern Mexico, home of the Zapotec people, four separate groups banded together to construct a new centre on the hilltop at Monte Albán around 500 BC. They laid out a number of shrines around a massive central plaza, with a royal palace at the northern end. Tombs were cut into the hillside below the sacred summit, while the lower slopes were covered with house compounds set on terraces, which by AD 100 accommodated up to 30,000 people. Other settlements throughout the Oaxaca valley housed the rural population of farmers and artisans. Among the first monuments erected in Monte Albán were stone slabs carved with designs of moving people. At first it was thought they were dancing, but they were actually sacrificed victims – writhing in agony or contorted in death. Each was accompanied by a name and date – almost the earliest use of writing that survives from Mesoamerica – and it is likely that they were the spoils of wars of expansion. Around AD 300 Monte Albán's expansion was checked by that of the rising state of Teotihuacán, but relations between the two states were generally peaceable, with traders from Monte Albán residing in a dedicated block in the great city of Teotihuacán.

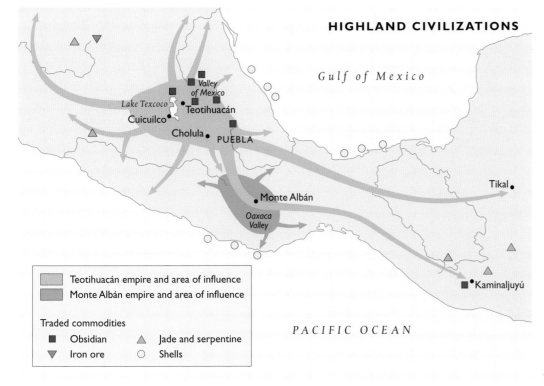

HIGHLAND CIVILIZATIONS

Gulf of Mexico

Valley of Mexico

Lake Texcoco

Teotihuacán

Cuicuilco

Cholula

PUEBLA

Tikal

Monte Albán

Oaxaca Valley

Kaminaljuyú

PACIFIC OCEAN

Teotihuacán empire and area of influence
Monte Albán empire and area of influence

Traded commodities
■ Obsidian   ▲ Jade and serpentine
▼ Iron ore   ○ Shells

1. The so-called 'Danzantes' ('dancers') reliefs from Monte Albán actually depict the agonies of tortured and sacrificed victims – presumably enemies captured in war. Names and dates on these slabs are among the earliest writing in Mesoamerica.

1. The Pyramid of the Sun was the principal shrine at the heart of the great city of Teotihuacán. The structures of the Ciudadela (in the foreground) were probably the ruler's palace.

2. Paintings showing mythological scenes adorned the walls of several of the palaces – vast residential complexes – that lay near the heart of Teotihuacán, housing the élite and their dependents.

The Valley of Mexico

Teotihuacán was the centre of an empire that began to develop around 400 BC in the Valley of Mexico. At first the city of Cuicuilco in the southern part of the valley was dominant, but Teotihuacán at the north end of the valley became the centre of the developing state when Cuicuilco was overtaken by volcanic eruptions between 50 BC and AD 150. The city of Teotihuacán was designed to represent the cosmos. Beneath it was a maze of caves and passages regarded as the portal to the underworld. Above the city towered temples set atop pyramids, touching the heavens. And the city itself was laid out in four quarters representing those of the universe. The centre, the religious heart of the city, was divided by a street running north–south (the Avenue of the Dead), with the Pyramid of the Moon at one end and the main administrative and economic complex, together with the temple of Quetzalcoatl, at the other. In the middle lay the great Pyramid of the Sun, a structure so sacred that it remained a place of pilgrimage long after the city itself had fallen. The Avenue of the Dead was bisected at right-angles by a street that led to the east and west ends of the city. All four road ends pointed to landmarks in the surrounding countryside that had special ritual significance.

The majority of people in the Valley of Mexico, numbering 100,000–200,000, lived within the city of Teotihuacán. At its centre were the palaces of priests and nobles, while the greater part of the city was composed of residential compounds arranged in districts. Several housed foreign merchants, such as those from Monte Albán, while others contained the homes and workshops of various craft specialists. On the outskirts of the city, in the smallest and simplest houses, dwelt the farmers who tended fields in the fertile valley around the shores of Lake

Texcoco. Teotihuacán was a great industrial centre, with specialized workshops producing fine pottery, obsidian tools, jade masks and figurines, and many other domestic, prestige and ritual objects, for domestic consumption and for foreign trade.

Teotihuacán's empire

Teotihuacán dominated and controlled trade and the extraction of raw materials throughout the highland zone, and its influence reached as far as the Maya lowlands. Though their own art portrays them in peaceful settings, the people of Teotihuacán are shown elsewhere as warriors, and their economic dominance and religious pre-eminence were probably backed by military force. Trading stations and customs posts were established along trade routes, and outposts were set up in distant areas to exploit and control important resources. For example, a colony was established at Kaminaljuyú (modern Guatemala City) to exploit the rich local sources of obsidian. Most communities around Kaminaljuyú, however, seem to have been little affected by the presence of people from Teotihuacán. Although Teotihuacán held sway over this empire for centuries, by AD 650 it was in decline and the city was destroyed by fire. It is uncertain whether those responsible were downtrodden local people in revolt or the discontented subject people of Cholula in the neighbouring Puebla valley.

THE MAYA

The Classic Maya civilization occupied the Yucatán peninsula, and flourished between AD 300 and 900. The heartland of the Maya lowlands is Petén, a region of dense rainforest, rivers and swamps at the base of the Yucatán peninsula. Today it is occupied by relatively few people, raising crops in small plots hacked out of the jungle; these plots only retain fertility for a handful of years before a new plot must be cleared. In Classic Maya times, however, this area was densely settled, for the Maya had devised many ways of increasing agricultural productivity. They constructed hillside terraces on which they farmed permanently cleared fields, and cut

 THE SACRED BALL GAME

The ball game was a strenuous contest with powerful religious significance, played by all Mesoamerican cultures, from the Olmec onward. It was played with a rubber ball on an oblong court with sloping edges like this I-shaped example at Xochicalco. Players had to keep the ball from landing on the court, although it could bounce against the sloping side walls. They could only hit it with their shoulders or hips – and paintings and reliefs often show them hurling themselves down on one knee or flat on their stomachs to reach the ball. Massive wooden yokes were worn around the hips both for protection and for hitting the ball, and protective leg-guards, armbands, gloves and helmets were also worn. After the game the Maya may have changed their wooden playing yokes for 'dress' ones of stone.

The rules of the game varied between cultures. Opposing teams probably had to drive the ball into specified parts of the other team's half. In some regions there were rings set on either side and the supreme object was to get the ball through a ring, thereby scoring a 'goal' that not only won the game but also entitled the scorer to the spectators' jewellery and clothes.

The ball game was an important ritual event. It seems that sometimes a captured enemy formed the ball, and in many regions the losing team (or at least its captain) would be sacrificed. Racks near the ballcourt displayed the skulls of defeated players.

★ The Classic Maya used intoxicating drinks as enemas to induce a state of trance in which they communicated with the gods.

canals from the rivers to water surrounding land. Most notably they constructed raised fields in the swamps by cutting a lattice of drainage channels and mounding up the dredged silt on the ground between. The regular cleaning of the drainage channels meant that rich silt was repeatedly deposited on these plots, maintaining their fertility. Fish teemed in the channels and edible snails thrived along their sides, providing two easily culled sources of protein. Here it was possible to raise not only staple crops like maize and beans but also cotton and cacao, which could not be cultivated elsewhere in the region. Cacao (used to make a chocolate drink) was like gold to the people of Mesoamerica: only the élite could consume it, and the Aztecs used the beans as money.

Many other commodities were also highly valued. Some – such as cotton cloth, seashells, salt, jade and the feathers of exotic birds like the quetzal – were produced within the Maya realms. Others, such as obsidian,

were imported from neighbouring regions. Trade was immensely important because many of these commodities – obsidian and stingray spines, for instance, which were used in bloodletting (▷ p. 184) – were essential for the performance of the rituals that the Maya and other Mesoamerican civilizations believed vital for the maintenance of society.

Religion and society

The Maya saw the world of the gods and that of humanity as inextricably intertwined. The gods maintained the world in existence and their actions determined everything that happened. For this reason it was supremely important to know what the gods were going to do, and this could be determined by constantly charting the movements of the sun, moon, stars and planets, all of which represented gods. The Maya became superbly competent astronomers through their detailed interest in predicting divine actions

1. Polychrome Maya pottery shows scenes from mythology or from the lives of individual rulers. Here a servant offers a container to a seated lord.

2. Figurines from the island of Jaina depict many aspects of Maya life – women weaving,

lords and ladies clad in ceremonial finery. Here, one lady is seen writing. Although they echo real life, these figurines probably represent deities.

3. Lady Xoc of Yaxchilan draws a rope set with thorns through her tongue to make a personal blood sacrifice.

3

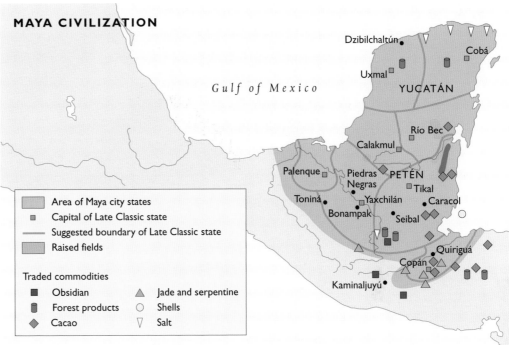

MAYA CIVILIZATION

Dzibilchaltún

Cobá

Uxmal

Gulf of Mexico

YUCATÁN

Río Bec

Calakmul

Palenque · Piedras Negras · PETÉN

Toniná · Yaxchilán · Tikal

Bonampak · Caracol

Seibal

Quiriguá

Copán

Kaminaljuyú

	Area of Maya city states
■	Capital of Late Classic state
—	Suggested boundary of Late Classic state
	Raised fields

Traded commodities

■	Obsidian	△	Jade and serpentine
▮	Forest products	○	Shells
◆	Cacao	▽	Salt

▷ MAYA WRITING

The people of Mesoamerica developed symbols that enabled them to record dates and names. Only the Maya developed this notation into a complete writing system capable of recording any spoken word. It has taken a very long time for scholars to unlock the secrets of the Maya script as it is extremely complex. Although largely phonetic, the script also has pictographic elements, and the ancient Maya delighted in using different 'spellings', combining and interchanging pictographs and phonetic signs, and elaborating the form of their highly ornate signs. Thus the name of the great king Pacal (whose inscribed sarcophagus is shown here) – Shield – could be written as a picture of a shield, or with the signs for the syllables 'pa', 'ca' and 'la', or by combining picture and syllabic signs. The various elements together formed a glyph, approximately square in shape. As a result, each Maya sign has to be individually deciphered. Although many glyphs can now be read, there are still many that cannot.

Most Maya texts record information about kings – their ancestry, birth, accession, personal blood sacrifices and death, and particularly their successes in battle and the inevitable sacrifice of war captives that followed.

1

(▷ pp. 206–7). The gods required humanity to construct ritual structures to communicate with them – pyramid temples spearing upward into the heavens, and ballcourts as portals to the underworld. The gods also required humans to provide sustenance for them – by offering precious materials, and, above all, the blood of kings.

Maya lords were both kings and priests. They sacrificed their own blood and fought wars to capture kings of other states to sacrifice. Under them were lesser lords – members of the royal family or their noble cousins – who ruled cities, observed and analysed the heavens, recorded the deeds of kings, and went as ambassadors to trade with the rulers of other regions. Craftsmen worked under the patronage of the lords, carving stone and making pottery, textiles and all the elaborate paraphernalia of the sacred life. At the bottom of the hierarchy the peasants

raised crops to feed the whole society. They also gave their labour, constructing great monuments and public works, secure in the knowledge that their rulers were ordering the world and supporting and communicating with the gods for their benefit.

Political life

Like Classical Greece, the Classic Maya were culturally united but politically divided, their lands a patchwork of city-states dominated by the great ceremonial centres. These centres not only had a religious function – with temples, ballcourts, plazas, stelae (inscribed slabs) recording the deeds of kings, and ancestral royal burials – they were also centres of population. Unlike highland Teotihuacán, the population was not neatly housed within a tight urban layout, but instead was scattered over a wide area, house compounds being interspersed

with gardens, fields, orchards and lakes.

The rulers of these states intermarried, and also fought each other. Initially wars were conducted with the sole aim of obtaining captives for sacrifice, but by AD 600 the rulers also struggled to dominate each other, so that cities such as Tikal, Calakmul, Palenque and Yaxchilán came to rule substantial states.

Around AD 800 things began to go wrong in the Maya lands. The population rapidly declined, and Petén in particular suffered serious depopulation. Disease was in part to blame, and environmental degradation may have been involved. It is also possible that the intensive conflict and competition between states may have pressed too hard upon the peasantry. When things went seriously wrong it was clear that the gods had turned away their favour, so the peasants left too, moving to regions like northern Yucatán where things were less difficult.

PUEBLOS AND MISSISSIPPIANS

Contacts were made over surprisingly long distances in the ancient Americas. Sometime before 1000 BC maize, beans and squash were introduced from Mesoamerica to the American Southwest, where agriculture gradually developed alongside hunting and gathering. Continuing links brought the introduction of characteristic Mesoamerican religious structures such as plazas and ballcourts, which appeared in settlements such as Snaketown around AD 700. Irrigation using canals may also be a Mesoamerican introduction, greatly increasing productivity in this arid zone. Mesoamerican traders were particularly interested in the turquoise mined at Santa Fe (in present-day New Mexico), and around AD 1400 may have taken over the town of Casas Grandes in the north of Mexico as a base from which to control trade in this

prized luxury. In exchange they supplied the people of the region with copper bells and fine feathers – and even live scarlet macaws.

Around AD 900 the people of the American Southwest began to construct pueblos – large complexes of adjoining dwellings with living rooms, store rooms and shrines (kivas) to which access was gained by descending a ladder. Walls surrounded some pueblos, while others were constructed on platforms cut into cliff faces. In one area fine roads were built crisscrossing the country and linking the pueblos together. Each of the smaller pueblos was probably a village housing related families, while the large pueblos may have been towns with a large resident population. Alternatively they may have functioned as religious centres, places of pilgrimage in which only priests dwelt permanently, but where the people of the surrounding villages stored their agricultural produce.

The large concentrations of population that gave rise to the pueblo towns grew up in

3

2

1. Magnificent temple pyramids and plazas form the ceremonial centre of the great Maya city of Palenque.

2. Sunken shrines (kivas) were an important part of the great Pueblo complexes of the American southwest, such as Pueblo Bonito in Chaco Canyon.

3. Portraits of warriors embossed on copper were a familiar feature of the 'Southern Cult' art of the Mississippian people.

⭐ Almost the only creature domesticated in Mesoamerica was the stingless bee, which produced beeswax and honey.

a relatively short-lived period of favourable climatic conditions with higher than average rainfall and fewer droughts. The climate began to return to less favourable conditions around AD 1150, after which some groups reverted entirely to hunting and gathering, while others continued farming, but lived in small communities, which were all the region could reliably support.

The Mississippians

The people of southeastern North America had cultivated local plants as well as hunted and gathered wild foods for many centuries. After AD 800 agriculture became much more important, with the introduction through trade of maize and later beans – crops that had been domesticated in Mesoamerica. Settlements were now concentrated in river valleys where cultivation was easy and agriculture could support the expanding and permanently settled population. In good

years productivity was high, and crops were supplemented by catching fish and waterfowl. However, both excessive floods and droughts were common, and the people of this so-called Mississippian culture region began to organize the storage of surplus agricultural produce under community chiefs. The chiefs were responsible for distributing this produce in lean years and using it for community feasts and festivals at appropriate times.

In some areas the local chiefs became subordinate to regional rulers based in substantial towns such as Cahokia and Moundville. These were regional religious centres with plazas, massive mounds and temples. The élite who resided there obtained luxuries such as obsidian and seashells through trade networks that also supplied everyday commodities such as salt and flint for hoes to the village dwellers. When they died the regional chiefs were buried in the great mounds, along with their most precious possessions and sacrificed members of their household.

CAHOKIA

Cahokia was the largest settlement of the Mississippian culture, located within an area of prime agricultural productivity, American Bottom, watered by the rivers Missouri, Mississippi and Illinois, and was at its peak around AD 1050–1250. It was laid out to symbolize the cosmos, and as an aid in observing the patterns of the stars.

Cahokia's thatched wooden houses may have accommodated as many as 30,000 people. Surrounded by a substantial log palisade, the settlement's centre occupied nearly a square kilometre (about 200 acres), with plazas around which were grouped many massive terraced earthen mounds topped by platforms. On the largest, 30 m (100 feet) high, was the palatial residence of the regional ruler. Smaller mounds bore various structures: mansions of nobles and priests, temples, and charnel houses in which dead bodies were laid out before burial. Many important individuals were interred in the mounds. Leaders were accompanied in death not only by valuable possessions, but also by human sacrifices.

THE TOLTECS AND THEIR SUCCESSORS

Northern Mesoamerica was arid land unsuitable for agriculture, inhabited by Chichimeca hunter-gatherers. Further south, poor lands were inhabited by related groups who mixed some farming with hunting and gathering. Deteriorating climatic and environmental conditions periodically drove these groups out of their traditional lands. One such group was probably ancestral to the Toltecs, who appeared on the Mesoamerican scene around AD 900. After wandering for a number of

years under the leadership of the legendary Topiltzin, they eventually settled north of the Valley of Mexico and built a new city, Tula. Topiltzin was a pacific ruler, to the dissatisfaction of followers of the warrior god Tezcatlipoca who drove out the king and his supporters. They fled, eventually reaching northern Yucatán, where, according to tradition, in AD 987 they established a state centred on Chichén Itzá. The Putun Maya from the Gulf coast of southern Yucatán were also involved in the establishment of this state, and the Toltecs may only have been their mercenaries. The new state had many highland

1. Huge figures of warriors, more than 4 m (14 feet) high, surmount the great pyramid in the Toltec capital at Tula. They are each armed with their characteristic weapon, the atlatl (spearthrower).

Mesoamerican features, which included chac-mools, sculptures of a god lying on his back clutching a bowl to his stomach – this was designed to hold the hearts of sacrificed victims. Human victims were also among the offerings thrown into the great Cenote (Well) of Sacrifice here, along with fine objects of jade, pottery and metalwork, although sacrifices in the well may only have started after the Chichén Itzá state collapsed in the early 13th century.

At Chichén Itzá, the newcomers constructed many buildings similar to those from Tula, aided by the local Maya people, who were skilled architects. These included a massive temple fronted by a great hall in which the pillars were carved with figures of warriors. Tula itself was badly damaged when the city was sacked around AD 1200. The most impressive of its surviving remains is the great pyramid temple on whose summit stand colossal statues of warriors, which once supported the roof. Many of Tula's portable remains were carried off by the Aztecs as treasured souvenirs – like many late Mesoamerican cultures, the Aztecs claimed to trace their ancestry back to the Toltecs, whom they regarded as craftsmen of exceptional skill. Although there is little to show for it, the Toltecs in their heyday probably ruled an empire that extended over much of highland Mexico, seized and maintained by military force.

Other kingdoms

The Zapotec state of Monte Albán in the Oaxaca valley had collapsed around AD 700. A new capital was founded at Mitla, the heart of a small kingdom dominated by its priesthood. Much of the Zapotec region was progressively overrun by their Mixtec neighbours from the west, where well-fortified city-states had been expanding for centuries. The Mixtecs gained control of the Oaxaca valley by AD 1350, but were eventually checked by Aztec expansion. They became particularly fine workers of gold and silver, developing metallurgical technology introduced from South America around AD 800.

The Tarascans who lived in Michoacán, a kingdom of fortified towns in central Mexico that successfully resisted Aztec attempts at conquest, were also fine workers in precious metals as well as in turquoise and obsidian. In the political vacuum left by the collapse of the early states many kingdoms rose and fell, including the many small city-states that appeared in northern Yucatán after AD 1450, successors to the Mayapan kingdom that had followed Chichén Itzá. The scale of warfare significantly increased after AD 900, providing some states, such as that of the Zapotec at Mitla, with huge numbers of war captives for sacrifice. Professional soldiers and standing armies appeared in some regions, while fortified settlements became common.

Some enterprising individuals in Mesoamerica 'forged' cocoa bean money by removing the beans' insides and carefully refilling them with mud.

1. (opposite) The great pyramid known as the Castillo dominates the centre of the Post-Classic city of Chichén Itzá, where traditional Maya architecture blends with themes derived from highland Mexico, including the Feathered Serpent, Kukulkan.

ASTRONOMY AND CALENDARS

People have always been intimately involved with the seasonal rhythms of the world they lived in. Hunter-gatherers needed to know the timing of bird and animal migrations or the appearance of food plants. Farmers had to prepare their fields and plant their crops at the appropriate time. So they had to learn the clues embodied in nature to enable them to identify key moments in the annual cycle of their world. This need led people to construct calendars. The regular movements of heavenly bodies provided an important means of doing so, and many cultures developed a detailed knowledge of these patterns – none better than the ancient Mesoamericans.

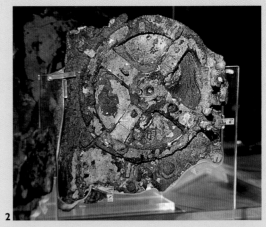

2. This remarkable bronze mechanism, discovered in an ancient shipwreck, puzzled scholars for many years. It was eventually identified as a clock-work calculator.

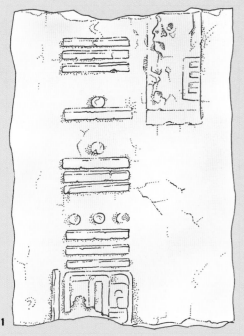

1. The Maya also used the Long Count, recording the number of days since its start in 3114 BC in blocks of kin (single days), uinal (20 days), tun (360 days), katun (7200 days) and baktun (144,000 days). This stele gives a Long Count date of 3 September 32 BC.

Marking time

The interrelationship of the positions and movements of sun, moon, stars and planets in the skies gave people a means of identifying particular moments in the annual passing of time – fixed points in the seasons – and of dividing time into recurring blocks – years. Many cultures reckoned their fixed points by the first rising of particular stars or constellations near the sun after a period of being invisible (their 'heliacal rising'). For example, the Egyptians used the heliacal rising of the bright star Sirius to mark the time when the waters of the Nile would begin to rise in the annual inundation.

Many cultures constructed their calendars of months timed by the phases of the moon, which take 29.53 days to complete a cycle. In Mesopotamia the appearance of the crescent moon denoted the beginning of a month, whereas the Egyptians started their months with the day on which the waning moon became invisible.

As the actual year is 365.2422 solar days, a year based on 12 lunar months of 29 or 30 days would soon get completely out of step with the seasons. Adding an extra month every few years or a number of intercalary (extra) days after 12 months allowed an adjustment to be made that brought the year length closer to actuality – but the accuracy with which this was done varied. The calendar brought in by Julius Caesar in 46 BC introduced the leap year, in which every fourth year had an extra day; with some modification, this is the basis of the calendar we use today.

The most elaborate calendar was that devised by the people of Mesoamerica. They used two calendars together to produce what is known as the 'Calendar Round'. Their 'Almanac Year' was 260 days long and combined the numbers 1 to 13 with 20 named days. Alongside this ran the 'Vague Year' of 365 days, which consisted of 18 months of 20 days each, followed by 5 extra days. Combining the Almanac Year and the Vague Year gave each day a four-element name that was repeated only once every 52 years.

Observing the heavens

The peoples of Mesoamerica studied the skies because they believed that certain things would take place at particular times, especially when certain planets (especially Venus), the moon and the sun were in particular places in the heavens and in certain relationships to each other. From these patterns they predicted what was likely to take place or determined appropriate days for important events, such as the investiture of the heir to a kingdom or a battle in which to take captives for sacrifice.

Other cultures, such as the ancient Egyptians, Etruscans and Indians, also believed that the stars and other heavenly bodies were manifestations of the gods, and that observing them would give an insight into what the gods were up to – and so allow them to determine the favourable time to perform certain activities. As a result, many of these ancient peoples came to have a very exact knowledge of astronomy.

A fascinating Greek mechanical device was discovered in a 1st-century BC shipwreck at Antikythera off Greece. This contraption, hailed as the first computer, demonstrated the movement of the sun, moon and principal stars over the course of four years, using a series of geared wheels. Indeed, the Greeks were among the first people to practise astronomy for mainly scientific reasons. In the 6th century BC Thales of Miletus is thought to have predicted a solar eclipse, while in the 3rd century BC Aristarchus of Samos realized that the earth turns on its axis and orbits the sun. However, in the 2nd century AD Ptolemy of Alexandria placed the earth at the centre of the universe, an error that was to dominate European astronomy for nearly 1400 years.

3. The extraordinary painted ceiling of the tomb of the pharaoh Seti I in the Valley of the Kings depicts the Egyptian view of the heavens. Red dots represent stars in the northern constellations, whose animal forms are shown.

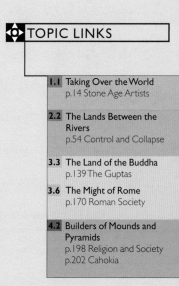

❖ TOPIC LINKS

1.1 Taking Over the World
p.14 Stone Age Artists

2.2 The Lands Between the Rivers
p.54 Control and Collapse

3.3 The Land of the Buddha
p.139 The Guptas

3.6 The Might of Rome
p.170 Roman Society

4.2 Builders of Mounds and Pyramids
p.198 Religion and Society
p.202 Cahokia

Farming communities developed in northern South America, the Andes and the Amazon Basin before 2000 BC. Ceremonial centres and elaborate goldwork characterized the chiefdoms that emerged in the northwest around 500 BC, while in the early years AD large villages ruled by chiefs appeared in the Amazon Basin. The central Andean region saw the flowering of civilization in South America, beginning around 1200 BC when the Chavín cult united disparate regional groups.

By around 200 BC this uniformity was gone, but the religion that underlay it – with its distinctive beliefs and practices – formed the basis for the later religions of the region, while the cultural life of the Chavín period set the pattern for Andean civilization. Some later Andean states, notably Nazca and Tiwanaku, may have owed their cohesion mainly to religious bonds, while in others, such as Moche and Huari, military force was added to divine sanction.

CHAVÍN AND ITS PRECURSORS

Many features of traditional Andean life were established by about 2000 BC. People lived in villages, often quite large, and exploited local resources and also those of other zones, obtained personally or by trade. Fishing was important on the coast – one of the richest marine areas in the world – while further inland farming and hunting were important. Different crops were grown at different altitudes, and guinea pigs were raised for food. In the high pastures alpacas were kept for wool and llamas for meat. Wool and cotton were used to produce fine textiles with geometric designs in the form of stylized animals and people, often with religious meanings. Already textiles were highly valued and were to become one of the most precious products of the Andean realms, along with gold, which was worked by cold hammering by 2100 BC. The dead were often buried wrapped in fine textiles and mats. There were few differences in the quality of offerings placed with them, showing that most people enjoyed equal status.

Nevertheless, society was becoming more organized. The Andean coastal plains are a desert in which rain never falls, and rivers running through the area provide the only water. By 2500 BC the local people were constructing irrigation channels fanning out from the rivers, and these allowed the surrounding area to be cultivated. Through time the channels became increasingly complex and required correspondingly greater community organization and cooperation. The gods were also honoured through communal efforts, large ceremonial complexes being constructed in the shape of a 'U': a large plaza surrounded on three sides by massive platforms of earth. The central platform often bore a pyramid, topped by a shrine. Plaster or stone religious decorations

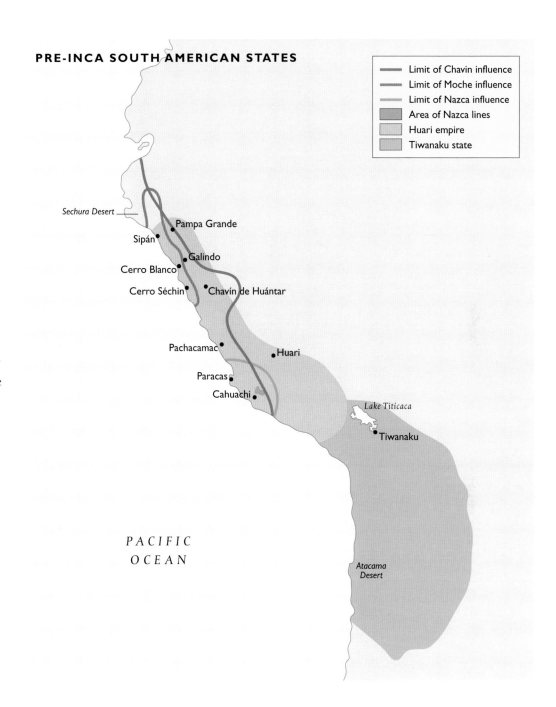

PRE-INCA SOUTH AMERICAN STATES

Legend:
- Limit of Chavin influence
- Limit of Moche influence
- Limit of Nazca influence
- Area of Nazca lines
- Huari empire
- Tiwanaku state

Sechura Desert
Pampa Grande
Sipán
Galindo
Cerro Blanco
Cerro Séchin
Chavín de Huántar
Pachacamac
Huari
Paracas
Cahuachi
Lake Titicaca
Tiwanaku
PACIFIC OCEAN
Atacama Desert

⭐ Charred human bones at the shrine of Chavín de Huántar suggest ritual cannabalism may have been performed here.

on these temple mounds depicted jaguars, alligators and other menacing beasts. At Cerro Sechín, on the north central coast of Peru, carved slabs depicted scenes of human torture and sacrifice, including a pile of severed heads, showing that a trophy-head cult – popular among later peoples in the region – was already practised.

Chavín

Considerable diversity characterized the early cultures of the Andes. Around 1200 BC, however, this began to change as local styles of shrines, pottery and other aspects of life gave way to a set of uniform cultural traits known as 'Chavín'. The reason behind this growing uniformity is believed to have been a religious cult that was adopted throughout the Andes. Beginning in the coastal region, by 850 BC it was also established in the highlands, where a great centre at Chavín de Huántar had become its principal shrine, an oracle and a place of pilgrimage.

At the same time social differences had emerged in Andean culture, reflected particularly in the burials. Most people were buried in pits in large cemeteries, accompanied by a few grave goods, which often included fine jars with a stirrup-shaped spout. In contrast, a few people were interred in much more elaborate shaft graves within the ceremonial centres. These individuals were the leaders of society, who probably combined the roles of priest and ruler. With them were buried the luxury products of the different regions: fine textiles, elaborate pottery vessels and jewellery made of gold and silver – metals that were symbolically linked with the gods.

Technology and trade

Important settlements grew up alongside the ceremonial complexes at Chavín de Huántar

1. This Chavín pottery figurine shows a man, probably a shaman, playing music on a pipe in order to summon spirits or work himself into a trance. Musical instruments, such as flutes and panpipes, are sometimes found in ancient Peruvian burials.

and other sacred sites: these were the first towns to appear in South America. Many of the inhabitants of these towns were specialist craft workers. The Chavín period saw many technological improvements and innovations. Beautiful three-dimensional figures were now made from gold, silver or an alloy of the two, constructed from pieces shaped out of thin sheet metal and skilfully soldered together. Textiles were decorated using a variety of techniques, including painting and tie-dyeing. Designs on metalwork, pottery and textiles echoed those on the temples, showing the all-pervading influence of the Chavín cult.

Interregional contacts became more developed, enabling the Chavín cult to spread widely. Llamas and alpacas began to be used as pack animals, carrying goods that previously had had to be borne by individuals themselves. Interregional trade and exchange were also encouraged by the construction of roads, made by clearing or adding stones to create a horizontal surface, often edged with stones and sometimes with substantial walls. Along these routes many commodities were carried – the various foodstuffs of different regions, textiles, and strombus and spondylus seashells from the Ecuador coast (outside the Chavín domains), which were important ceremonial objects. There was also lapis lazuli from the Atacama Desert in the south, obsidian from the south-central highlands, and many other luxury, ritual and everyday goods.

The Chavín legacy

Though the unity of the Chavín cult broke down by 200 BC, the ideas and practices endured, to re-emerge in many guises in later Andean cultures. The Chavín period saw the crystallization of many features that were to be standard in later Andean civilizations. Diverse regional cultures were united by a shared set of religious beliefs, with deities whose attributes were drawn from the natural world, centred around the Supreme Being, a fanged, smiling deity combining the features of a man and a jaguar, holding a staff in each hand. This fearsome-looking god was nevertheless seen as benevolent, preserving the balance of the universe. Gold and other metals and textiles not only reflected wealth and status, but were also ritually important. The temple was the major focus for the people of town and country. Some later Andean civilizations were united by shared religion, while others were created by military conquest – but their leaders were all intimately involved in religious practices, and were often buried in temple mounds.

 CHAVÍN DE HUÁNTAR

Chavín de Huántar became the centre of Chavín religious activity around 850 BC. It probably drew pilgrims from all over the Andean realms. The original complex (the Old Temple) follows the traditional U-shaped layout of early Andean shrines. Later the New Temple was constructed, adding a large mound on either side of the original platform and including a huge plaza. Religious carvings decorated the stonework of the complex, depicting supernatural creatures, severed heads, jaguars and the Supreme Being. The interior of the Old Temple was a maze of narrow winding galleries in which it would have been easy to get lost. One branch led to a chamber in which people left offerings.

Canals ran through the complex, creating a great roaring noise in the galleries. The intention was probably to confuse and terrify visitors so that when they reached the shrine in the heart of the platform they would be in the proper, awe-inspired frame of mind. Here at the centre they could consult the oracle: a massive granite carving of the Supreme Being, the ends of the carving anchored in the ceiling and floor of the chamber, like a cosmic pillar holding together heaven, earth and the underworld.

⭐ Moche pottery depicts almost every aspect of life, from childbirth and a great variety of sexual practices to portrait busts of individuals and lively animals.

PARACAS AND NAZCA

On the southern Peruvian coast, contemporary with the Chavín culture but little influenced by it, lived the Paracas people. Grave goods in the burials of Paracas chiefs reveal their skill as potters and weavers. The dead were probably smoked to preserve their bodies, then tied tightly in a foetal position along with pots, food offerings and often gold objects, wrapped in a cloth and placed in a basket with other offerings, including cotton textiles. Everything was then wrapped in a huge mantle. These were of woven cloth beautifully embroidered in many colours with designs that reflect Paracas religious beliefs and practices. The designs include strange god figures, trophy heads, and many birds, animals and plants.

Nazca

The Nazca, successors of the Paracas culture, flourished in the region from around 250 BC to AD 600. They too made fine textiles using similar designs, but their most beautiful creation was their pottery. Decorated in many colours, sometimes eight on a single vessel, these jars and bowls show creatures such as humming birds, foxes, monkeys, cormorants and killer whales. These creatures all had their place in the mythology and symbolism of the Nazca religion. Other pots were designed like sculptures. One, for example, is in the form of a fisherman swimming through the sea, placing fish in baskets strapped around his waist. Others are shaped like trophy heads, their eyes closed and their dead lips pinned together. Real trophy heads, with holes to hang them on a rope, have been found in the graves of Nazca people. It is likely that taking enemy heads was thought to enhance the power of an individual.

1. This Andean pottery vessel takes the form of a trophy head. Such preserved heads of defeated enemies were common grave goods.

2. This Moche warrior modelled in clay is armed with a small shield and a club with which to knock his enemies on the head.

The Nazca had religious centres that, like the earlier Chavín centres, were places of pilgrimage. The most important was Cahuachi, where a great pyramid was the chief shrine of the Nazca people. Smaller mounds around it were probably the shrines of individual communities or kinship groups. Many of the dead were brought to these centres for burial, and periodically there were major religious festivals attended by thousands of people. The pilgrims camped at the site during the festival, and scrupulously cleaned away every trace of occupation before returning to their homes. Other religious rituals were performed in the Nazca Lines (▷ p. 214), adjacent to Cahuachi.

The sanctity of Cahuachi may be related to the natural springs that occur here, for in the Nazca people's desert home every drop of water was precious. Many of the gods were linked to rain and fertility, and many rituals were performed to produce and maintain water supplies. Irrigation from the rivers and from underground watercourses made it possible to cultivate the area. By late Nazca times, perhaps under the influence of the Huari people from the adjacent highlands, sophisticated underground aqueducts were being constructed to carry water over long distances without loss through evaporation. So well designed were these that they are still in use today, 1400 years later.

⭐ The Nazca women occasionally wove huge pieces of cotton cloth on a ground loom through which a team of weavers passed the shuttle back and forth.

3. Sacrificed retainers surround the central coffin of the Moche Lord of Sipán, who was laid to rest clad in a magnificent array of ornaments and weapons made of gold and other materials valued by the Moche.

MOCHE, HUARI AND TIWANAKU

Far to the north of Nazca lived the warlike Moche people, who emerged after the Chavín decline around 200 BC. Concentrated initially along the valleys of the Virú, Moche and Chicama rivers, the Moche expanded by military conquest to control a state covering the north Peruvian coast. An outpost on the Piura river beyond the Sechura Desert was also occupied by the Moche from early times. Many of their fine painted pots depict scenes of warfare in which warriors armed with maces and clubs fight others similarly armed – presumably other Moche – or poorly armed people, the inhabitants of regions conquered by the Moche. Captives were taken for later sacrifice, their throats being cut to obtain blood that was drunk by the ruler – who was also the chief priest – in important religious ceremonies. These ceremonies also involved the offering of spondylus seashells to the gods for their nourishment.

Royal graves

After their death, Moche rulers were buried in great mud-brick mounds. Marks on the bricks show that the mounds were constructed by labour gangs drawn from different communities. Labour on community projects was a form of tax in Moche and other Andean states: not only sacred mounds but also long and complex systems of irrigation canals and fine roads were built in this way. The summit of these mounds was topped by a shrine, and Moche lords were buried within them with a fabulous array of offerings – their ritual robes and paraphernalia, made of feathers, fine cotton cloth, turquoise, copper, silver and gold. The craftsmanship these display is staggering. For example, one lord wore a tiny nose ornament in the form of a warrior figure made of gold and turquoise. This figure itself wore an elaborate headdress and a minute moveable nose ornament – the whole a masterpiece in miniature. Some pieces were of copper

 THE NAZCA LINES

Between the Nazca and Palpa rivers a vast area of desert – some 500 square km (193 square miles) – is covered with strange designs, known as the Nazca Lines. Made by removing the dark stones from the desert's surface to expose the light soil beneath, the Lines include vast representations of animals, birds and geometric patterns, as well as lines that radiate out from a central point. Many of the designs are very similar to those the Nazca painted on their pots. The figures are so huge that their makers could never have seen what they looked like, and so many absurd theories have been put forward about how they were made. The most ridiculous suggest that they were the work of aliens from space. In fact experiments have shown that they are easy to create as a scaled-up version of a small, visible design. From the air they can be seen in all their magnificence, and they may have been intended for the gods to view. Shamans, believed to leave their bodies during drug-induced trances, might also be expected to see them. Many of the figures were created using a single continuous line, and these were probably regarded as sacred paths along which worshippers would walk to deposit offerings. Some of the designs, dating from an extended drought in the later Nazca period, are wedge shapes, and have been interpreted as invoking the descent of water from the mountains to which they point. Local people continue to place offerings along the Nazca Lines in times of drought.

1. (opposite) The huge figure of a hummingbird flies across the landscape – one of the famous Nazca lines. Birds were regarded as messengers between humanity and the gods, and the hummingbird was particularly associated with the sun.

1. Among the most magnificent garments that have survived from ancient South America are capes and tabards made of feathers. This Nazca or Huari example was created using the brightly coloured feathers of macaws.

South American shamans were believed to be able to transform themselves into other creatures or to leave their bodies and fly as spirits.

electroplated with gold, using a chemical process. These rulers were accompanied to the grave by sacrificed dogs, men and women, including warriors also furnished with gold jewellery. A frequent subject in Moche art is the god known as 'the decapitator', who in one hand holds a severed head and in the other a special sacrificial knife.

Martial states

The early Moche state had its capital by the mountain of Cerro Blanco, situated at the mouth of the river Moche. Here two massive mounds were constructed, the Pyramid of the Sun and the Pyramid of the Moon, in which royalty were buried and on which were

erected shrines, palaces and probably administrative buildings. In the area around and between them lay a huge city. Major disasters led to the destruction of this capital in the 6th century AD: a major El Niño, the warm current that periodically devastates Peru's coasts, was followed by a prolonged period of reduced rainfall and drought. Cerro Blanco was covered in sand and the capital shifted up the valley to Galindo. From around AD 600, however, the centre of political power shifted north to the Lambayeque valley, probably under a new ruling house, who established a new capital at Pampa Grande. This endured until about AD 700, when it was entirely destroyed by fire, probably deliberately.

In the mountains of southern Peru a culture known as the Huari had emerged by AD 600, lasting until around 800. Huari prosperity was based on the cultivation of maize on finely engineered terraces, watered by sophisticated networks of long irrigation canals – probably devised in response to the great drought of the previous century. From its heartland in the Ayacucho region, the Huari state expanded by military force over the entire Andean highlands, compelling the local people to construct terraced fields and irrigation canals. Huari officials lived in fortified outposts along with their soldiers, supervising the subject peoples and collecting taxes in food and probably textiles. The Huari also gained some control over coastal regions, probably giving impetus to the construction of Nazca's underground aqueducts, but their authority was looser in this region. Their city of Huari, rigidly divided into zones housing the different classes of people, gives an impression of the tight control exercised by the Huari rulers in their upland empire.

Tiwanaku

Farther south, in the region of Lake Titicaca, a highly stratified state emerged around AD 400, with its religious centre at Tiwanaku. This city, which may have housed 40,000 people, was formally laid out with residential blocks along avenues. At its heart lay a ceremonial complex of plazas, statues, gateways and pyramids, built of huge, carefully dressed blocks of imported stone, many of them covered in gold. One monumental gateway bears a carving of the staff god who had been worshipped since Chavín times, and who was later revered by the Inca as Viracocha the creator. The cult of the Tiwanaku staff god spread far beyond the regions under Tiwanaku's control, becoming the religion of the vast Huari empire and reaching even to Ecuador.

In the swampy grounds on the shores of Lake Titicaca the Tiwanaku people constructed a maze of drainage channels and raised fields, where agriculture was enormously productive. The presence of water raised night-time temperatures, preventing frost damage to crops. Fish and wildfowl attracted by this environment added protein to the diet of the Tiwanaku people. Their rulers controlled craftsmen and peasants in a small, closely knit state. Beyond its borders the Tiwanaku established trading outposts over a substantial area, enabling them to obtain the products of other regions, and in turn supplying these regions with fine craft products such as pottery, textiles and goldwork. The administrators who supervised these outposts were buried locally with many fine examples of such objects as grave offerings. Roads were constructed linking these centres, and along them caravans of llamas carried many goods.

2. The sunken courtyard of the Kalasaya temple precinct lies at the heart of the city of Tiwanaku, decorated with stone sculptures.

3. This Moche pot depicts two fishermen with a jar of beer. A large fish alongside their reed boat shows they have been successful.

TEXTILES

The manipulation of fibres – by twisting, plaiting and weaving – is very ancient. Early people undoubtedly made items such as ropes, baskets and nets. Bone and ivory needles were used in Upper Palaeolithic times to sew together pieces of material (animal hide or tree bark) to make clothing or containers.

Textiles, however, are a feature of settled farming communities. The first textiles were made around 7000 BC in the Near East by peoples who had developed the loom – a device that greatly simplifies the weaving process. Looms were also used by 2000 BC in the Andean region. By Inca times, wealth here was measured in textiles, which were used as currency and collected as taxes, as they were by the Aztecs in Mesoamerica.

2

1. This scene on a South American Moche pot shows two weavers using backstrap looms. They are working under supervision in an official weaving shed.

2. This embroidered bird adorns a Chinese silk found in a tomb at Pazyryk – probably owned by a Chinese princess sent as a bride for a steppe nomad lord.

1

Collect your fibres

The first fibres to be used for making textiles were those obtained from the stems of plants such as flax, hemp and nettles, and in the Americas from cactuses. Flax – from which linen is made – was one of the first non-food crops to be domesticated, by about 6000 BC. Stem fibres are long and strong, but they make a fairly coarse cloth that can be uncomfortable against the skin. Cotton, a plant that produces much shorter and softer fibres, was domesticated in at least three locations – in India and Mesoamerica by 4300 BC and in Peru by about 3500 BC.

Stem fibres do not take dye easily and it is difficult to produce strong colours. Cotton, wool and silk take dyes much more easily, and the value of such textiles was often enhanced with coloured designs. Ancient peoples used a large variety of vegetable, animal and mineral products to dye fabrics. Substances that produced strong, long-lasting colours could be worth their weight in gold, and were traded over great distances.

Animal fibres, as opposed to animal skins, did not become important until about 3400 BC when the woolly sheep, with a fleece that could be sheared off, was developed in the Old World. Before this, wool had to be collected by combing animals, which made the resulting fibres and cloth almost prohibitively expensive. The production of woollen cloth, prized not least for its warmth, became a major industry in several ancient civilizations. The wool of domestic alpacas and hunted vicuñas was used by Andean peoples both to embroider decorations on cotton cloth and to make woollen textiles. Cotton and woollen textiles became the main vehicle of Andean artistic creativity. In about 2900 BC the Chinese domesticated the silkworm, the source of a very high-quality textile that was to remain their monopoly throughout the ancient period.

Spin and weave

Before fibres can be woven into a textile they must be spun – twisted together to form long, continuous threads. At first this was done by hand, but people soon invented tools to help with this process. The most common was the spindle whorl, which was spun like a top, twisting the fibres together and leaving the user's hands free to guide the fibres accurately.

A loom is basically a frame that allows the user to manipulate a set of parallel fibres held under tension, so that other fibres can be woven into them. Two basic types were developed, the ground loom and the vertical loom. A ground loom is held under tension by pegs hammered into the ground, and the cloth is woven parallel to the floor. A vertical loom is set upright, usually against a wall, and the cloth is woven at right angles to the ground. Weights are used to keep the fibres under tension. In South America most weavers used a backstrap loom, with one end tied to a tree or wall and the other end attached to a belt around the weaver's waist.

The quality of the cloth was determined when setting up the initial set of fibres on the loom – some of the fabrics produced by the Paracas people of southern Peru were woven as closely as 120 fibres per centimetre (300 per inch). By varying the initial setting of the loom, variations in texture were introduced into the cloth and patterns produced. The Chinese invented the satin weave, which produces a very smooth-surfaced textile.

Not all textiles were woven. The nomads of Central Asia made felt by dragging bags of damp wool behind their horses. With sufficient pounding the wool fibres became matted together into a thick, warm fabric that could be cut and sewn.

3

3. This shirt, found in the tomb of an ancient Egyptian aristocrat, is thought to be the oldest surviving garment in the world. It was made around 2800 BC and was carefully ironed and pleated so that it would fit closely around the shoulders.

◆ TOPIC LINKS

FLOWERY WARS AND CONQUERORS

The 14th and 15th centuries AD saw the emergence of two great empires in the New World, those of the Aztecs in Mexico and the Inca in the Andes. Both owed their success to their effective military organization and capable administration. However, Aztec rule was extremely harsh, weighing heavily on their subject peoples, and the institution of ritual warfare to obtain human sacrificial victims took a great toll of their traditional enemies. The Spaniards who invaded in 1519 therefore made many willing native allies. By contrast, Inca rule was designed to encourage integration. Unfortunately, the Inca empire was barely created before it was destroyed by the Spaniards. Religion played an important role in both areas, the ruler having divine status as the direct representative of the gods. A complex ritual calendar controlled life in Mesoamerica, as it had done since Olmec times. The Inca empire was equally the heir to indigenous traditions.

THE AZTECS

After the fall of the Toltec city of Tula around AD 1200 (▷ p. 205), a number of small states emerged in and around the Valley of Mexico (the area around modern Mexico City). Latest to arrive in the valley were a barbarous and uncouth people from the north who called themselves Mexica, but who are better known as the Aztecs. Initially they worked as labourers and mercenaries for the valley's states, founding their own city of Tenochtitlán on a small island in Lake Texcoco in 1345, but in 1427 they turned on their former employers and began a wave of military conquests that ended in their domination of a huge part of Mesoamerica.

AZTECS

Aztec empire c. AD 1519

Taxes and sacrifice

Early in their rise the Aztecs entered into an alliance with the neighbouring states of Texcoco and Tlacopan against Tlaxcallan and other adjacent states, beginning the institution of formal set-piece battles in which they fought to take captives for sacrifice. The Aztecs called these engagements the 'Flowery Wars', comparing the flow of blood and the deaths of warriors to falling blooms. They believed that human blood was needed to enable the sun to rise each day, and daily sacrifices were therefore made on the altars of the Great Temple at Tenochtitlán, the priests cutting the heart from the living breast of human victims. Bound up with their vision of the world and the gods, it seemed right and appropriate to the Aztecs that they should die in battle or as captive sacrifices, giving their lives to ensure the continuation of their world, as the sun god had himself done, and they faced their end with pride. Warriors who died in battle or as sacrifices and women who died in childbirth went to the heaven of the sun god – everyone else was doomed to

1. The Aztecs created magnificent mosaic masks of turquoise, shell and other valued materials. This example depicts Quetzalcoatl, the Feathered Serpent, god of the wind and one of the principal Aztec deities.

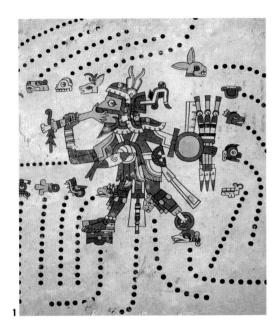

1. The supreme Aztec deity, Tezcatlipoca, represented royalty and fate. He is shown here eating the hand of a sacrificed victim.

2. The Aztecs believed they had to sacrifice people, cutting out their living hearts, in order to nourish the gods and sustain the world.

ultimate extinction in the gloomy underworld, with the exception of the drowned, who went to the heaven of the rain god.

While the Aztecs themselves might accept their harsh destiny, their subject peoples found it hard. Conquered regions were administered by Aztec or subject rulers backed by Aztec military force, and were expected to deliver a heavy, twice-yearly tribute of produce, such as foodstuffs and textiles, and to perform forced labour on public works. The Aztecs, although they did not have true writing, kept careful records of these taxes in pictures depicting the items and quantities to be delivered by each community. Some of the tax produce went to maintaining the rulers and élite of Tenochtitlán, while some was used to trade with other regions through the pochteca merchants (▷ p. 225).

The Aztec capital

Tenochtitlán was constructed on an island, with canals as highways of communication. Three causeways connected the city to the mainland. In the city's heart was the walled ceremonial complex housing the Great Temple (dedicated jointly to the sun god and the god of rain), other temples, the priests' residence, a great ballcourt and a huge rack for displaying the skulls of sacrificed victims. Several royal palaces lay immediately outside the precinct walls, home to the two Aztec rulers and their entourage. The emperor or Huei Tlatoani ('great speaker') was responsible for external affairs, such as trade, warfare and foreign relations, while his co-ruler, known as the Cihuacoatl ('female serpent', although he was a man), conducted internal affairs. Adjacent to

★ The Inca had rigid rules about the quality and type of cloth that could be worn by different ranks of people in society.

the palaces was the great plaza in which markets were held. The surrounding city was a patchwork of small islands on which stone and wooden houses were built. In all, the city housed at least 200,000 people, a far larger population than any European city of the time.

All round the city's more solid centre and over much of the western part of Lake Texcoco were innumerable chinampas – 'floating gardens'. These were constructed of layers of reeds and silt and were stabilized by stakes around their outside and willows planted at their edges. These plots were intensively cultivated, producing several harvests a year of maize, beans, vegetables and other crops. The houses of their cultivators, simple structures of cane, mud and thatch, were also constructed on the chinampas. In the canals that ran between them lived fish, salamanders and tadpoles – all of which the Aztecs ate.

Aztec fathers taught their sons to carry burdens such as firewood and water, to fish and to practise their own crafts such as potting, while girls learned from their mothers how to spin, weave and cook. From a certain age Aztec children attended school until they reached adulthood. The children of the élite were trained for the priesthood or high administrative office, while in the schools for commoners the boys learnt military skills and the girls ritual practices such as singing and dancing.

CHIMÚ AND INCA

In the Andean region the Moche in the Lambayeque valley (▷ pp. 214–16) were succeeded around AD 700 by the Sican culture, great irrigation farmers, whose best known remains are the magnificent royal tombs in the ceremonial centre at Batan Grande. To their south, the Chimú culture developed from a small core in the Moche and Chicama valleys around AD 900 to a great military state, which by 1475 controlled the coast from Ancón in the south to Tumbes in the far north. The Chimú built on the success of the Moche in constructing irrigation works that had brought great fertility to the river valleys, adding canals such as the incomplete 65 km (39 miles) long example intended to link the Moche and Chicama valleys.

The Chimú kings had their capital at Chanchan. Each king constructed a great compound including admininistrative

4. Massive walls of adobe (mudbrick) surrounded the royal compounds in the Chimú capital at Chanchan. These were often created in open-work geometrical shapes of diamonds and checkerboard squares.

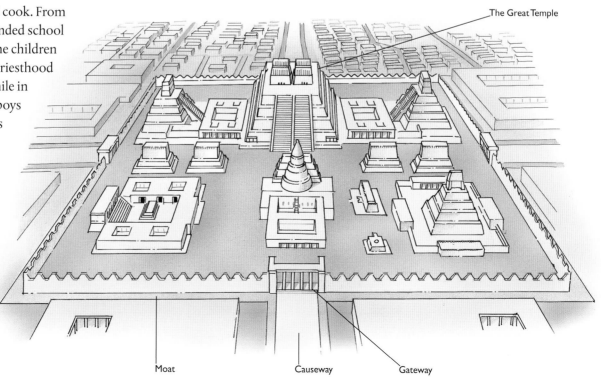

The Great Temple

3. A huge pyramid crowned by a twin temple to the gods of sun and rain dominated the sacred walled precinct at the heart of the Aztec capital, Tenochtitlán.

3

Moat   Causeway   Gateway

Relative values: the conquistadors sought primarily gold, but the Inca were much more upset about the loss of their highly prized textiles.

buildings, a royal palace, storerooms and shrines. On his death, the king's body would be mummified and his compound would become the centre of rites connected with his cult. His successor would construct a new royal compound. Chanchan has ten of these royal compounds, surrounded by the housing and workshops of lesser members of society.

The Inca

Contemporary with Chimú, small states existed in many other Andean regions. Among the highland states was that of the Inca, focused in a small southern area. Around 1410 the Inca began to expand, seizing the neighbouring areas from 1437. Under Pachacuti and his son Topa Inca, a combination of military conquests and astute political alliances created an empire which stretched from Ecuador in the north far down into the south. This empire, covering 4200 km (2500 miles) down the west side of South America, was larger than any previous Andean empire. By 1527 the Inca realms had reached their greatest extent, but the sudden death of the emperor led to a civil war over the succession. The war was won by Atahualpa who, however, had no time to consolidate his state before it was overrun by European adventurers.

The Inca ruled by establishing administrative outposts in conquered lands, garrisoned by their efficient army. A heavy tax burden was placed on the subject people, who were required to hand over a high proportion of their agricultural produce as well as textiles and other craft products. They were also required to perform unpaid labour cultivating government land and constructing and maintaining roads, irrigation canals and buildings. Although the Inca did not devise a writing system they used a complex system of knotted cords (called quipu) to record figures such as taxes due and paid. Recalcitrant

INCA AND CHIMÚ EMPIRES

— Limit of Chimú empire c. AD 1475
▨ Inca empire c. AD 1525

Quito

Sechura Desert — Huancabamba
Cajamarca
Chanchan

Pachacamac
Machu Picchu
Cuzco
Vilcas

Lake Titicaca

Atacama Desert

PACIFIC OCEAN

Talca

groups were likely to be forcibly resettled in areas unswervingly loyal to the Inca, where they could do little harm, and many fine craftsmen, including in particular the skilled goldworkers of Chimú, might be required to take up residence in the Inca capital at Cuzco to serve the emperor.

On the other hand, the sophisticated system of terraced fields supplied with irrigation water greatly raised agricultural productivity throughout the Inca realms, and the Inca interfered relatively little with the native culture of their subject peoples. They came to an early alliance with the great shrine and oracle at Pachacamac and encouraged the founding of Pachacamac branch oracles in subject areas, which acted as spies for the Inca. The Inca tolerated local religions as long as the subject peoples accepted the worship of the Inca royal line.

Inca builders

The Andean region had a long tradition of road building and the Inca brought this to a peak, constructing major highways along the high ridge of the Andes and through the coastal lands, and connecting these two highways at intervals. Impressive rope suspension bridges spanned chasms. The roads were for official business only – for carriers of tribute goods, subject groups being relocated, soldiers and officials, but not casual travellers. Rest houses were built along the roads one day's journey apart (on foot, as the Native Americans had no wheeled transport). The rest houses might include storerooms for tax goods, administrative buildings and accommodation for soldiers – all features of the larger garrison towns from which regional governors administered subject areas. Public

1

1. The Inca did not have writing but kept administrative records using a complex arrangement of knotted strings and cords known as quipu.

A variety of knots were used to record numerical information, and differences in the length, colour and position of the cords encoded other data.

▷ POCHTECA MERCHANTS

Special merchants called pochteca conducted long-distance Aztec trade. Unlike ordinary market traders, the pochteca were of high status, and answerable directly to the emperor. Membership of the pochteca guilds was hereditary, and merchants could rise through their ranks. The emperor issued the pochteca with trade goods, in particular, fine textiles received in taxes and goldwork made by royal craftsmen. They not only obtained valued commodities for the emperor, but also undertook spying missions in foreign and potentially hostile lands, acting on occasion as agents provocateurs to assist the Aztec takeover of other states.

Mainly, however, the pochteca operated as private traders, often becoming extremely wealthy. Successful merchants were expected to share their wealth by giving feasts to other guild members. They travelled to lands as distant as the Maya regions in the southeast, source of valuable quetzal feathers, exotic animal skins and cacao, used by the Aztecs as money. Some groups also traded in slaves, for domestic use and particularly for sacrifice. Travelling in distant lands was dangerous, at risk from both disease and hostile foreigners, and so, like warriors, the pochteca enjoyed the privilege of going to heaven on their death.

buildings were constructed in a distinctive style, with trapezoidal doorways, windows and niches, and massive walls of finely worked irregular blocks fitting so closely together that a knife blade could not be inserted between them. One of the largest blocks could take a team of 20 men a year to make, shaping it by pounding with stone hammers and grinding with wet sand. The size of the blocks and quality of the architecture reflected the importance of the buildings: royal palaces, fortresses and shrines were constructed of massive stones, the houses of nobles of smaller stones and adobe (sun-dried mud brick) and the dwellings of peasants of the traditional cane, mud and thatch.

Cuzco

The name of the Inca capital, Cuzco, means 'navel' – it was at the centre of Tahuantinsuyu, the Inca 'world of the four quarters'. Cuzco was unlike most cities in that only the upper echelons of society dwelt there, although the surrounding area was inhabited by craftsmen and peasants. Overlooking the city was a massively built ritual complex, known as Sacsahuamán, sacred to the sun. At the centre of the city lay the Holy Place from which four roads led out, dividing the city into four parts that reflected the empire's division into north, south, east and west quarters. In the city were the chief shrines, including the Temple of the Sun, its doors and walls coated in gold. Each Inca emperor constructed a royal palace, that of his predecessor being turned into a shrine

1. The fortress walls of the Inca city of Machu Picchu, high in the mountains, surround houses, temples and other public buildings built of massive stone blocks. Terraced fields cut into the slopes below provided the city's livelihood.

⭐ The Aztecs gathered the scum of spirulina algae that grew on Lake Texcoco as a welcome source of protein. They pressed it to form cakes.

1. This kero – a traditional Inca wooden beaker – was made after the Spanish conquest and is painted with designs showing both Inca people and foreigners, perhaps including Pizarro himself. Many traditional crafts continued to be practised under Spanish rule, though some skills were lost.

for the deceased god-emperor's mummy cult, following earlier Andean tradition.

Storerooms housed the tribute brought in from distant subject lands – foodstuffs, textiles and essential ritual goods such as seashells from Ecuador. Tribute was used not only to support the inhabitants of Cuzco, the army, officials and so on, but also to provide for the people of the empire during natural disasters, such as when the terrible El Niño current periodically brought devastation to the coast.

Another important building in the heart of Cuzco was the Acllahuasi, a nunnery housing beautiful virgins who spent their days weaving the finest textiles of vicuña wool for the emperor – but who might also be chosen as royal concubines or as sacrifices. Textiles were the major item of wealth in Inca society and were a frequent offering at Inca shrines. There were strict laws defining the types of textiles that could be worn by different ranks in society. Sacrificial victims, who were often children, were offered in shrines or holy places on the summits of the Andes, drugged and killed or left to freeze to death, along with fine figurines of gold and silver, fit offerings to the gods.

THE CONQUISTADORS

After Columbus reached the West Indies in 1492 the Spaniards began to explore the Americas, searching in particular for gold. In 1519 Hernán Cortés landed at Veracruz on the Gulf coast, leading an expedition sent by the Spanish governor of Cuba. Cortés repudiated the latter's authority and set off inland. After a brief period of hostilities against Tlaxcala, the Aztecs' enemies in the Flowery Wars, the Spaniards and Tlaxcala joined forces. Marching inland to Tenochtitlán the Spaniards were at first received hospitably by the Aztec emperor

Motecuhzoma II (Montezuma) as representatives of an important alien power. With their superior weapons the Spaniards quickly made Montezuma a virtual prisoner, and an uneasy truce reigned. In 1520 the governor of Cuba sent an expedition against Cortés, who returned to the coast. In his absence his deputy and followers began to pillage Tenochtitlán. Although Cortés rapidly returned, the situation soon deteriorated. Montezuma was murdered by a stone thrown by one of his own subjects, and the Spaniards, deprived of their hostage, fought their way out of the city along one of the causeways, losing into the waters of Lake Texcoco many of their number and virtually all the treasure that they had amassed. Reinforced by the Tlaxcala and other enemies of the Aztecs, they succeeded in 1521 in besieging and taking

Tenochtitlán, the signal for a campaign of looting and violence throughout Mexico.

Rumours of a still more wealthy kingdom in South America inspired another Spaniard, Francisco Pizarro, to mount an expedition, which landed in Ecuador in 1532. Welcomed by the Inca, Pizarro's army of only 180 men marched on Cuzco, where by a ruse they took the emperor Atahualpa prisoner and massacred many thousands of his nobles. They demanded a huge ransom for the release of the emperor, which the pious Inca subjects raised, but when it had been paid the Spaniards executed Atahualpa and commenced a period of rapine and looting. The immense wealth in gold and silver of South America served only to inflame the greed of the Spanish conquistadors, and the civilizations of Central and South

America crumbled before them. Torture and revolting cruelty attended both their quest for precious metals and jewels and their attempts to convert the natives to Christianity. They destroyed many of the fine native works of art, but some of the missionaries also recorded the native way of life and their legends and history, providing us with a second-hand literary source that has been invaluable in understanding American civilization. Even more devastating than the Spaniards' rapacity, however, were the epidemic diseases that they introduced, such as smallpox and measles and even the common cold, to which native Americans had no immunity. Within a few decades the population of these two densely settled regions had crashed to a fraction of its former size.

SOUTH AMERICAN GOLD

Gold and silver had a special ritual importance in South America. The Inca regarded them as the sweat of the sun and the tears of the moon. Gold was obtained from rivers or mined, and other metal ores were also widely available. Gold was often alloyed with silver (producing electrum) and copper (making an alloy called tumbaga). The colour of gold was considered of prime importance, so many objects were gilded. Tumbaga objects could be gilded by using chemicals to remove the surface copper from the alloy – depletion gilding. The Moche dipped copper objects into a heated solution of gold and minerals, and fixed the thin layer of gold that was thus deposited by heating briefly to a high temperature.

Andean cultures often made fine figurines and jewellery from sheets of metal hammered into shape, then soldered together. The Inca inlaid gold objects with other materials, including stone and silver. The sophisticated techniques used in the chiefdoms of the northwest (right) included lost-wax casting (▷ p. 45) and granulation – decoration built up from tiny beads of gold attached to an object's surface. Gold offerings to the gods were placed in shrines or thrown into sacred lakes, such as Lake Guatavitá in the north. Many Andean cultures buried gold objects with royalty – the Moche burials recently found at Sipán (▷ p. 213) are furnished with a huge selection of gold ornaments and ceremonial armour.

MEDICINE

Although the bacteria and viruses causing illness were not identified in the ancient world, most cultures had a good practical knowledge of diseases and how to deal with them. In fact, many plants used then are still part of the modern pharmacopoeia.

Physical treatment often took place alongside ritual practices to discover the supernatural causes of the illness or injury – such as the displeasure of a god – and to promote the effectiveness of the cure. Such beliefs did not necessarily interfere with treatment – for example, the Aztecs set broken limbs extremely competently, while reciting chants against the mythological quails that were blamed for the injury.

2

Treating illness

Most early cultures had some knowledge of herbs that could be used to treat illnesses. Medicinal plants found in Guitarrero cave in the Andes are among the earliest cultivated plants in South America, around 6500 BC. The botanical gardens planted by the Aztec emperor Motecuhzoma I included medicinal trees that greatly interested Spanish botanists after the conquest. The ancient Egyptians employed a wide range of herbal remedies, many of which were adopted by the Greeks. Medicines made from a variety of herbs and minerals are described in medical treatises found in a Chinese tomb of the 2nd century BC at Mawangdui and many of these are still in use in China. The treatises also describe the Chinese medical practice of acupuncture, and needles for performing this have been found in other ancient Chinese tombs. The recent discovery of a frozen man in the Alps suggests that acupuncture was also practised in pre-historic Europe around 3300 BC.

The dangers of infection were often appreciated. For example, one of the 18th-century BC Mari letters (▷ p.51) discusses measures taken to prevent the spread of a highly contagious disease, by ensuring that no one used the same cup, seat or bed as the invalid.

Surgery

One important use of drugs was as an anaesthetic accompanying surgery. Such drugs included opium and coca leaves, but also such powerful poisons as datura – and it says much for ancient medical skill that patients survived. An impressive range of operations was successfully performed. These ranged from amputation, perhaps practised as early as 50,000 BC, to the removal or couching of eye cataracts by both Roman and Indian (and probably Babylonian) surgeons, using special fine needles. The late BC Indian medical pioneer Sushruta also describes the performance of plastic surgery, grafting facial skin to form a new nose or earlobe.

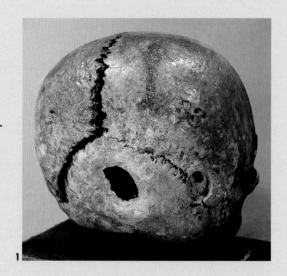

1

2. This collection of Roman medical equipment includes forceps, a variety of probes, scalpels, spoons and spatulae, and a cup for taking blood, a regular practice in treating patients. A compartmented box held medicines.

kit used by the Romans for trepanation was found in Germany.

Other Roman surgical instruments included scalpels, saws and forceps, all of which were manufactured to a very high standard. Indian surgeons used a huge repertoire of steel instruments, while in Mesoamerica and other cultures without metal tools, the incredibly sharp edge of obsidian blades made effective surgical knives.

Studying people

The Greeks were perhaps the first to take a scientific interest in anatomy, finding out the detail by dissecting not only corpses but also live animals and condemned prisoners. The Chinese also developed an accurate knowledge of many aspects of human anatomy. The best known Greek physician was Hippocrates (c. 460 – c. 380 BC), to whom Western medicine owes the greater part of its ethical code. He made careful notes on the patients he attended and their progress. He also espoused the idea of preventive medicine, encouraging such things as fresh air and walking to promote health.

Sometimes the skill and knowledge of the physician was not enough. Many societies imposed harsh penalties for what they saw as medical negligence. Failure in delicate eye operations was punishable in Babylonian times by the amputation of a hand. A South American Moche healer whose patient died was liable to be staked out for the birds to peck to death.

1. The dangerous operation of trepanation was carried out in many parts of the world – this skull comes from Canada. This individual, who lived around 2000 years ago, underwent the operation twice. The first was successful and bone grew back over the hole, but the second was not completed.

One of the most extraordinary and dangerous operations was trepanation. This involved grinding down, cutting out or drilling a circle of bone from the skull. This may have been performed to relieve brain tumours or pain induced by head injuries in battle, though equally it may have been done for ritual reasons. Trepanation was practised in many areas, from ancient Peru to Neolithic Europe. Some patients had it performed as many as seven times, new bone growth showing that they had survived. A 2nd-century AD tool

◆ TOPIC LINKS

3.3 The Land of the Buddha
p.139 The Guptas

Afterword

The success of a handful of Europeans in bringing down the two great empires of the New World, despite the martial experience of the Aztecs and the Inca, highlights several key issues in the development of civilizations.

THE ROLE OF TECHNOLOGY

One crucial factor was the role of technology. Since the early days of humanity, people have been overcoming their physical limitations and gaining control over their environment by devising technological solutions to the problems of survival. Sometimes these were in the shape of tools – stone implements for cutting in the beginning, and later a whole range of different tools invented to cope with specific activities. Materials employed in these devices could be natural substances in an unmodified form – boulders used in construction, for instance – or sophisticated man-made substances whose production required considerable knowledge and expertise, such as metal alloys or glass.

Nature could be harnessed to human needs in other ways too – by selectively breeding plants and animals, for example, to provide food and clothing, or by using the strength of animals to pull vehicles or to carry loads. The elements were made to serve humanity: water diverted to irrigate crops, or to operate machinery; fire to cook food, to warm and defend dwellings, and to transmute materials, such as clay into pottery.

Technology not only allowed societies to conquer nature but also to conquer each other. The guns used by the Spanish against the Aztecs and Inca were only the latest in a long line of weapons designed to give one culture mastery over others.

CULTURAL VARIETY

But there were also other crucial factors. The arrival of the Spanish in the New World brought about the first meeting between two great cultural blocs. Each had been developing independently along different paths and each comprised a number of cultures, past and present, that had interacted in many ways – particularly trading and fighting – for thousands of years. Within each bloc, many things were shared to a greater or lesser degree – technological innovations, religious beliefs, cultural attitudes – and diseases. The clash of cultures in the 16th century was between peoples whose whole outlooks were profoundly different. The people of the New World were at a disadvantage to those of the Old many times over – in technology, in resistance to disease and in the rules they played by.

This pattern was repeated several times in subsequent centuries, and it is familiar from the past too, Old and New World empires seizing control of the lands of their 'backward' neighbours.

Why was there this disparity in development between regions? Conquerors often put it down to their own innate superiority. But the reason was more fundamental. The world is not uniform in the opportunities it offers – it varies locally and regionally in climate, environment, topography and natural resources. This uneven spread of opportunities made it possible for the inhabitants of different regions to develop at different rates. The uniqueness of cultures lay in the use to which each one put these opportunities – a potentially infinite diversity of responses to a great variety of situations.

Glossary

acropolis The upper part of an ancient Greek city, often situated on a hill or outcrop and usually fortified (capitalized, the Acropolis refers to Athens). The term is also used to refer to similar features in other ancient cities.

agate A variety of the semi-precious stone chalcedony (a form of the mineral quartz), which is characterized by concentric bands of different colours. Agate may be cut and polished to make jewellery and decorative vessels.

agora The public open space that was the centre of an ancient Greek city's social and commercial activity (capitalized, the Agora refers to Athens). Buildings around the agora often housed the city's administration as well as shops and business offices.

alloy A mixture of two or more metals. Alloys are made either to improve the qualities of the finished metal e.g. by adding tin to copper to make bronze, or to dilute a precious metal e.g. by adding copper to silver.

amphitheatre A large circular or oval building in a Hellenistic or Roman city, with tiered seating around a central open space. Initially used for public sporting contests and ceremonial games, in Roman times they became associated with gladiator fights.

amphora An ancient Greek or Roman pottery vessel with two handles (▷ p. 112). Amphorae were used for storing and transporting a range of mainly liquid commodities and ranged in capacity from a few to dozens of litres.

Anatolia The upland plains that extend over much of central and eastern Asia Minor. Parts of Anatolia had similar environmental conditions to the 'Fertile Crescent' and this region adopted farming at an early date.

Asia Minor The large peninsula bounded by the Black Sea and the Mediterranean Sea. The narrow entrance to the Black Sea at the north-western corner of Asia Minor has traditionally marked the frontier between Europe and Asia.

ball game A ritual game played on specially constructed ballcourts by Mesoamerican cultures from about 1000 BC. The game was played between two teams, and players could only strike the ball, which was usually made of rubber, with their knees or hips.

Brahmi script A script developed in India about 500 BC based on one of the alphabetic scripts then used in the Near East. After about AD 500 Brahmi script spread, along with other elements of Indian culture, to parts of Southeast Asia.

Buddhism An Indian religion established by the teachings of Siddhartha (Gautama; 563–483 BC) as an alternative to Hinduism. After AD 200 Buddhism spread to China, Japan and Southeast Asia, while its popularity in India had declined by AD 500.

carnelian A variety of the semi-precious stone chalcedony (a form of the mineral quartz), characterized by a red to reddish-brown colour, sometimes with white streaks. Carnelian has been used to make beads and gems for rings and brooches since ancient times.

casting A technique by which metal is shaped by being poured molten into a mould and allowed to cool. The first moulds were simple shapes cut into pieces of stone; the later development of clay moulds enabled the casting of intricate shapes.

Central Asia A vast, sparsely populated region of mountains, deserts and steppes, located north of the Himalaya, west of China and east of Iran. Inhabited by mainly nomadic peoples, Central Asia has been a major crossroads for trade and technology exchange since prehistory.

chinampa A so-called 'floating garden', constructed by the Aztecs in and around their capital Tenochtitlán on Lake Texcoco in Mexico. Chinampas were made of layers of reeds and silt and supported houses as well as intensively cultivated plots producing several harvests a year.

cist A box-shaped burial structure made of stone slabs stood on edge. Cist burials have been made by various cultures throughout history. Cists, both plain and decorated, were often constructed at the bottom of a pit with a mound raised above.

city-state A political unit consisting of a city and its surrounding farmland. City-states developed in the Near East after 3000 BC and later became established as the basic units of ancient Greece, early Roman Italy, and Mesoamerica in the Maya period.

civilization The collective term for a group of cultural attributes (generally including city-building, writing, political hierarchy and social responsibility) which characterize the large, centrally administered and economically advanced states that first emerged in the Old World about 3000 BC.

Classic In Mesoamerican history, the term Classic refers to the period from around AD 200 when civilizations such as Monte Albán, Teotihuacán, and the Maya were at their height. The Classic was preceded by the Pre-Classic and followed by the Post-Classic.

clay token A small distinctively shaped or marked piece of baked clay made by ancient peoples and used either as part of pre-literate counting and accounting systems, or as gaming pieces in board-type games of skill or chance.

Confucianism The official philosophy of the Chinese state for most of the historical period. Confucianism arose from the teachings of Confucius (Kongfuzi, 551–479 BC), who emphasized respect for ancestors and obedience to authority.

cuneiform The distinctive writing system of Mesopotamia, consisting of wedge-shaped impressions made by pressing the end of a cut reed into wet clay, that was developed about 3200 BC and was widely used in the Near East over the following two thousand years.

Daoism A Chinese philosophy that is attributed to the teachings of the teacher Lao Zi, who lived about 500 BC. Daoism had a mystical strain from the outset, and later incorporated a great number of local superstitions.

domestication The process (by means of conscious or unconscious selective breeding) by which wild plants and animals became genetically altered as a result of being cultivated or husbanded by early farming cultures.

dynasty A group of successive rulers of a state or empire, often hereditary or closely linked by kinship. China was ruled by a series of emperors in named dynasties until 1911; the pharaohs of ancient Egypt are divided into dynasties numbered 1–31.

empire An extensive territory (usually incorporating conquered states or 'foreign' lands) under the overall control of a single individual – the emperor or empress. The term also refers to areas under the domination of a particular group or city.

evolution The natural process by which organisms change their characteristics through adapting to their environment. The term is also used figuratively to refer to cultural change within human societies occurring over relatively short periods of time.

felt A type of matted woollen cloth made by rolling and compressing wet wool fibres, which may have been first woven together. Eurasian steppe nomads made felt by dragging bundles of wet wool behind their horses.

forum The public open space that was the main centre of a Roman city's social and commercial activity (capitalized, the Forum refers to Rome, where several emperors enlarged and rebuilt the city's forum district adding new buildings).

glyph A 'word' in the semi-pictorial writing system developed by the Maya. Each glyph is self-contained and approximately square in shape, and consists of a pictorial element with additional phonetic symbols.

grave goods Objects placed with human remains in a burial. The objects may consist of supplies for an afterlife journey, or objects intended to denote the status of the deceased, or both. Ancient rulers were often buried with enormous quantities of grave goods.

Hellenistic The final named period in the development of ancient Greek art and architecture. Hellenistic also refers to the period from about 330 BC to 100 BC when Greek language, art and culture had their widest influence in Europe and Asia.

hieratic The first Egyptian script, developed by priestly administrators as a shorthand form of hieroglyphics in about 2500 BC. Hieratic continued to be used by Egyptian priests for sacred writings long after the introduction of the even more simplified demotic script.

hieroglyph Ancient Egyptian picture writing first developed about 3200 BC. Although superseded for many purposes by more easily written scripts, hieroglyphics remained in use in Egypt for monumental inscriptions until the Roman period.

hunter-gathering The universal method of human subsistence before the development

and adoption of farming, and still practised in some regions. Food is obtained by hunting or trapping animals and fish, and collecting the edible parts of wild plants. Such a lifestyle usually imposes a nomadic existence.

Ice Age A period of global cooling. The most recent began about 40,000 years ago and ended about 10,000 years ago. During this period much of the northern continents were covered by a glacial ice-sheet up to 2 km (1¼ miles) thick.

Indo-European languages One of the world's largest language families. A group of related languages that includes all the modern European languages, except Basque, Finnish, and Magyar (Hungarian), together with some Iranian and Indian languages.

Iron Age The period of history in much of the Old World during which iron came into widespread use for tools and weapons. In western Asia and southern Europe the Iron Age began about 1000 BC, and about 700 BC in western Europe.

irrigation The provision of water for crops in regions where rainfall is insufficient. The principal methods are: retaining water with banks and dams; distributing water along canals and channels; and lifting water with a variety of devices.

jade Refers to any of several semi-precious, hard, fine-grained rocks, often green in colour, that are used for jewellery and other carved objects. Ancient Chinese and Mesoamerican societies in particular considered jade to be especially valuable.

Jainism An Indian religion established by the teachings of Mahavira (599–527 BC) at approximately the same time as Buddhism, and rooted in a similar reaction against conservative Hinduism and the caste system.

lacquer The sap of the lacquer tree. Chinese craftworkers painted layers of lacquer, often coloured with pigments, onto wooden objects, such as bowls and boxes, to form a waterproof, heat-resistant and highly decorative finish.

lapis lazuli A semi-precious stone with a deep blue colour, sometimes containing gold-coloured flecks of pyrite. Highly prized for jewellery by ancient peoples, lapis lazuli was traded over thousands of kilometres.

Levant The region along the coastline of the eastern Mediterranean between Asia Minor and Egypt; and roughly equivalent to present-day Syria, Lebanon, Israel, Jordan and Palestine, together with the island of Cyprus.

Levantine script The first alphabetic script, with consonants only and no vowels, devised about 1700 BC by Semitic-speaking inhabitants of the Levant, who began to use Egyptian single-consonant symbols to write down words in their own language.

Linear A script A syllabic script, in which symbols stand for syllables rather than individual letters, used by the Minoan civilization. Linear A has not yet been deciphered and the language it was used to write remains a mystery.

Linear B script A script devised by the Mycenaeans, and adapted from Minoan Linear A, to write their own language. Linear B has been translated, and the Mycenaean language identified as an early form of Greek.

lost-wax process A metal-casting technique in which the object to be cast is first modelled in wax. A mould is made by packing sand or clay around the model, and the wax is melted away. The mould can then be filled with molten metal.

manioc Also known as cassava. A South American plant with a starch-rich root, manioc has been cultivated since ancient times. Before cooking, it must be carefully peeled, grated and squeezed to remove the natural poisons it contains.

Mesoamerica A term used by prehistorians to refer to the cultural region consisting of Central America (especially present-day Guatemala and Belize) and Mexico during the period before the Spanish conquest.

Mesopotamia The region between the rivers Tigris and Euphrates, which flow from Asia Minor into the Persian Gulf; the region is roughly equivalent to present-day Iraq. The earliest civilization, that of the Sumerians, developed in southern Mesopotamia.

Middle East A large region consisting of North Africa, the Levant, Asia Minor, the Arabian Peninsula and Iran. Although it had several distinct civilizations in ancient times, the Middle East has mainly had a single, unified culture since the establishment of Islam.

Middle Kingdom The period of Egyptian history that began with the accession of Mentuhotep II in about 2050 BC and ended with the Hyksos takeover in about 1750 BC. It was a time of general prosperity and unrivalled artistic achievement.

native metal An occurrence of raw, nearly pure, metal at the earth's surface. Certain metals, notably copper, silver and gold, sometimes occur as native metal, and these were the first to be exploited by the earliest metalworkers about 5500 BC.

Near East A region within the Middle East consisting of Asia Minor, the Levant, Egypt and Mesopotamia. This region is roughly equivalent to present-day Asiatic Turkey, Syria, Lebanon, Israel, Jordan, Palestine, Egypt, and Iraq.

Neolithic In Eurasian history, the final period of the Stone Age (approximately 8000–3000 BC) during which farming was developed and adopted. The term is not usually used with reference to Africa or the Americas.

New Kingdom The period of Egyptian history that began with the reign of Ahmose I in about 1550 BC and ended about 1070 BC. During this period Egyptian pharaohs ruled an empire that extended from the Levant to Nubia.

Nubia Egypt's southern neighbour. The traditional frontier between Egypt and Nubia was the 1st cataract of the Nile. Nubia was under Egyptian domination for most of the ancient period but later emerged as the independent state of Meroe.

obsidian A form of natural volcanic glass that was highly prized by ancient peoples because it could used to make extremely sharp blades, mirrors and other desirable objects. Obsidian was traded over distances of hundreds of kilometres.

Old Kingdom The period of Egyptian history that began with the pharaoh Zoser about 2700 BC and ended about 2200 BC. This was the 'pyramid age' in Egypt, the most famous of which are the Giza pyramids built between 2650 and 2550 BC.

oracle bones Animal bones that were used by the Shang people of China to commune with their gods. Questions were scratched onto the bones, which were then heated and the resulting cracks interpreted as answers.

Palaeolithic The earliest period of the so-called Stone Age, from about 2 million BC to about 10,000 BC. The final part of the Palaeolithic period, the Upper Palaeolithic (about 40,000–10,000 BC) is marked by technological and artistic developments.

pastoralism A type of agriculture based on animal herding, with crops being of minor importance. Pastoralists often follow a nomadic lifestyle as they move between seasonal pastures for their flocks and herds.

pictographic writing Picture writing – the earliest writing systems, such as those of

Mesopotamia and Egypt, used simple pictures to convey words and ideas. For example, the word for water might be indicated by a series of wavy lines.

prehistory The whole of human history before the development of written records in about 3000 BC. The term is often used to refer to the period of human cultural history between about 30,000 BC and 3000 BC.

primary civilization A civilization that developed independently, rather than as a result of contact with other civilizations. There were six areas of primary civilization: Mesopotamia, Egypt, the Indus Valley, China, Mesoamerica, and the Andes region of South America.

pyramid A large, geometrically shaped structure of stone or bricks. Pyramids were constructed by a number of ancient peoples, either as monumental tombs (as in Egypt) or within ceremonial and religious centres (as in Mesoamerica and Mesopotamia).

reflex bow A composite bow made of laminated wood and horn. It was bent back on itself when strung, producing a characteristic double curve. The reflex bow was smaller and more powerful than conventional ancient bows.

relief A piece of stone or clay wall panel that has been decorated by carving or moulding with a design or picture that stands out from the background surface. Reliefs were a popular method of adorning ancient palaces and temples.

seal A small object made of stone, pottery or metal that is used to impress a design into clay or wax. Seals were used from the Neolithic period to identify the owners of property, and later to authenticate written messages.

Semitic languages A group of related Middle Eastern languages of which Arabic and Hebrew are the most prominent modern examples. The ancient Akkadian, Amorite and Phoenician languages belonged to the Semitic language group.

shaduf A water-raising device widely employed in ancient Egypt and elsewhere, consisting of a bucket attached to one end of a counterweighted beam. An operator dipped the bucket into water, the counterweight lifted the filled bucket, and the operator emptied it.

shaman Tribal priest in the ancient cultures of Central Asia and the Americas (and perhaps prehistoric Europe). Shamans claimed the power to communicate with the spirit world and often used fasting or drugs to induce a state of trance.

Silk Road The overland route (actually a network of several routes) by which silk was transported by pack animals across Central Asia from China to the west. Other commodities, including ideas, also travelled the Silk Road between east and west.

smelting The process of heating ore to extract the metal content – the first stage of metal production. The initial discovery of smelting copper from its ores probably occurred as a result of of peoples' increasing skill at firing pottery.

steatite Also popularly known as soapstone. A soft, easily worked stone, usually greyish in colour. Steatite was popular with ancient peoples for making both large vessels and monumental carvings, seals and small beads for jewellery and adorning clothing.

stele Also stela, plural stelae. A single block or pillar of stone set upright in the ground and decorated with a carved design and/or an inscription. The term is generally used to refer only to stones carved by literate peoples.

Stone Age The period of human history, from about 2 million BC to about 4000 BC, before metal tools came into use. It is sub-divided into the Palaeolithic, the Mesolithic (about 10,000–8000 BC) and the Neolithic.

stupa A large Buddhist monumental shrine often dome-shaped, with four ceremonial gateways at the cardinal points. Stupas originated with the mounds built over the Buddha's ashes after they had been widely distributed by his disciples.

technology Any of the processes that human beings use to manipulate their physical environment; or the distinctive products thereof. Pottery, irrigated fields, edible manioc, domesticated animals, stone tools, painted murals and ocean-going ships are all products of different technologies.

terracotta Unglazed baked clay (literally 'cooked earth') with a reddish-brown colour. The term normally excludes pottery used for making containers and tableware, but includes objects such as loom weights, figurines, statues, tiles and bricks.

ziggurat A Mesopotamian type of stepped pyramid constructed of mud-brick and forming the base for a temple. The first true ziggurat was constructed about 2100 BC; before this time Mesopotamian temples were built atop simple raised platforms.

Picture credits

BBC Worldwide would like to thank the following for providing photographs and for permission to reproduce copyright material. While every effort has been made to trace and acknowledge copyright holders, we would like to apologize should there have been any errors or omissions.

CIVILIZATIONS

Index

Published by BBC Worldwide Limited, Woodlands,
80 Wood Lane, London W12 0TT

First published 2001
Copyright © Jane McIntosh and Clint Twist, 2001
The moral right of the authors has been asserted.

ISBN 0 563 55191 7

Commissioning Editor: Joanne Osborn
Academic Consultant: Professor Robin Dennell
Development Editor: Susan Watt
Project Editor: Khadija Manjlai
Art Editor: Lisa Pettibone
Designer: Kathryn Gammon
Copy-editor: Ian Crofton
Picture Researcher: Deirdre O'Day
Cartographer: Olive Pearson
Illustrator: Chris Forsey

Set in Albertina MT and Gill Sans

Printed and bound in Britain by Butler & Tanner Ltd,
Frome and London

Colour separations by Radstock Reproductions Ltd,
Midsomer Norton

Jacket printed by Lawrence Allen Ltd, Weston-super-Mare